APOSTOLIC
IMAGINATION

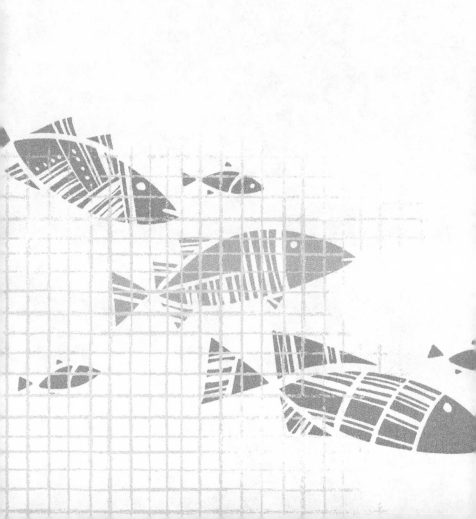

APOSTOLIC IMAGINATION

Recovering a Biblical Vision

for the Church's Mission Today

J. D. PAYNE

B
Baker Academic
a division of Baker Publishing Group
Grand Rapids, Michigan

Published by Baker Academic
a division of Baker Publishing Group
PO Box 6287, Grand Rapids, MI 49516-6287
www.bakeracademic.com

Library of Congress Cataloging-in-Publication Data
Names: Payne, Jervis David, 1974– author.
Title: Apostolic imagination : recovering a biblical vision for the church's mission today / J. D. Payne.
Description: Grand Rapids, Michigan : Baker Academic, a division of Baker Publishing Group, [2022] | Includes bibliographical references and index.
Identifiers: LCCN 2021035446 | ISBN 9781540962553 (paperback) | ISBN 9781540965325 (casebound) | ISBN 9781493434923 (ebook) | ISBN 9781493434930 (pdf)
Subjects: LCSH: Missions. | Mission of the church. | Missions—History—Early church, ca. 30–600.
Classification: LCC BV2061.3 .P39 2022 | DDC 266—dc23
LC record available at https://lccn.loc.gov/2021035446

Baker Publishing Group publications use paper produced from sustainable forestry practices and post-consumer waste whenever possible.

22   23   24   25   26   27   28   7   6   5   4   3   2   1

To the One
from whom the imagination comes

And to Sarah

Contents

Introduction

Before I owned a GPS device or smartphone, I was passing through Nashville one evening traveling to Louisville. It was dark, and I was distracted by the lights of the city and construction signs on the interstate. Thinking I was in the correct lane to continue North on I-65, I somehow ended up traveling Northwest on I-24. I am embarrassed to write this, but I drove the interstate for two hours before realizing I was lost and in the wrong part of Kentucky! The sad truth is I had traveled the three-hour I-65 route from Nashville to Louisville on numerous occasions. Yet, my mind was elsewhere. I was distracted, busy, believing I was traveling the proper path but going in the wrong direction. Eventually I arrived at my destination. Eventually. Unfortunately, matters of distraction and busyness are not limited to my story but have also become part of the Church's present reality.

During the first three centuries, the Church experienced rapid and widespread growth.[1] What was seen as a sect of the Way, consisting of troublemakers who "turned the world upside down" (Acts 17:6), eventually became one of the recognized religions of the Roman Empire. While a great deal of attention has been given to the movement of Christianity toward the West, for centuries preachers also traveled East.[2] Much expansion of the faith occurred through the work of

---

1. Throughout this book, I refer to the universal, denominational, national, or regional Church with a capital C. I use a lowercase *c* when referring to the local expression of the Church.

2. Philip Jenkins in *The Lost History of Christianity: The Thousand-Year Golden Age of the Church in the Middle East, Africa, and Asia—and How It Died* (New York: HarperOne, 2008) provides a fascinating account of an aspect of Christian history's first millennium that often receives little attention in the West.

missionary monasticism from AD 500 to 1500.[3] The Reformation, Pietism, colonialism, Moravians, and Great Awakenings contributed to developments that brought the Church into the "Great Century of Missions" (1792–1910), with the remarkable development of mission societies. The twentieth century saw numerous conferences and congresses that addressed world evangelization. The century was also marked by a fantastic amount of discussions and publications regarding the theology of mission. This reality coincided with many people being sent into the world. By the early twenty-first century, it was estimated that 1.6 million US citizens were going on annual short-term trips.[4] The past seventy years also included the Church Growth Movement, the Lausanne Movement for World Evangelization, and the Missional Church Movement, all bearing on the task of the Great Commission.

By the twenty-first century, scholars had produced a wealth of studies on the amazing growth of the Church throughout Asia, Africa, and Central and South America. The Church throughout the Majority World is now both larger and growing faster than the Church throughout the traditionally Western contexts.[5] Missions is no longer understood to be from the West to the rest of the world, but from wherever the Church is located to all places on the planet.[6] The new catchphrase: missions is from everywhere to everywhere.

Lack of Clarity

Yet, with all the discussions, publications, and *missions* taking place, a great deal of confusion remains. The language of mission is unclear.[7]

3. Edward L. Smither, *Missionary Monks: An Introduction to the History and Theology of Missionary Monasticism* (Eugene, OR: Cascade, 2016).

4. Robert J. Priest, "Introduction," in *Effective Engagement in Short-Term Missions: Doing It Right*, ed. Robert J. Priest (Pasadena, CA: William Carey Library, 2008), ii.

5. Philip Jenkins drew much attention to this growth in *The Next Christendom: The Coming of Global Christianity*, 3rd ed. (New York: Oxford University Press, 2011).

6. Patrick Johnstone, *The Future of the Global Church: History, Trends, and Possibilities* (Downers Grove, IL: IVP, 2014); and Jason Mandryk, ed., *Operation World: The Definitive Prayer Guide to Every Nation*, 7th ed. (Downers Grove, IL: IVP, 2010).

7. Michael W. Stroope, *Transcending Mission: The Eclipse of a Modern Tradition* (Downers Grove, IL: IVP Academic, 2017).

Is missions found in passing out gospel tracts in China or overseeing food distribution in Nicaragua? Is missions fulfilled by church planting in Iraq or constructing a building for a church in Russia? Does missions include all of these examples and others as well? Identity is unclear. Is every Christian a missionary, or only those who relocate their lives to a remote location overseas? Are doctors and teachers actually missionaries, even if they do not share the gospel verbally, or are evangelists the only missionaries? The purpose and priority of missions is unclear. Do missionaries go to serve people with great physical needs? If so, what is the difference between missionaries and any NGO workers? Do missionaries go and share the gospel and do nothing related to social justice? Is priority given to evangelism or meeting social needs? Or, is there no overarching priority, but rather multiple priorities related to the individuals who go and not the Church as a whole? Practices are unclear. What are missionaries to do on the field? Are they to be involved in church-planting activities? Are they to be involved in relief and development? Are they to be involved in training leaders? Caring for the environment? Freeing those captive to human traffickers? Alleviating poverty?

How should funding and sending structures be established? Should the Church spend most of the offering money at home or abroad? Should people be sent to reached or unreached areas of the world? Or are all locations equal? How should pastors lead church members to reach the nations?

People are making inquiries about the Church in the West. Is the West a mission field?[8] If so, it is unlike anything that has been traditionally labeled a mission field. If the West is a mission field, then how should the Church, which operates from a pastoral approach to ministry, function in contexts that demand *apostolic work*? What

8. Many books have been published on this topic. A good place to begin is searching for resources connected to the Gospel and Our Culture Network. In both the UK and US, this group led an early charge related to mission in a post-Christianized context. Drawing much influence from the work of Lesslie Newbigin, the group influenced the thinking of many in what became the Missional Church Movement, which was birthed with the publication of *Missional Church: A Vision for the Sending of the Church in North America*, ed. Darrell L. Guder (Grand Rapids: Eerdmans, 1998). Both this network and this movement have experienced diminishing influence in North America in recent years.

about the role of the Church in the West in a postcolonial age?[9] If the Church is larger and growing at a faster rate in the Majority World, then how should Western churches consider the future of their kingdom labors? What does biblical partnership look like in the twenty-first century?

My reason for writing this book is because the Church has become lost in the disciple-making task. The Church has ventured away from the apostolic path and continues down a road involving numerous important and good activities labeled as missions. The need of the hour is to ask, What is the apostolic imagination that influenced much of the first-century labors, and how does it affect the Church's global task today?

Apostolic Imagination

By its very nature, the Christian faith is apostolic. Without this defining element, it ceases to be the Christian faith. The good news of the redemption and restoration of all things in the Messiah was meant to be proclaimed to both Jew and Gentile. While the Church has made missions a complicated matter, such was not the case in the first century. The movement of sending, preaching, teaching, planting, and training was unquestioned in the Scriptures. While challenges arose over matters such as the Gentile inclusion, food distribution, team conflict, and persecution, the Church's raison d'être and modus operandi were clear.

The disciples had a deep sense of living out the eschatological fulfillment of God's mission. The last days had arrived, as confirmed with the Messiah and the outpouring of the Spirit (Acts 2:16; Joel 2:28–32). The ingathering of the Gentiles had begun in earnest (Acts 13:47; Isa. 49:6). They would glorify God for his mercy (Rom. 15:8–13), provoking Israel to jealousy until salvation arrived (Rom. 11:11–12). The next event on God's calendar was the judgment and restoration of all things. Now was the day of repentance and faith (Acts 2:20; 17:31). Now was the time to go and share the good news.

9. Paul Borthwick, *Western Christians in Global Mission: What's the Role of the North American Church?* (Downers Grove, IL: InterVarsity, 2012).

A new imagination guided the disciples. Although it was not for them to know the times and season of the restoration (Acts 1:7), they were sent into the world (John 20:21) to give priority and urgency to being a witness (Luke 24:48; Acts 1:8), preaching the gospel (Mark 13:10; 14:9; Luke 24:47), making disciples of all nations (Matt. 28:18–20). The evangelization of Jew and Gentile was emphasized throughout the Gospels. Those who came to faith in the Messiah were to be gathered into newly formed kingdom communities and taught how to live the kingdom ethic, which instructed them in their relations with God, other kingdom citizens, and those outside the kingdom. These local expressions of Christ's body were to act justly, love mercy, and walk humbly in their societies (Mic. 6:8; cf. Deut. 10:12–13). The book of Acts, Pauline and General Epistles, and the Apocalypse testify to a prioritization and urgency of certain tasks found in the apostolic imagination. The God who created was about to restore all things, but the good news was to be communicated throughout the world so that Christ might become "wisdom from God, righteousness and sanctification and redemption" to those who had not yet heard the gospel (1 Cor. 1:30).

This book is an attempt to understand the imagination that the Spirit and the Word created and shaped, which resulted in the multiplication of disciples, churches, and leaders. This imagination motivated them to fill Jerusalem with the teachings of Christ (Acts 5:28). This imagination "turned the world upside down" (Acts 17:6). This imagination resulted in our conversions. And this imagination will continue to take the Church to the nations until the parousia.

Always Reforming

Every generation must continually return to the Scriptures to make certain they are aligning themselves with "the faith that was once for all delivered to the saints" (Jude 3). Part of our journey to understand the apostolic imagination is to examine the imperatives in the Scriptures. Other times, the method is to study the indicatives and story line. Actions frequently come from thoughts and considerations. This approach is not an act in wishful thinking, an attempt to recreate ancient Middle Eastern cultures among contemporary audiences or to read contemporary rationale into the minds of the first disciples. Although there are challenges with this approach to research, it is absolutely necessary for the life and health of the Church. The desire should be to believe what they believed and to contextualize practice based on what they modeled. This is an act in wise stewardship. The claim that only orthodoxy should be imitated and not orthopraxy belittles the apostolic Church while practicing hermeneutical gymnastics. It is a detrimental inconsistency to assume that the Church is to be constantly reformed by the Word of God yet the Church's practices are to go without evaluation. Just because the Church has done what the Church has done does not mean Christians should continue doing the same. Context is critical, but not king. Sometimes a slight revision is all that is needed in contemporary expressions. Other times, a radical overhaul is necessary. Although we cannot revise the past, the Church should not sit idly by, believing that past practices must bind Christians today.

I read student course evaluations with a bit of fear and concern. I think all professors do. After a nondenominational course that addressed church-planting strategy and challenged the students to understand biblical principles and consider their application within their contexts, one student's evaluation read, "What Dr. Payne taught will never work in my denomination! This class was a waste of my time." I started asking myself: Was the class content unfaithful to the biblical text? If not, and such practices for disciple making are impossible amid contemporary ecclesiology, then what must change? The Scriptures? The denominational structure? Or should the denomination embrace pragmatism and take a cafeteria approach to the Scriptures by picking and choosing what to embrace and what to avoid? Should the denomination write off the weight of biblical truth for such ministry and give more credibility to present context built upon history? If such is the case, does this mean the cultural manifestation of ecclesiology trumps a biblical model if the latter is unable to connect with the denominational structure? Or maybe my class indeed was irrelevant and a waste of time.

On another occasion, I was in a conversation with a Southern Baptist theologian regarding a biblical expression of local churches. Without considering either the strengths or limitations of my propositions, he quickly voiced his opposition: "This will not support the Southern Baptist Convention!" No biblical rebuttal was provided. His reaction revealed the location of his heart, which was cemented into an unquestioned manifestation of a cultural preference, opposing a possibly more excellent way. When the Church is unwilling to return to the Scriptures in constant evaluation and reformation for *both* doctrine *and* practice, then the Church has revealed a most pathetic stewardship. Such a Church may be a hearer and a doer of the Word, but the doing is limited to the letter of the law of tradition and not the Spirit of mission. The weightier matters have been neglected as five billion people remain outside the body of Christ.

This book is not an attempt to argue for a return to the first century. Such is an impossibility. Neither is this work a case for disregarding historical developments and contemporary contexts and blindly attempting to apply first-century practices to the present. However, lest I be misunderstood, there is much to learn from the Bible in addition to doctrine. Principles and methods of apostolic actions can be discerned from the biblical descriptions. While some questions remain unanswered, practices should not be glossed over or discarded.

This journey into the imagination of those who are millennia removed from the present is no easy task. I expect to fall short and beg your pardon in advance. Yet the work is worth the risk. Something is not right in what the Church has come to call missions. Without certainty and definition, the Church drives through a fog, doing a multitude of activities, believing everything is fine. Actions and distractions are dangerous and often lead to taking the wrong highways and neglecting the expectations of Christ.

Some readers will conclude that this book is an attempt to send fewer people to the field (cf. Matt. 9:37; 13:38). Such is neither my purpose nor what I believe will be the outcome. It is my desire that more and more people will commit their lives to global disciple making. Neither do I write this book to question others' callings or ministries or to belittle their service. This book is not an attempt to reduce the value and importance of the multitude of ministry activities that are being conducted throughout the world. Many people have made *great* sacrifices for the kingdom. I rejoice in such actions and praise God for such servants, even those who disagree with my conclusions. It is my desire that more and more churches will become involved in sending more people to participate in caring for widows and orphans, ending human trafficking, teaching English, conducting medical clinics, feeding and sheltering the poor, developing businesses to provide sustainable jobs and make profits for communities, caring for the environment, and serving in a multitude of other ministries. In this, God is most glorified. The body of Christ is diverse and rightly manifests diversity in ministry activities at home and abroad. My concern, however, is that the Church, while involved in many important activities, may be neglecting a weightier matter.

This book is written to call the Church to accountability and more faithful service. If five billion people remain without the Savior, then an "anything goes" attitude toward the apostolic task is insufficient. The task is great, and the Master has not returned. The Church does not need a GPS but indeed has the living Word and dynamic Spirit. There is no time to be traveling in the wrong direction, believing that we will soon arrive at the proper destination.

It has been a delight to have a partnership with colleagues at Baker Academic. I am thankful for the friendship and hard work of Dave Nelson and others at Baker who collaborated with me on this project. I take full responsibility for any shortcomings of this work. As always, I greatly appreciate the prayers and encouragement that came from my family throughout this project. Sarah, Hannah, Rachel, and Joel, you are the greatest! I am so thankful for you!

PART 1

FOUNDATIONS

CHAPTER 1

What Is the Apostolic Imagination?

Imagination is a gift from God. Unfortunately, it is often referenced in relation to childish thoughts and actions. Adults make comments such as these: "He has an active imagination, thinking there are monsters under the bed." "She really uses her imagination when playing with toys." Their statements reveal the belief that fiction is the substance of one's imagination. While there is definitely an element of truth here, it is limited to a small area of what constitutes the imagination and has no relation to this book.

Imagination in the Bible is frequently connected to evil and stubbornness (Gen. 6:5; 8:21; Deut. 29:19; Jer. 3:17; 7:24; Prov. 6:18; Luke 1:51; Acts 17:29; 2 Cor. 10:5). The unregenerate heart is not concerned with the things of God. Jeremiah describes it as deceitful (Jer. 17:9). Without divine transformation, the imagination is apart from Christ and capable of nothing of eternal value for the kingdom (John 15:4–5).

However, Paul writes that believers are to "set [their] minds on things that are above, not on things that are on earth" (Col. 3:2). Every thought is to be shaped in obedience to Christ (2 Cor. 10:5). This is no command to overlook daily reality and fixate on a date when time is expected to cease. God's mission is to be executed by and through his people. Their relationship with Christ has transformed their position before God, and holy living should be the result (Col. 3:3–17). The apostolic imagination is a mind that is set on the things of Christ and his kingdom (Matt. 6:33; 11:29; 22:37; cf. Deut. 6:4). It recognizes the limitations of the world and understands people's relation to God and one another (Rom. 1:21; 8:8). It rests in the peace that only God can provide (Isa. 26:3). The apostolic imagination is a mind that is set on the Spirit (Rom. 8:6) and reflects a ministry led by that Spirit into a broken world. This imagination was found in the Great Apostle (Heb. 3:1), who did nothing from selfish ambition or conceit. Rather, Jesus Christ's imagination established a vision of God's mission and the cross (Heb. 12:2), which would reveal divine humiliation, servanthood, and exaltation so that the mission may be fulfilled (Phil. 2:3–11). The imagination assists with the application of knowledge to life and ministry. The divinely given wisdom that saturates the imagination assists with problem-solving and the ability to be a wise steward with what has been received.

During the first century, the apostolic imagination was a Spirit-transformed mindset that helped facilitate urgent and widespread gospel proclamation, disciple making, church planting, and leadership development. That imagination established a mental framework related to strategy. To use a contemporary expression, it offered the apostolic teams a "score card" to evaluate their labors in light of God's expectations. Christ had commanded the good news to be shared and believers to be taught obedience to his commands. This was the way in which the kingdom ethic would be understood and lived out among the nations. They knew the Master would soon return to evaluate their stewardship of his mission (Matt. 25:14–30; Luke 19:11–27). Just as the people of Israel were to manifest the coming kingdom of God to the world (Exod. 19:5–6; Deut. 4:4–8), now the people of God were the Messiah's called-out ones to provide a foretaste of the kingdom come. The downfall of strongholds would come about through a supernatural work that was not waged against flesh and blood (2 Cor. 10:3–5; Eph. 6:12). As the day of the Lord approached, the Spirit and Word would sanctify communities, thus transforming life, culture, and civilization. This was not a plan to create a utopia on earth, but rather to bring in the full number of Jews and Gentiles before the day in which the dwelling place of God would be found among his people (Rom. 11:25–27; Rev. 21:3). A judgment would arrive, but the Church, wherever localized, was to proclaim to the world, "If you want to see where the future is going, then look at us and join our community!"[1]

Past and Present

The apostolic imagination is connected to history and present reality. It demands returning to the first century and asking questions related to both belief *and* practice. It calls to the Church in the present to be a wise steward with available time and resources in light of God's mission. The apostolic imagination does not neglect Church life after the first century but challenges the Church in every age to evaluate the predecessors and practices. There is much to learn, but not everything learned is worth applying in the present.

Scriptures Reveal Contextual Approaches

It is a scary and humbling experience to read a review of one's book. After evaluating one of my church-planting texts, a reviewer concluded by asking, "How does Payne know how the first-century believers planted churches?" His point was that we cannot be certain of the biblical methods. Although I am still surprised by this question, given the general descriptions in Acts alone, it leads to an important point: the Scriptures were *not* written to teach us how to plant churches. In fact, the Scriptures were *not* written to teach us how to do a great deal of things. However, many principles are applied and practices described in the Bible that later generations may learn and contextualize to their settings.

Jesus modeled actions before the Twelve and sent them into communities to repeat what they saw (Matt. 10:5–8). This approach was

1. Goheen declares that this should have been Israel's attitude throughout the Old Testament. Michael W. Goheen, *A Light to the Nations: The Missional Church and the Biblical Story* (Grand Rapids: Baker Academic, 2011), 51.

used with the seventy-two (Luke 10:1–12). Their ministries comprised evangelizing, teaching, healing, and exorcisms. This model is described after the ascension throughout the book of Acts. The Pauline Epistles sometimes shed additional perspective on unmentioned details in the Acts narrative. Though the Bible is not a how-to manual, the Church is not left in the dark regarding apostolic practice. Each generation has enough details to examine and make wise applications, adjusted to their contexts. Paul clearly expected churches to imitate him in practice and thus in ways beyond merely right belief (1 Cor. 11:1–2; Phil. 3:17; 4:9; Col. 4:2–6; 1 Thess. 1:6–7; 1 Tim. 4:12–15).

History and Contexts Are Not Kings

The apostolic imagination welcomes the study of history. Outstanding kingdom work did not occur only in the first century.[2] However, the Church's activities at times have fallen short of manifesting apostolic imagination. Though the New Testament was produced in first-century cultures and contexts, such is no excuse for setting aside apostolic practices. Just as the principles of exegesis can lead to an excellent understanding of the texts for doctrine, this process provides clarity into an understanding of actions as well. It is illogical to advocate the ability to recover one without the other. The difficulty lies within the Church in any age. Will the Church always adjust and conform Christian doctrine and practices to the Word of God? This is the challenge. The apostolic imagination recognizes that a great deal of latitude is permitted for life and ministry, but continual evaluation is part of stewardship. The Church's heart and mind often embrace apostolic doctrine, but the ecclesiology often rejects apostolic practice.

Stewardship in the Present

The apostolic imagination is concerned with leveraging both historical knowledge and contemporary opportunity. Everything granted

2. For an important and outstanding historical study, see David Bosch, *Transforming Mission: Paradigm Shifts in Theology of Mission*, 20th anniversary ed. (New York: Orbis, 2011).

to the kingdom citizen is under the Church's stewardship. Time, knowledge, vocation, education, finances, influence, opportunities, gifts, interests, passions, talents, and skills are blessings given "from the Father of lights" (James 1:17) and are to be enjoyed and used for his glory in the world. The story of God's people is a story of God's blessings. He bestows good gifts for his people's delight *and* work. God blesses his people to be a blessing to others. The Church has no problem grasping the truth that blessings are for enjoyment. Yet the actions required to bless the nations are frequently neglected. Blessings were extended to Abram that "all the families of the earth shall be blessed" (Gen. 12:3). The psalmist desired God's blessings that his "way may be known on the earth," his "saving power among all nations" (Ps. 67:1–2). In every age, the Church is confronted with a kingdom stewardship intimately connected to God's mission in the world during the time in which Church members live and move and have their being. The apostolic imagination calls attention to the past and present for the advancement of the good news to the nations.

Rooted in the Mission of God

The evangelists drew attention to how Christ's advent and ministry fulfilled Old Testament prophecies pointing toward the redemption of God's people and restoration of the cosmos. Luke referenced many texts to explain first-century occurrences described in the Acts narratives. The gospel advanced as imaginations were developed and supported by Old Testament passages. The coming of the Spirit fulfilled Joel's prophecy (Acts 2:16) for global mission. Psalm 2 emboldened hearts to preach the good news even amid persecution (Acts 4:25–26). Isaiah shed light onto the apostolic labors among the Gentiles in Pisidian Antioch (Acts 13:47). Amos (9:11–12) helped resolve the conflict at the Jerusalem Council and fueled future work among the Gentiles (Acts 15:16–17). Paul referenced Isaiah (52:15) for the rationale of preaching where a foundation was not established (Rom. 15:21). The Apocalypse, with over 350 allusions to the Old Testament, exhorted churches to endure as God's mission was expressed in the world through their actions (Rev. 13:10; 14:12). Even in the face of death, they conquered Satan by "the blood of the Lamb and the word

of their testimony" (12:11) and became part of that grand multiethnic, multinational gathering around the throne (5:9–10; 7:9–10). It is
this connection to God's mission that enables Christian imagination
to have a vision of the possible in light of numerous global challenges.

Vision of the Possible

Paul's desire was to take the gospel to those who had never heard it
(Rom. 15:20). His imagination included the logical acknowledgment
of the foolishness of this task. Gentiles quickly claimed the folly of
the gospel message. Jews saw it as a scandal and an absurdity. The
message was clearly a stumbling block to many (1 Cor. 1–2). The news
of repentance toward God and faith in the Lord Jesus (Acts 20:21)
did not make sense to the heart and will unmoved by the Spirit. Yet
the apostle's imagination also included a conviction in the power of
God. Isaiah declared that God would destroy the wisdom of the wise,
and Paul held on to this truth (1 Cor. 1:19; Isa. 29:14). His imagination understood that the message proclaimed was the power of God
(1 Cor. 1:18) and that God was pleased to work through such folly
to bring the nations to himself (1 Cor. 1:21).

Paul's declaration that he and his team had the "mind of Christ"
is significant to the point at hand. He understood that the Spirit of
God alone knew the thoughts of God and that the apostolic team
had received this Spirit. What they were teaching the Church was
guaranteed to be from God (1 Cor. 2:11–13). The apostolic imagination has a vision of God's possibilities in the world because it is
intimately connected with the Spirit. This imagination does not see
a future day based merely on luck, wishful thinking, speculation,
or guesswork. Rather, the sanctified mind understands the dynamic
work of the Spirit in the world, in times past and present, and is able
to imagine a future possibility of redemption and transformation.
The following are a few possible futures that belong to the apostolic
imagination.

Salvation of others. Divine election is not only required for salvation; it is also a guarantee that redemption will occur through gospel
proclamation. From Genesis to Revelation, God's sovereign will is
displayed and actualized in time when people respond with belief (cf.

Acts 13:48). For example, the psalmist imagines a time when Egypt, Babylon, Philistia, Tyre, and Cush will know the Lord (Ps. 87:3–7). The first-century disciples were able to see a future with men and women who represented Jews, Samaritans, God-fearing proselytes, and Hellenistic Gentiles entering the kingdom of God. They knew that God sent the Son to save people from their sins (John 3:16–18). It was this perspective, as related to his own calling to salvation and apostleship, that led Paul to make significant sacrifices in order that some might be saved from the judgment to come (1 Cor. 9:22–23).

Sanctification of believers. The commission from Jesus was to make disciples, not converts. While disciple making begins with evangelism and conversion, such is the tip of the Great Commission iceberg. Growth in faith, thought, and actions is the result of healthy discipleship. The apostolic imagination expects such transformation within local contextualized expressions of the body of Christ. Summarizing the work and vision of his apostolic team, Paul wrote, "Him we proclaim, warning everyone and teaching everyone with all wisdom, that we may present everyone mature in Christ" (Col. 1:28). The Lord "gave the apostles, the prophets, the evangelists, the shepherds and teachers, to equip the saints for the work of the ministry, for building up the body of Christ . . . to matur[ity]" (Eph. 4:11–13). Whenever Paul discerned that the sanctification of the saints was not occurring in an appropriate fashion, he was quick to state his concern. After eighteen months in Corinth, he was unable to address them "as spiritual people" but had to feed them "with milk, not solid food," for they were still walking in the flesh (1 Cor. 3:1–3). The apostolic imagination recognizes the power of the Spirit and the Word in the life of a church and formulates a vision of what sanctification might bring in the near future.

Commitment of new churches to the Spirit and Word. Apostolic teams were not permanent fixtures attached to newly planted local churches. Just as Jesus did not abandon his disciples in Jerusalem but provided leaders for the new church and sent the Spirit, apostolic teams also prepared churches for the future. Paul would return and visit the congregations or send others to visit. He would work with those churches to have their own elders (Acts 14:23; Titus 1:5). Sometimes he would send letters to instruct, encourage, rebuke, exhort, and answer questions. The apostolic imagination understood that the new believers were filled with the Spirit and were to be released to live out the kingdom ethic in their contexts and beyond.

Partnership with new churches. The apostolic imagination has a future vision of partnership in the ministry. It is this mindset that sees a future in which unbelievers not only become disciples and form local churches but those churches also become partners in advancing the gospel. After Paul departed from Macedonia, the Philippian Church partnered with him in his apostolic work in other locations (Phil. 4:15). Paul asked the Colossians to pray for his team as they preached the gospel (Col. 4:3). Though he had not yet met the Roman Church, his letter sought their assistance as he made plans to work in Spain (Rom. 15:24). The New Testament letters acknowledge numerous flaws in the first-century churches, yet there is no evidence of paternalism in the relationship between the apostolic teams and the churches. Even the language of spiritual fathers and children was not used to represent the restrictive elements found in later Church history, but to demonstrate the community found within the family of God.

Multiethnic Church around the throne. Racial and ethnic prejudices were widespread in the first century. Jews and Samaritans avoided one another (John 4:9). Devout Jews refrained from certain interactions with Gentiles (Acts 11:3; Gal. 2:11–14). God's election of Israel was never to exclude the nations from his shalom. Rather, it was the means by which the nations would come to know God. A "mixed multitude" fled Egypt along with the Hebrews (Exod. 12:38). Torah welcomed Gentiles into the community of Israel (Exod. 12:49; Lev. 19:34). Rahab and Ruth were examples of a historical incorporation of Gentiles (Josh. 6:17; Ruth 1:16). Solomon dedicated the temple with a prayer that Gentiles would come to the God of Israel and fear him (1 Kings 8:41–43, 59–60). In what has been called "one of the clearest Old Testament statements on the theme of missionary outreach," Isaiah prophesies that the Lord will gather the nations to himself (Isa. 66:18–23).[3] James (the brother of Jesus) drew attention

---

3. Andreas J. Köstenberger and Peter T. O'Brien, *Salvation to the Ends of the Earth: A Biblical Theology of Mission* (Downers Grove, IL: InterVarsity, 2001), 52.

to Amos's prophecy that Gentiles would be included in the "tent of David" (Acts 15:16; Amos 9:11–12). Paul recognized that the Jew and Gentile relationship with God and one another was a mystery revealed in Christ as he removed "the dividing wall of hostility" to create one fellowship (Eph. 2:14–16). With this Old Testament backdrop, one wonders if John was surprised to view the diversity around the throne (Rev. 7:9).

Elders overseeing churches. The local expressions of the universal body of Christ came into existence as the Church engaged in apostolic activities. What began with Jesus in Jerusalem resulted in the increase of churches across the Roman Empire. It was out of a disciple-making movement that these churches were planted. The early believers carried an imagination with them that saw unbelievers coming to faith, being gathered as local churches, and developing their own pastoral leadership. These communities of saints, living and expressing the gospel in their locales and beyond, were not governed by a heavy hand from afar. Jerusalem or Antioch did not micromanage their ministries. The apostolic teams served these groups in such a way that when they departed to begin work elsewhere, the churches could continue with the stewardship they had received.

Gospel spreading rapidly and with honor. The apostolic imagination understood the gospel as capable of rapid dissemination across a people. Throughout Acts, Luke periodically pauses and offers a summary of the widespread distribution of the message and the multiplication of disciples (Acts 2:41, 47; 4:4; 5:14; 6:7; 9:31; 16:5; 19:20). Paul was encouraged by the example of the Thessalonians, how "the word of the Lord sounded forth from" them throughout Macedonia and Achaia (1 Thess. 1:8). He later requested their prayers so that, through the apostolic team, "the word of the Lord may speed ahead and be honored, as happened among" them (2 Thess. 3:1). The disciples' imagination included a vision of a global community of believers, made possible through the proclamation of the gospel along the highways and hedges of societies. This vision was imbued with an urgency since the anticipated time was short. Even though opponents would work to slow and stop the communication, gospel advance continued in spite of threats (Acts 4:19–20), imprisonments (16:16–34; 28:31; Phil. 1:12), and violence (Acts 11:19–21; 12:1–24).

Model imitated and reproduced. The apostolic imagination sees beyond self to the involvement of new believers in kingdom work. The apostles' work accomplished on the frontier did not reflect well-established ministries of churches that had been in existence for years. What existed in microcosm within the apostolic team was to be magnified in the local church. Development would come with time. Apostolic teams did not come into a new community with complexity, but rather with a simple example that could be imitated. They did not bring highly detailed evangelism and justice ministries that would take years for new believers to understand and facilitate. It was a simplicity of method, empowered by the Spirit, that Paul attributed to the gospel sounding forth from Thessalonica. He reminded them that they knew "what kind of men we proved to be among you for your sake. And you became imitators of us and of the Lord" (1 Thess. 1:5–6). In the imagination that transforms the Church's mission, not everything ends with apostolic teams. This perspective can see beyond the present to a near future when new believers and young churches are able to manifest wise stewardship and carry out the ministry of Christ. Such imagination recognizes that these churches are able to carry the gospel farther and faster within their contexts than the outside teams. These churches are able to stand for justice and show mercy within their communities in more relevant ways than the itinerant workers.

Motives

Before concluding this chapter, it is necessary to inquire about the motives connected to the early imagination that moved the Church beyond local ministry in Jerusalem, Antioch, Thessalonica, and other cities.[4] The initial believers operated from a trinitarian drive. God is both transcendent and immanent. He is "a gracious God and merciful, slow to anger and abounding in steadfast love" (Jon. 4:2). He loved so much that he sent the Son to save people. Jesus humbled himself and gave his life as an atonement for sin, so that the unrighteous

---

4. Johannes Verkuyl's work was most helpful in crafting this section. I do not address all the motives he provided, yet I do adapt portions from his classic work *Contemporary Missiology: An Introduction* (Grand Rapids: Eerdmans, 1978), 163–75.

may become righteous (2 Cor. 5:21). Christ had sent his people into the world to represent him and replicate what he modeled before them. The Spirit was sent as a seal of God's confirmation and to empower his people for global witness. The following is not a mutually exclusive or exhaustive list, but rather a general representation of those early motives.

Doxology. Johannes Verkuyl writes, "This motive of *gloria Deo* [glory to God] is not only present in virtually every theoretical treatment of the motives for mission, but it also inspired the life and work of many missionaries themselves who during the centuries have participated in the missionary enterprise."[5] The early believers were motivated to see God's glory among the nations. Throughout the Old Testament, God frequently acted so that the nations would know he is the true God (Exod. 9:14, 16; Deut. 4:6–8; Hab. 2:14; Mal. 1:11). Their imagination was filled with prophecies of the kingdom established on the earth, with the nations streaming to Zion (Mic. 4:1–3). The psalmist's words echoed in their minds: "Let the peoples praise you, O God; let all the peoples praise you!" (Ps. 67:3, 5). "Let everything that has breath praise the LORD!" (Ps. 150:6). This grand view was likely behind the desires that "every knee should bow" before Jesus and "every tongue confess" him as "Lord, to the glory of God the Father" (Phil. 2:10–11; cf. 1 Pet. 4:11).

Gratitude. Michael Green described gratitude as the most significant motivator for the first disciples.[6] They had been called to Christ and had been entrusted with "the ministry of reconciliation" (2 Cor. 5:18). Deeply moved by their conversion experiences, they took the gospel to the nations.

Obedience. Jesus told his disciples that they would show their love for him by obeying his commands (John 14:15; cf. 1 John 2:3). As obedient disciples, they were not to be "conformed to the passions" of their "former ignorance" (1 Pet. 1:14) but were to comply with Jesus's expectations. John rejoiced when he heard of believers "walking in the truth," just as the apostles had been commanded by the Father (2 John 4). The Matthean Great Commission involved Jesus's

---

5. Verkuyl, *Contemporary Missiology*, 165.
6. Michael Green, *Evangelism in the Early Church* (Grand Rapids: Eerdmans, 1970), 236–43.

disciples teaching new disciples to obey all that Jesus commanded (Matt. 28:20). As the Twelve extended the gospel and taught others, they were part of what would become a cyclical process. The new disciples would be taught the commands of Christ related to making disciples and were expected to obey, showing that obedience with their actions.

Obedience was often connected with calling. Paul frequently introduced his letters by mentioning his calling to be an apostle (e.g., Rom. 1:1; 1 Cor. 1:1). He recognized that his apostolic task came with expectations (1 Cor. 1:17). These responsibilities were critical in bringing about "the obedience of faith . . . among all the nations" (Rom. 1:5; 15:17–18). Paul identified his ministry as "a stewardship" (1 Cor. 9:17), which compelled him to preach the good news to both Jews and Gentiles (1 Cor. 9:16–19).

Parousia and judgment. The biblical worldview was that time moved in a linear direction with beginning and ending points. Though the Old Testament vision of the last days had a hard and definite terminus immediately followed by the restoration of all things (Joel 2:28–32), New Testament revelation provided a more detailed perspective. The present age and the age to come blended together in history. The initial coming of Christ and the Spirit transitioned the world into the last days. The kingdom was already, but not yet (Matt. 6:10). Revealing an Old Testament eschatology, prior to the ascension, the disciples asked Jesus if he was going to "restore the kingdom to Israel" (Acts 1:6). His response was that they should not be concerned with the timing; instead, they were to bear witness to him throughout the world. The end was yet to come for the gospel had not been proclaimed to all nations (Matt. 24:14; Mark 13:10; 14:9).

The parousia became imminent *and* was intimately connected to the advancement of the gospel. Jesus's delay did not become an excuse for going to the nations but was a manifestation of God's patience toward the unrepentant (2 Pet. 3:8–10). David Bosch was correct in writing, "It is not true that, in the early church, mission gradually *replaced* the expectation of the end. Rather, mission was, in itself, an eschatological event."[7] David's fallen tent had to be rebuilt with

---

7. Bosch, *Transforming Mission*, 42.

Jew and Gentile before "the kingdom of the world" became "the kingdom of [God]" (Rev. 11:15). The enemies of Christ would eventually become his footstool (Ps. 110:1); for now the Church was to be significantly involved in the redemption and restoration of all things. The disciples believed that the day of salvation had arrived for all. Repentance and confession of Christ was the proper response to the good news of the kingdom, protecting believers from the judgment (Acts 2:38; 16:30–34; 20:21). Life was like a mist that would quickly vanish (James 4:14). The day of the Lord would come like a thief at night (1 Thess. 5:2).

A holy respect for God motivated the first-century churches. The judgment and wrath of God were shown numerous times throughout the Old Testament. God could "destroy both body and soul in hell" (Matt. 10:28). The disciples recognized God's wrath as an awesomely terrible thing against ungodliness (Rom. 1:18). They also knew that God would judge his people, and it would be "a fearful thing to fall into the hands of the living God" (Heb. 10:30–31). Everyone was to appear before the judgment seat of Christ to give an account of their actions. This future image, impressed on the apostolic imagination, motivated the early disciples to go and sacrifice themselves to "persuade others" to follow Jesus (2 Cor. 5:10–11).

Affection. Love, mercy, and compassion also fueled the drive to reach the nations. The disciples understood what it meant to be in the kingdom of darkness and then transferred into the kingdom of God (Eph. 2:1–10; Col. 1:13). Knowing that they were once children of disobedience and that their neighbors remained in that state, early Christians were no doubt motivated to action.

Great affection for new believers also motivated the early disciples to develop them into healthy churches. Paul's reflections on his time in Thessalonica reveal that he and his team "were ready to share with you not only the gospel of God but also our own selves, because you had become very dear to us" (1 Thess. 2:8). He wrote to the Philippians of his love and longing for them, describing them as "my beloved" (Phil. 4:1).

Blessings. Blessings came to those who walked faithfully with God. If the sinful parents of this age knew how to give good gifts to their children, then God was clearly able to give immeasurably greater gifts to those who asked him (Matt. 7:7–11; cf. Eph. 3:20). The citizens of the kingdom were a blessed people (Matt. 5:3–12). This was especially true in relation to the Church's apostolic work. After describing his willingness to make great sacrifices to save others, Paul declared, "I do it all for the sake of the gospel, that I may share with them in its blessings" (1 Cor. 9:23). Even after threats and abuse, the apostles found joy that they were able to suffer for Christ (Acts 5:40–42). The Church was engaged in disciple-making efforts and took delight and satisfaction in knowing that those efforts were in partnership with the God of creation. The early Christians were blessed to be living during a time that the prophets foresaw and engaged in divine actions that would usher in the new heaven and the new earth.

QUESTIONS TO CONSIDER

1. How would you summarize the apostolic imagination in your own words?
2. What is the value of studying the Church's history in relation to the global work of the Church in the present?
3. Which of the motives addressed in this chapter are most pronounced in your life? What are the limitations of being motivated by only one motivator?

CHAPTER 2

Challenges to the Imagination

The Church faces several challenges to the development of an apostolic imagination. Alan Hirsch argues that the Church should rediscover the "forgotten ways" that prevailed in the early dynamic disciple-making movements.[1] The Church's original "Apostolic Genius" was not limited to the first century. The problem is a forgotten past. Hirsch writes, "Apostolic Genius (the primal missional potencies of the gospel and of God's people) lies dormant in

---

1. Hirsch has written extensively on the topic of apostolic thought and functions. He has been involved in developing the influential APEST model for ministry based on Eph. 4:11–12, where the acrostic stands for *a*postle, *p*rophet, *e*vangelist, *s*hepherd, and *t*eacher. Hirsch is a strong advocate for the presence of each of these roles in the Church today. For example, see Michael Frost and Alan Hirsch, *The Shaping of Things to Come: Innovation and Mission for the 21st Century Church* (Peabody, MA: Hendrickson, 2003); Alan Hirsch, *The Forgotten Ways: Reactivating the Missional Church* (Grand Rapids: Brazos, 2006); Alan Hirsch and Dave Ferguson, *On the Verge: A Journey into the Apostolic Future of the Church* (Grand Rapids: Zondervan, 2011); and Alan Hirsch and Tim Catchim, *The Permanent Revolution: Apostolic Imagination and Practice for the 21st Century Church* (San Francisco: Jossey-Bass, 2012). For another early twenty-first-century perspective on the apostolic function, similar to Hirsch's, see Neil Cole, *Organic Church: Growing Faith Where Life Happens* (San Francisco: Jossey-Bass, 2005).

you, me, and every local church that seeks to follow Jesus faithfully in any time. We have quite simply forgotten how to access and trigger it."[2] Other scholars argue that such a return is not needed or even impossible. Two thousand years of history and contemporary contexts should be allowed to have much bearing on expressions of mission. Bosch writes, "I suggest, then, that the solution to the problem presented by the present failure of nerve does not lie in a simple return to an earlier missionary consciousness and practice. Clinging to yesterday's images provides solace, but little else."[3]

While large segments of the Church have forgotten this history and do not realize that certain matters are untranslatable, there are many challenges to the development and maintenance of the apostolic imagination. In this chapter, I attempt to address ten of those barriers.[4] Though they are complex in nature and often include a long history, recognizing the challenges is a necessary first step toward a more excellent way.

Mission and Missions

Since the twentieth century, there has been no shortage of literature on the mission of God.[5] A great deal of attention has been given to addressing the distinction between the words *mission* and *missions*. Bosch writes: "Attempts to define mission are of recent vintage. The

2. Hirsch, *The Forgotten Ways*, 22.

3. David Bosch, *Transforming Mission: Paradigm Shifts in Theology of Mission*, 20th anniversary ed. (New York: Orbis, 2011) 7.

4. In 2019, I wrote an article in which I addressed five "currents of change" that have brought the Church to a point in history where anything the Church does is considered missions. Portions of that article have been adapted for this chapter. For the original work, see J. D. Payne, "Currents of Change: How Did Everything Become Missions?," *Mission Frontiers* 41, no. 6 (November–December 2019): 28–31 (used with permission). The article was also included as a chapter in *Conversations on When Everything Is Missions: Rediscovering the Mission of the Church*, ed. Denny Spitters and Matthew Ellison (n.p.: Bottom Line Media, 2020), 11–19.

5. A couple of recent works with extensive citations and bibliographies related to the mission of God include Christopher J. H. Wright, *The Mission of God: Unlocking the Bible's Grand Narrative* (Downers Grove, IL: IVP Academic, 2006); and Mike Barnett, ed., *Discovering the Mission of God: Best Missional Practices for the 21st Century* (Downers Grove, IL: IVP Academic, 2012).

early Christian church undertook no such attempts—at least not consciously. . . . More recently, however, it has become necessary to design definitions of mission in a more conscious and explicit manner. Since the nineteenth century such attempts have been legion."[6]

Contemporary discussions of mission began with the work of Karl Barth, yet in the 1930s Karl Hartenstein was the one who began using the term *missio Dei* (mission of God) to address the eternal Trinity's mission, distinct from a mission developed by the Church. The International Missionary Council held in Willingen, Germany, in 1952 was a significant turning point in mission thinking. Mission moved from an ecclesiocentric understanding to a theocentric understanding in the minds of many theologians and missiologists. Mission had been viewed as belonging to the Church, with the Church and/ or world establishing the agenda. Willingen emphasized the Trinity as the source of mission: the Church should engage in mission by witness in the world during the last days. Mission involved a wide range of activities, not a narrow few. Greatly influenced by the work of Johannes Hoekendijk (1912–75), ecumenical voices by the 1960s argued that the locus of God's activity is in the world rather than in the Church.[7] Hoekendijk criticized an ecclesiocentric approach to mission and insisted that the Church is of secondary importance for the *missio Dei*, which is about the kingdom of God in the world and the establishment of shalom through service, fellowship, and preaching. God's primary concern is with the world. For Hoekendijk, everything is mission.[8] The scholarship of Johannes Blauw, Georg Vicedom, and Gerald H. Anderson also resulted in important works calling the Church to recognize that mission belongs to God.[9] As

6. Bosch, *Transforming Mission*, 523. The twentieth century saw several large global ecumenical and evangelical gatherings attempting to address definitions of mission.

7. Rodger C. Bassham, *Mission Theology, 1948–1975: Years of Worldwide Creative Tension—Ecumenical, Evangelical, and Roman Catholic* (Pasadena, CA: William Carey Library, 1979), 33–34.

8. Henning Wrogemann has written an outstanding work on mission theologies. Here I am indebted to his research on Hoekendijk. Henning Wrogemann, *Theologies of Mission*, trans. Karl E. Böhmer (Downers Grove, IL: IVP Academic, 2018), 73–86.

9. Gerald H. Anderson, ed., *The Theology of the Christian Mission* (Nashville: Abingdon, 1961); Johannes Blauw, *The Missionary Nature of the Church: A Survey of the Biblical Theology of Mission* (London: Lutterworth, 1962); Georg F. Vicedom,

Vicedom notes, "God becomes not only the Sender but simultane-
ously the One who is sent."[10] For him, the goal of *missio Dei* is discipleship and not merely "shalomatization of the world."[11] Mission
originates within and extends from God,[12] who enters into his world
and calls the Church to engage in the task.

This understanding of God's mission is applied to the Church
yet further distinguished from the term *missions*. A. Scott Moreau,
Gary R. Corwin, and Gary B. McGee observe that, on the one hand,
"*missions* has been relegated to the specific work of the church and
agencies," but on the other hand, "*mission* is broader, referring to
everything the church is doing that points toward the Kingdom of
God."[13] Since God's mission is broad and involves redemption and
restoration of all things, the Church must engage in God's mission
through a wide array of activities (i.e., missions).

This understanding has often failed to take into consideration and
address two important matters. First, many activities in the Scriptures
are exclusively reserved for God. Justification, sanctification, reconciliation, glorification, and the restoration of creation are just a few
matters that extend well beyond the Church's jurisdiction. Second, it
is true that mission applied to the Church requires diversity. Indeed,
missions are expressed through the Church in a variety of means.
Engaging in God's mission includes caring for those with physical
needs and planting churches; it involves social justice and evangelism.
But here is the point of confusion.

The Church has wrongly assumed that since God's mission and
the Church's missions are wide and diverse, then nothing is to be
prioritized. All activities are equal in God's eyes, and emphasis is not
to be placed on any aspect of the Church's work. An examination

---

The Mission of God: An Introduction to a Theology of Mission (St. Louis: Concordia, 1965).

10. Vicedom, *The Mission of God*, 7.

11. Wrogemann, *Theologies of Mission*, 89–91.

12. Wrogemann reports that, at Willingen, it was understood that mission "un-
folded purely on the basis of God's being." Wrogemann, *Theologies of Mission*, 68.

13. A. Scott Moreau, Gary R. Corwin, and Gary B. McGee, *Introducing World
Missions: A Biblical, Historical, and Practical Survey*, 2nd ed. (Grand Rapids: Baker
Academic, 2015), 17. Wrogemann notes that by the sixth world missionary conference
in Accra, Ghana (1958), "mission was being defined more and more comprehensively."
Wrogemann, *Theologies of Mission*, 72.

of the New Testament, however, reveals specific attention given to *apostolic* labors. An equivalence of actions was not found in the first-century Church. A prioritization was the expectation.

Language and Definition

Closely related to the aforementioned challenge is the modern use of the language of mission. Andreas J. Köstenberger is correct in writing, "Any understanding of a *biblical* theology of mission must derive its contours from the biblical material itself rather than being submerged by extrabiblical definitions."[14] But what if the modern language of mission is not found in the Bible? Chapter 5 will present more on the history of missional language, reviewing modern expressions. As André Seumois reports, Ignatius of Loyola was using variations of the term *missions* in 1540, applying the term to the Jesuits.[15] The language of *mission* and *missions* is used in Ignatius's *The Constitutions of the Society of Jesus*, which was first approved by the first General Congregation in 1558, with such terminology referring to being sent into the world "for the greater glory of God and the good of souls, whether among the faithful or unbelievers."[16] While God's glory may have been part of the motivation behind such kingdom endeavors, a great deal of Catholic (and eventually Protestant) missionary activities became closely connected with European military and colonial expansion. Christianization and civilization were often two interrelated goals for both Church and country. The sacred and the secular often had an intimate union, which resulted in confusion.

Whenever the Church lacks exegetical support for theology, then extrabiblical terms can result in concepts with a variety of meanings. Since there is no Hebrew or Greek word for *mission, missions,* or

14. Andreas J. Köstenberger, "The Place of Mission in New Testament Theology: An Attempt to Determine the Significance of Mission within the Scope of the New Testament's Message as a Whole," *Missiology* 27, no. 3 (July 1999): 357.

15. André Seumois, *Théologie missionnaire: Délimitation de la fonction mission-naire de l'Église* (Rome: Bureau de Presse O.M.I., 1973), 9.

16. John W. Padberg, ed., *The Constitutions of the Society of Jesus and Their Complementary Norms: A Complete English Translation of the Official Latin Texts* (St. Louis: Institute of Jesuit Sources, 1996), 281.

missionary, who is to say that any definition is more accurate than another one?[17] Church cultures and contexts become most important as defining factors of mission. Given this relativistic understanding, Bosch writes that "mission remains undefinable; it should never be incarcerated in the narrow confines of our own predilections. The most we can hope for is to formulate some *approximations* of what mission is all about."[18] Michael W. Stroope describes *mission* as a "broad river in which there is space for many usages and meanings" and considers *mission* to be a term "quite elastic in its meaning."[19] Such fluidity exists partially due to meaning and activity being socially constructed in the moment or developed into a paradigm across an epoch.

A great deal of the present reality has been described in Bosch's work *Transforming Mission: Paradigm Shifts in Theology of Mission.*[20] According to Bosch, the historical-contextual situation is the key to a proper understanding of mission. Though he claims a high view of the Scriptures and calls for their importance in mission theology, the influence of higher critical scholarship is found throughout his work. While he denies a relativistic approach to mission, the freedom he grants to culture over revelation is troubling. For Bosch, mission evolves with the contextual factors of the present.[21] The historical gap is so great that the Church is unable to return to the Scriptures to determine what should be done currently. He writes: "The Bible is not to be treated as a storehouse of truths on which we can draw at random. There are no immutable and objectively correct 'laws of mission' to

17. Some will say there is no biblical word *Trinity* either. However, a major difference is that the Church has a definitive understanding of the Trinity. Any definition that differs from this orthodox statement is considered heterodox. The Church has no equivalent standard for *missions* or *missionary*.

18. David J. Bosch, *Transforming Mission*, 9.

19. Michael W. Stroope, *Transcending Mission: The Eclipse of a Modern Tradition* (Downers Grove, IL: IVP Academic, 2017), 4.

20. Vanhoozer listed Bosch's work as one of five "essential theology books of the past 25 years." Kevin J. Vanhoozer, "5 Picks," *Christian Century*, October 3, 2010, https://www.christiancentury.org/reviews/2010-09/kevin-j-vanhoozer-5-picks. In his extensive review, James A. Scherer described the work as Bosch's "*magnum opus*" and "an indispensable tool" for the missions community. James A. Scherer, "Transforming Mission: Paradigm Shifts in Mission Theology; A Review Article Commemorating an Important Missiological Event," *Missiology* 19, no. 2 (April 1991): 153–60, here 153, 159.

21. Bosch, *Transforming Mission*, 511.

which exegesis of Scripture gives us access and which provide us with blueprints we can apply in every situation. Our missionary practice is not performed in unbroken continuity with the biblical witness; it is an altogether ambivalent enterprise executed in the context of tension between divine providence and human confusion."[22]

For example, any attempt to understand the mind of the apostle Paul and expect any methodological continuity "is a task fraught with danger." The Church is "tempted to draw hasty conclusions and apply these to our contemporary situation, forgetting that Paul developed his missionary theology and strategy in a very specific context." Bosch's solution to this problem is that the reader should allow Paul to "'fertilize' our imagination and, in dependence on the guidance of the Holy Spirit, to prolong, in a creative way, the logic of Paul's theology and mission amid historical circumstances that are in many respects very different from his."[23] According to Bosch, some of the biblical writers contradict one another regarding the notion of mission. Instead of each providing a facet of a multifaceted gem regarding mission, they are simply in disagreement. Just as Matthew differs from Paul, the medieval Roman Catholic missionary paradigm differs from the post-Enlightenment Church. The present becomes the determining factor for definition and practice. Within each contemporary context, the Church provides the hermeneutic by which to understand Jesus and mission.[24]

However, in an almost contradictory fashion, Bosch observes that even though Paul was a unique person with a specific context, the contemporary reader should still seek to understand what Paul's Letters mean today. The modern task is to "bridge the gap between the then and the now." After all, Bosch writes, Paul projected "his vision and image of mission to his fellow-workers and to the churches."[25]

Such esoteric, and even contradictory, writing creates a quagmire. Should the Church trust the Scriptures for missionary practice? How can the Church understand not only missionary activity in the first century, but also discover what, if anything, is translatable into the

22. Bosch, *Transforming Mission*, 9.
23. Bosch, *Transforming Mission*, 170.
24. Bosch, *Transforming Mission*, 22.
25. Bosch, *Transforming Mission*, 171.

present? According to Bosch, certain biblical aspects are not applicable while other portions are. His method of dividing the former
from the latter is unclear. While the Church can and should learn
from the New Testament (somehow), the Church's context is king for
understanding language and definitions. The first century is unlike
the fifth, fifteenth, or twenty-first; therefore, mission understanding
and practice will evolve.[26]

In 2008, for example, I attended a breakout session of the Evangelical Missiological Society to hear Ralph D. Winter (1924–2009)
present a paper. Winter, known for his pioneering work on mission
to unreached peoples and emphasis on cross-cultural evangelization,
was one of the most influential missiologists in the late twentieth
century. I was eager to hear this living legend for the first time. To
my surprise, along with several others in the room, Winter spent his
time addressing the need to destroy the works of the devil as part of
the mission of the Church.[27] This destruction was primarily defined
in terms of eradicating disease from humans caused by "evil working
parasites." He writes the following in the widely distributed *Perspectives on the World Christian Movement*, used as part of the Perspectives course that has been taught to over 230,000 people since 1974:[28]
"But, is the total eradication of evil microbes part of, and essential
to, the task of winning souls and reaching unreached peoples? Is *the
mission of the Kingdom* that broad? If so, is it not ominous that
neither our sermons nor conventional missiology seriously reflect
this dimension of the task? Do we know what it means to 'destroy
the works of the devil'? Is that a mission frontier?"[29]

26. In his review of Bosch's book, William J. Nottingham wrote, "Paradigms of
mission are not equally worthy, and some must be judged self-serving and false or even
demonic." Wise words. Just because the Church is able to do something does not mean
that such liberty should be exercised. Everything is not a reflection of wise kingdom
stewardship. William J. Nottingham, review of *Transforming Mission: Shifts in Theology
of Mission*, by David J. Bosch, *Mid-Stream* 33, no. 1 (January 1994): 125–30, here 128.

27. Robin Dale Hadaway was also in the room that day and briefly reflected on his
experience in *A Survey of World Missions* (Nashville: B&H Academic, 2020), 277.

28. From https://www.perspectives.org/About#/HTML/our_history_and_min
istry_vision.htm.

29. Ralph D. Winter, "The Mission of the Kingdom," *Perspectives on the World
Christian Movement: A Reader,* ed. Ralph D. Winter and Steven C. Hawthorne, 4th
ed. (Pasadena, CA: William Carey Library, 2009), 572–73, here 573.

Or, consider the field of ecology. Scholars have recently drawn attention to the relation of environmental issues and the work of the Church. Allan Effa refers to this as the "Greening of Mission."[30] Neil Darragh represents the perspective of a growing number of people that "God loves all of creation and that the mission of the Christian community is not restricted to human beings alone. Eco-missiology, a missiology that is concerned with the whole of creation insofar as human beings [*sic*] impact upon it, has begun to make a shift from a purely human-centered to Earth-centered mission. Eco-missiology is about the part that human beings may play in the reconciliation, characterized by interdependence, among all of God's creation."[31]

In his concern for a better environment, Darragh notes that missionaries are commonly "associated with over-consumers," and therefore "the integrity of mission comes further under question." His solution? Missionaries need to share a message that involves the value of God's creation and the use of resources and reduction of waste. A failure of the Church to shift from a human-centered approach to an earth-centered mission "constitutes the most significant hazard to the integrity of Christian mission today."[32]

In his highly influential work *The Mission of God: Unlocking the Bible's Grand Narrative*, Christopher J. H. Wright believes that the ecological sphere has implications for the Church and must be included in understanding the mission of God. Though Wright's perspective is not as extreme as Darragh's, he declares that creation care must be included in the Church's mission: "Those Christians who have responded to God's call to serve him through serving his non-human creatures in ecological projects are engaged in a specialized

30. Allan Effa, "The Greening of Mission," *International Bulletin of Missionary Research* 32, no. 4 (October 2008): 171–76.

31. Neil Darragh, "Hazardous Missions and Shifting Frameworks," *Missiology* 38, no. 3 (July 2010): 271–80, here 278. Ross Langmead describes "ecomissiology" as "an approach to mission that sees the mission of God in terms of reconciliation at all levels," which could be called "missionary earthkeeping." Ross Langmead, "Ecomissiology," *Missiology* 30, no. 4 (October 2002): 505–18. J. Andrew Kirk included a section on environmental care in his book *What Is Mission? Theological Explorations* (Minneapolis: Fortress, 2000), 164–83.

32. Darragh, "Hazardous Missions," 278.

form of mission that has its rightful plane within the broad framework of all that God's mission has as its goal."[33]

Consider a Barna Group study of the views of US Christians regarding missionary service. Their findings revealed that 29 percent of younger Christians (18–34 years old) and 23 percent of older Christians "say a missionary and 'someone else who does work to fight poverty and injustice' are *very similar.*" Almost half of younger Christians (47%) want missionaries to save lives. This service expectation exceeded their other expectations of missionaries being involved in evangelism (44%) and discipleship (40%).[34]

In the year 2000, J. Andrew Kirk summarized the inevitable result of unclear language and definitions: "Slowly, and somewhat painfully, mission is becoming uncoupled from its association with the previous Western movement of evangelism and church planting and being redefined to cover the calling of the Church, at every level and in every place, to be part of God's mission in the world."[35] What Kirk observed then has become reality now. Mission, and missions, is no longer defined in such narrow terms: it includes a great deal of diversity and actions.

Theological Shifts

Theological shifts in the eighteenth through twentieth centuries moved the Church away from historic orthodox teachings regarding inspiration, theology proper, Christology, and personal and cosmic eschatology, to mention a few areas. The Bible was subjected to critical study, often with an anti-supernatural bias. Ethical monotheism was viewed as the result of societal evolution. Jesus's life became a moral example to follow, while the significance of his penal-substitutionary

33. Christopher J. H. Wright, *The Mission of God: Unlocking the Bible's Grand Narrative* (Downers Grove, IL: IVP Academic, 2006), 416.

34. Barna Group, *The Future of Missions: 10 Questions about Global Ministry the Church Must Answer with the Next Generation* (n.p., 2020), 21–22, 44. These numbers reflect "engaged Christians," defined as those who attend a Protestant Church at least once a month, involved in ways beyond just attending services, have a commitment to Christ, and say their faith is very important in their lives (108).

35. J. Andrew Kirk, *What Is Mission? Theological Explorations* (Minneapolis: Fortress, 2000), 24.

atonement and honor/shame removal act was relegated to the dustbin in some circles. Sin, judgment, and hell were seen as psychological burdens, to be discarded as quickly as possible.

During this period, pluralism—and inclusivism—was growing in influence. For some, humanity became the center of mission. The Church, Jesus, and God existed for the improvement of society. Missionary activities were to improve quality of life but should "never violate the sanctity of human personality."[36] Religions became equals.

The publication of William Ernest Hocking's *Re-thinking Missions* revealed how humanism and liberal theology have influenced missionary thought and practice in certain circles: "If the conception of hell changes, if attention is drawn away from the fear of God's punitive justice in everlasting torment of the unsaved, to happier conceptions of destiny, if there is a shift of concern from other-worldly issues to the problems of sin and suffering in the present life, these changes will immediately alter that view of the perils of the soul which gave to the original motive of Protestant missions much of its poignant urgency. Generally speaking, these changes have occurred."[37]

Many mission leaders spoke against liberal and neoorthodox theologies; yet over time, aspects of such theological systems began to trickle down from the academy and influence local churches and mission agencies. Conversionistic missiology and the exclusivity of Christ were sometimes avoided for more palatable practices that encouraged more people to participate in mission activities; many believed it would be possible to witness through presence alone. The value of the Church's apostolic labors diminished significantly.

Evangelism and Social Justice

The evangelism and social justice debate has had a long history in the twentieth and twenty-first centuries. In 1931, Charles R. Watson

36. R. Pierce Beaver, "North American Thought on the Fundamental Principles of Missions during the Twentieth Century," *Church History* 21, no. 4 (December 1952): 352.

37. William Ernest Hocking, *Re-thinking Missions: A Laymen's Inquiry after One Hundred Years* (New York: Harper & Brothers, 1938), 19.

gave an address to a US audience in which he challenged listeners to a new consideration of missions that moved away from evangelization: "In approaching a non-Christian people is it not the part of wisdom to approach them along the line of their conscious needs? Has the Christian movement no helping hand to offer, no message of guidance, no service to render, along these and other lines? Do we not need to rethink missions in regard to the scope of the movement?"[38]

This challenge was felt even as recently as 2010 during the Third Lausanne Congress on World Evangelization. During a plenary session, John Piper acknowledged the tension and asked, "Could Lausanne say? Could the Global Church say this: 'For Christ's sake, we Christians care about all suffering, especially eternal suffering'?"[39]

The world has always been filled with areas of significant physical and spiritual need. Christians have always been moved with the desire to take bandages and the gospel to the world. Such is the right way of the kingdom citizen. However, faced with such global needs, the Church does not naturally gravitate toward gospel proclamation, but drifts away from it and toward care for those who suffer on a physical level. Eyes and hearts are often more in tune with the temporal than the eternal. Both should be a concern, but both are not equivalent.

John Stott brought much attention to these issues among evangelicals. However, the language found in a section of his influential book *Christian Mission in the Modern World* creates an opportunity for the Church to neglect gospel proclamation due to the ubiquitous realities of suffering and social injustices:

> To see need and to possess the remedy compels love to act, and whether the action will be evangelistic or social, or indeed political, depends on what we "see" and what we "have."
>
> This does not mean that words and works, evangelism and social action, are such inseparable partners that all of us must engage in both all the time. Situations vary, and so do Christian callings. As for situations, there will be times when a person's eternal destiny is the most

---

38. Charles R. Watson, "Rethinking Missions," *International Review of Mission* 21, no. 1 (January 1932): 106–18, here 110.

39. Bible Exposition: Ephesians 3—John Piper (Part 2)—Cape Town 2010, https://www.youtube.com/watch?v=1a5V1O4M4rU.

urgent consideration, for we must not forget that men without Christ are perishing. But there will certainly be other times when a person's material need is so pressing that he would not be able to hear the gospel if we shared it with him. . . . If our enemy is hungry, our biblical mandate is not to evangelize him but to feed him (Romans 12:20)![40]

Such language communicates that there are *times* when eternal matters are not ultimate. In his noble attempt to draw attention to the truth that the pain of suffering can rightly hinder one from hearing the gospel and thus demands immediate social action, Stott opened a door for missions to avoid identifying with proclamation. I cannot help but think that many people have taken such words and thoughts to an unhealthy end—one unintended by Stott. Instead of Christians expecting the "other times" to be *exceptional*, when urgent relief is necessary to save a life, the Church has come to view these times as *expectations* and has adjusted strategy and methods to support a multitude of activities, often at the expense of disciple making.

Pastoral Hegemony

My initial calling into vocational ministry was to the pastorate. I had no plans to do otherwise. Although the Lord has led me to serve in a variety of ministerial roles, I spent nineteen years as a pastor and more than that amount of time training pastors through theological education. Presently, I serve as professor of Christian Ministry at Samford University in Birmingham, Alabama, where I train students for a variety of ministries, especially for pastoral ministry. Paul wrote, "and he gave . . . pastor-teachers" (Eph. 4:11, my trans.). That passage alone is sufficient to demand the utmost respect, value, and need for pastoral ministry. Service as an elder is a "noble task" (1 Tim. 3:1).

Ministry, especially in the West, is primarily understood as pastoral ministry. Aside from acknowledging evangelists and missionaries, the pastoral has developed a hegemony throughout the world. Ministerial activities are filtered through a pastoral framework. This

40. John R. W. Stott, *Christian Mission in the Modern World* (Downers Grove, IL: InterVarsity, 1975), 28.

matter is not to make a claim against pastors (i.e., elder, overseer). It is a statement of reality.

However, viewing life and ministry primarily through pastoral lenses has greatly hindered the dissemination of the gospel across the world. There is a reason for diversity in the body of Christ. Pastoral functions are different from apostolic functions. Pastors should serve primarily as shepherds and teachers overseeing local churches, which involves disciple making; thus their primary activities are not apostolic in nature and function. Pastors are called and expected to be pastors. The pastor is called to care for and guard the sheep (Acts 20:28). While pastors are leaders, they are primarily concerned with the sanctification of the saints and equipping them for ministry (Eph. 4:11–12) through well-established churches.[41] Pastors mainly find themselves working with people who are not voicing the Philippian jailer's question, "What must I do to be saved?" (Acts 16:30), but rather asking, "How do we now live as followers of Jesus?"

Even throughout Majority World contexts, the shift from the apostolic to the pastoral has been well noted. Following centuries of the expansion of the Church into formerly pioneer territories, the definition of missions shifted from proclamation of the gospel and planting churches to the development of the churches that have been planted. Like all churches, contextualized issues both within and outside the faith community challenged health and development. Missionaries who had previously operated in pioneer contexts now felt themselves faced with another challenge: How do those of us from the West relate to these young churches? The question loomed so large in the minds of some missional leaders gathering in Mexico City in 1963 that the World Council of Churches in its Congress on World Mission considered changing the label of missionaries to "fraternal workers."[42] The proposal never received widespread attention. They kept the label "missionaries" but changed the functions. One could be a missionary and function in a pastoral capacity.

41. Including equipping for *apostolic* ministry.
42. Ralph D. Winter, "The Meaning of Mission: Understanding This Term Is Crucial to the Completion of the Missionary Task," *Mission Frontiers*, March 1, 1998, https://www.missionfrontiers.org/issue/article/the-meaning-of-mission-understanding-this-term-is-crucial-to-the-completion.

Societies and agencies shifted from apostolic to pastoral labors. Missionaries became less involved in cross-cultural evangelism and church planting and more engaged with Christians. They assisted with structural development, ministry needs, community development, and leadership education. And once Western organizations found themselves participating in these never-ending tasks, they found stability, predictability, and longevity; they *also* found it difficult to return to desired apostolic work. Reflecting on this development, Ralph D. Winter notes: "Today 90% of all missionaries are helping churches around the world in a whole range of technical and educational capacities. The future of this kind of mission is indistinguishable from the mission of the church at home, to its own society. Thus, now all of a sudden, there is no apparent need for, nor is there a separately existing category for, the term 'missionary.'"[43]

As churches developed greater levels of complexity, pastoral leadership developed accordingly. Over time, the apostolic mindset found in Jesus and the Twelve and modeled by the first-century apostles transitioned to a pastoral mindset, with little concern for the apostolic. The result was that the default model for missions often became a pastoral model.[44]

The pastoral approach trends toward maintenance and the conservation of structures and organizations. Such work is a good and necessary matter for elders and established churches.

Unfortunately, when this approach is applied to contexts where the gospel has not been well established (or contexts that have experienced significant cultural shifts away from the faith), the Church attempts to use methods and strategies designed for long-term kingdom citizens. The result is often the planting of congregations by gathering Christians from other churches and a great deal of paternalism. Although there are exceptions, a pastoral approach maintains control rather than empowering and releasing others to be and function as pastors. Pastors are to be permanent fixtures with churches; apostolic teams are to be scaffolds until the work is complete.

43. Winter, "The Meaning of Mission."
44. The irony in this matter is that *pastoral* assumes a church to pastor. Today some missionaries are called *pastors* and yet do not have a local flock to shepherd.

The apostolic imagination is one that includes an awareness of the pastoral imagination, with its care for the edification of the saints. The apostolic teams brought not only the message of regeneration to people but also the message of sanctification. The apostolic imagination extends far beyond the point of conversion. Anyone who claims that the apostolic imagination is only concerned with conversions and planting new churches has woefully failed to understand the minds and hearts of the writers of the New Testament.

Theological Training

Theological education has roots in both the Old and New Testaments. Theologians and teachers who influenced more formalized training may be found as early as the second and third centuries. As the Church grew and societies developed, the need for such training increased. Though some institutions saw the need to educate missionaries, most were devoted to pastoral development.

The Reformation brought many wonderful transitions. However, the general mentality that the Great Commission was already fulfilled hindered the advancement of the gospel and the development of the apostolic imagination. If the first-century apostles had already made disciples of all nations, then there was no reason to go to the lost with first-century zeal. Instead, the goal was to continue the pastoral nurture of the churches that already existed, with the hopes that they would evangelize those within their communities.[45]

If the world could be divided into jurisdictions under ecclesiastical authority, then any country with an expression of the body of Christ needed pastoral ministry. The country had received the gospel; the Church had been planted. Evangelism and teaching were to continue through the established ministry of the Church.

Although Protestant theological education had to develop apart from Catholic institutions, the structures, courses, and processes were derived from medieval theological education. Walter C. Jack-

---

45. Though there were exceptions in the sixteenth and seventeenth centuries (even among the Reformers), it was the Danish-Halle Mission, the Moravians, and colonial work in the North Atlantic states that significantly influenced Protestant missionary expansion in the eighteenth and nineteenth centuries.

son writes, "Small schools for the education of ministers began to appear among post-Reformation denominations in Europe and in North American settings in the eighteenth and nineteenth centuries. From these beginnings, the Protestant seminary movement began. As the Protestant denominations became able to do so, they produced their own colleges, universities, and seminaries, but they largely imitated the educational patterns of the great universities of their cultures."[46]

People imitate what they know, and they know what is modeled before them. Schools often focused on intellectual development at the expense of the practical.[47] "Practical theology" courses eventually developed, with many schools offering field-based training throughout the twentieth century. By the close of the century, many institutions had chairs, departments, schools, degrees, and courses dedicated to missiological subject matters.[48] Whenever such training has developed, it has most often been an afterthought. Although great strides have been made in formal missiological training over the last seventy years, a great deal of theological education is not applicable to apostolic workers since its core identity is rooted in pastoral training.

For example, the definition of preaching today is almost exclusively viewed as that which occurs within the safe confines of a worship gathering, with students being taught how to communicate in this environment. Such is often *not* the location of preaching for apostolic teams. This reconceptualization of the sphere of preaching is not an attack on safe worship gatherings. Rather, it is a challenge to consider how the pastoral worldview has influenced the formal training of apostolic teams.

46. Walter C. Jackson, "A Brief History of Theological Education Including a Description of the Contribution of Wayne E. Oates," *Review and Expositor* 94 (1997): 503–20, here 511.

47. There were exceptions, particularly with missionaries delivering theological education in Majority World countries.

48. For an extensive study of academic missiology through the mid-twentieth century, see Olav Guttorm Myklebust, *The Study of Missions in Theological Education: An Historical Inquiry into the Place of World Evangelisation in Western Protestant Ministerial Training with Particular Reference to Alexander Duff's Chair of Evangelistic Theology*, 2 vols. (Oslo: Forlaget Land og Kirke, 1955–57).

All Evangelism Is Equal

The shifting of evangelism into the church's worship gathering as the primary avenue for preaching fosters the view that all evangelism is equal. While the gospel is the same to both Jew and Gentile, the means by which it is communicated differs greatly. Most churches fail to recognize this matter. Their imaginations assume that as long as the good news is being shared without compromise, then Great Commission work is being accomplished. While this view contains an element of truth, the concern is related to the evangelistic activity of the church in view of the global needs. For example, if members of a church only share the gospel with their children, is that an evangelistic church? In one sense, the answer is yes. Members are attempting to live out the principles of Deuteronomy 6 and Matthew 28:18–20. But is this to be the extent of the disciple-making labors of the church when the Scriptures also place emphasis on proclamation to the world (Mark 13:10)?

The overwhelming majority of unreached people in any country will not be reached by local churches offering evangelistic invitations every Sunday. Given geographical and cultural gaps, preaching must be taken to the modern-day highways and hedges. The greatest need for evangelism today is intercultural evangelistic labors, both across the street and across the world.

This is not a novel concept. Ralph Winter called for such evangelistic activities during the 1974 Lausanne Congress on World Evangelization. His presentation, "The Highest Priority: Cross-Cultural Evangelism," brought attention to the hidden peoples of the world, living down the street, on the nearby island, or across world.[49] Unless the churches of Indonesia, France, or the United States cross into and reach their own differing cultural contexts with the gospel, then the peoples will remain unreached.

During the later twentieth century, a general typology for evangelistic activities was developed to communicate that not all evangelism is equal in scope. Thus E-0 evangelism characterized evangelistic activities done within the cultural context of a church's gatherings.

---

49. Ralph D. Winter, "The Highest Priority: Cross-Cultural Evangelism," in *Let the Earth Hear His Voice: International Congress on World Evangelization, Lausanne, Switzerland*, ed. J. D. Douglas (Minneapolis: World Wide Publications, 1975), 213–41.

An invitation at the conclusion of a worship gathering is an example of this type. Then E-1 evangelism involved evangelistic activities that occurred among people of the same culture as the evangelist, but outside a church's gathering. Whenever someone shares the gospel with a likeminded coworker or neighbor, E-1 frequently occurs. Winter called for E-2 and E-3 evangelism in order to reach unreached peoples of the world. These two ministry expressions require the gospel to be communicated among people of a slightly different cultural context (E-2) or a radically different cultural context (E-3) when compared with those proclaiming the gospel. Winter's presentation was a watershed moment in mission history; yet long before 1974, Jesus called the Church to such activities.

The introduction to the book of Acts outlines the general global movement of gospel expansion. The emphasis on "Jerusalem, . . . Judea and Samaria," and "ends of the earth" (1:8 CSB) is more significant than simply the geographical expansion. The apostolic work of the church happens in Jerusalem as well as at the ends of the earth. There is no dichotomy between home and abroad, no modern understanding of domestic and international. As the gospel fills the earth (geographical expansion), it will encounter cultural barriers until the nations are blessed through Abraham.

Domestic and International Dichotomy

The ethos of Christendom created an atmosphere in the West that resulted in a clouded imagination related to Christians and non-Christians. Christians, understood as those born within regions whose leaders were blessed and influenced by papal authority, were different from heathen in distant lands. Christians were in the geographical boundaries of Christian lands where the Church and State were intimately connected. Pastoral and evangelistic labors were necessary to disciple those in such contexts. Non-Christians were those in distant regions or lands, often reached by traveling long distances. Missions came to be understood as that which occurred "overseas" and not within the "Christian" nations.

This dichotomy of national and international (what used to be called "home missions" and "foreign missions") is an innovation not supported from the biblical text. Whenever the imagination understands the Great Commission primarily in terms of national and international, then the notion of apostolic work will always be "over there" and evangelism will be "over here," with the latter executed through established church ministries. The apostolic imagination fails to recognize such artificial divisions. Apostolic labors are both here and there.

Globalization and migration have also revealed the flaws of such thinking. The United States is home to the third largest number of unreached people groups in the world; Canada is home to the sixth largest number.[50] Apostolic labors are necessary to reach many of these groups in North America, as would be the case in their countries of birth. Throughout the world, the lines are now blurred between foreign and domestic. However, the Church continues to allow geography, rather than cultural contexts, to define and limit the Great Commission labors.

Good Intentions Plus Technological Advancements

Kingdom citizens are caring, serving, and giving people. This is proper and expected. However, many began to recognize that any good they could do at home was something that should be done abroad, in needier areas. With the domestic-international dichotomy shaping the understanding of the location of mission, churches simply transferred their good deeds from service done at home to good deeds done abroad, now labeled *missions*.[51]

Communication developments, diminished costs and speed of international travel, and more safety while spending time in other countries resulted in large numbers of Western Christians going to serve the nations. The Church in the West recognized that intercultural engagement could become the practice of the many and not

---

50. J. D. Payne, *Strangers Next Door: Immigration, Migration and Mission* (Downers Grove, IL: IVP, 2012).

51. Even this thinking has broken down in recent years as special good deeds are being defined as *missions* done at home. For example, church members who volunteer during a designated weekend to serve at a homeless shelter in their city are now described as participating in a weekend mission trip.

something exclusively for the few.[52] By 2005, some 1.6 million US adult church members were participating in international short-term mission trips.[53] While short-term teams often help in apostolic endeavors, many serve in other areas. A. Scott Moreau found that a larger percentage of short-term workers, sent by US agencies from 2001 to 2005, chose to participate in relief/development and education/training rather than primary activities of evangelism and discipleship.[54] The large numbers of those going and serving are to be welcomed and encouraged. However, this increase in equating any good deeds done away from home as missions has diverted attention from the need and significance of apostolic labors among unreached peoples.

Value of Instant Gratification

The Western drive for quick results emerged from a value system that facilitated immediate and quantifiable accomplishments. The Church, with global engagements, quickly accommodated to this worldview as short-term missions increased. A roof could be added to a church's building faster than a church could be planted among an unreached people. Antibiotics could be distributed much easier than the gospel could be shared in a different language. Things could be accomplished and measured quickly. Since the application of good service to other countries became known as missions work, the Church now became aware of how such global activity could happen with great speed.

In his research on short-term missions, Edwin Zehner observes that by the early twenty-first century, immediate gratification was a growing value among evangelicals: "Yet overall by 2007, especially in North America, there had been a subtle shift to new rhetoric and

52. This has led to much discussion about the "amateurization" of missions. See David J. Hesselgrave, *Paradigms in Conflict: 10 Key Questions in Missions Today* (Grand Rapids: Kregel, 2005), 203–41.

53. Robert J. Priest, "Introduction," in *Effective Engagement in Short-Term Missions: Doing It Right*, ed. Robert J. Priest (Pasadena, CA: William Carey Library, 2008), i–ix, here ii.

54. A. Scott Moreau, "Short-Term Missions in the Context of Missions, Inc.," in *Effective Engagement in Short-Term Missions: Doing It Right*, ed. Robert J. Priest (Pasadena, CA: William Carey Library, 2008), 16.

expectations, including greater interest in practical action and more realistic notions of what short-term efforts can accomplish."[55] If teams (short- or long-term) could do good activities in the name of Jesus and experience quick results, then why not develop and give more attention to methods and strategies to support such actions? Instant gratification dwarfs apostolic labors that often require much time. If a church can participate in *missions* by doing many good acts that offer quick results, then the apostolic imagination will be smothered by a great deal of activities that, nevertheless, encourage Christians at home and abroad.

QUESTIONS TO CONSIDER

1. Which of the challenges have you experienced in the Christian community?
2. Can you think of other challenges to the apostolic imagination that were not discussed in this chapter?
3. Which of the challenges do you agree with (if any)? Disagree with? Why?

---

55. Edwin Zehner, "On the Rhetoric of Short-Term Mission Appeals, with Some Practical Suggestions for Team Leaders," in *Effective Engagement in Short-Term Missions: Doing It Right*, ed. Robert J. Priest (Pasadena, CA: William Carey Library, 2008), 188.

CHAPTER 3

Apostolic Identity in the New Testament

I t is necessary to examine the concepts of apostolic identity and
function in order to understand the apostolic imagination and its
relevance for today.[1] This chapter addresses identity; chapter 4 is

1. Although a great deal of literature exists among New Testament scholars regarding apostolic identity and function, a small but growing body of literature is
being produced by missiologists and other mission thinkers. For additional study, see
doctoral works by Donald T. Dent, "The Ongoing Role of Apostles in Missions,"
DMiss diss., Malaysia Baptist Theological Seminary, 2009; and Stephen Bruce Addison, "The Continuing Ministry of the Apostle in the Church's Mission," DMin, Fuller
Theological Seminary, 1995. Book-length treatments by missiologists include these:
Donald T. Dent, *The Ongoing Role of Apostles in Missions: The Forgotten Foundation*
(Nashville: Westbow, 2019); Alan Hirsch and Tim Catchim, *The Permanent Revolu-
tion: Apostolic Imagination and Practice for the 21st Century Church* (San Francisco:
Jossey-Bass, 2012); Alan Hirsch and Dave Ferguson, *On the Verge: A Journey into the
Apostolic Future of the Church* (Grand Rapids: Zondervan, 2011); Alan Hirsch, *The
Forgotten Ways: Reactivating the Missional Church* (Grand Rapids: Brazos, 2009);
Alan R. Johnson, *Apostolic Function: In 21st Century Missions* (Pasadena, CA: Wil-
liam Carey Library, 2009); Christopher R. Little, *Mission in the Way of Paul: Biblical
Mission for the Church in the Twenty-First Century* (New York: Lang, 2005); C. Peter
Wagner, *Apostles and Prophets: The Foundation of the Church* (Ventura, CA: Regal,
2000); C. Peter Wagner, *Apostles Today* (Ventura, CA: Regal, 2006); David Cannistraci,
*Apostles and the Emerging Apostolic Movement: A Biblical Look at Apostleship and
How God Is Using It to Bless His Church Today* (Ventura, CA: Renew, 1996); and

47

devoted to examining apostolic function in the New Testament. For now, there are three questions worth considering. How does recent scholarship understand the term *apostle*? Who was an apostle in the New Testament? Was the apostolic category limited to the Twelve or extended to a wider audience?

Background for *Apostolos*

There has been much debate on the origins of the concept *apostle*. While *apostolos* is frequently used in the context of the Church, it was a rare word in secular Greek. The LXX (Greek version of the Old Testament) uses it once, describing a messenger (1 Kings 14:6). However, in the New Testament, the word is found seventy-nine times, with 80 percent of the usage by Paul and Luke.[2] Francis H. Agnew claims that scholars should pay special attention to this word in the New Testament: "Terms that rise to importance with a movement are ordinarily of special significance to it, and it is clear from the NT usage that this is true of the term *apostolos*."[3] It is not the purpose of this chapter to address the strengths and limitations of scholarship surrounding the development of the apostle concept. Readers are directed to the citations for additional study. Nevertheless, it is important to understand the general background addressed in New Testament research.

Modern scholarship concerning *apostolos* began with J. B. Lightfoot's 1865 commentary on Galatians, where he argues that the Jewish community was already familiar with the Hebrew *shaliakh*, indicating a messenger sent by an authority; in the Gospels, Jesus uses the Greek equivalent and is "not introducing a new term, but adopting

Larry W. Caldwell, *Sent Out! Reclaiming the Spiritual Gift of Apostleship for Missionaries and Churches Today* (Pasadena, CA: William Carey Library, 1992).

2. Here is the statistical breakdown of the New Testament's use of the term *apostle*: Paul, 34×; Luke-Acts, 34× (Luke, 6×; Acts, 28×); Mark, 1×; Matthew, 1×; John, 1×; Hebrews, 1×; 1 Peter, 1×; Jude, 1×; 2 Peter, 2×; Revelation, 3×. See K. H. Rengstorf, "*apostellō (pempō), exapostellō, apostolos, pseudapostolos, apostolē*," in *Theological Dictionary of the New Testament*, ed. G. Kittel and G. Friedrich, trans. and ed. W. Bromiley (Grand Rapids: Eerdmans, 1964), 1:398–447, here 420–21.

3. Francis H. Agnew, "The Origin of the NT Apostle-Concept: A Review of the Research," *Journal of Biblical Literature* 105, no. 1 (1986): 75–96, here 75.

one which from its current usage would suggest to His hearers the idea of a highly responsible mission."[4] Approximately a hundred pages into the work, Lightfoot offers a brief excursus titled "The Name and Office of an Apostle."[5] Following this publication, New Testament scholars have provided extensive study concerning the topic, with frequently contradictory conclusions.[6] K. H. Rengstorf's influential article "Apostolos" attempted to build upon Lightfoot's view.[7]

A second theory, however, rooted the origin of *apostolos* in Gnosticism. By the twentieth century, some scholars began questioning the *shaliakh* theory and argued that the Christian understanding came primarily from a Gnostic perspective. Walter Schmithals was a leading advocate for this view.[8] However, his position found little support and is almost universally rejected.[9]

A more recent perspective recognizes that the *shaliakh* origin is related more to sending a messenger for legal matters, while *apostolos* is more akin to religious issues. Attention is given to the sending language of *shalakh* in the Old Testament and *apostellein/pempein* in the New Testament. The relationship between the sending of messengers and prophets with that of New Testament apostles is being reconsidered. Robert W. Herron Jr. concludes that the origin of the apostolate is found with the historical Jesus and that the *apostolos* category underwent a radical change following the resurrection.[10]

4. J. B. Lightfoot, *St. Paul's Epistle to the Galatians*, 2nd ed., rev. (London: Macmillan, 1866), 94.

5. Lightfoot, *Epistle to the Galatians*, 314–23. An extensive list of the older literature may be found in Rengstorf, "*apostellō (pempō), exapostellō, apostolos, pseudapostolos, apostolē.*"

6. Andrew Kirk argues that "the diverse ways of presenting the apostolic ministry within the New Testament reflect a fundamental unity." J. Andrew Kirk, "Apostleship since Rengstorf: Towards a Synthesis," *New Testament Studies* 21, no. 2 (1975): 249–64, here 249. For a viewpoint that the New Testament writers have contradictory perspectives, see Rudolf Schnackenburg, "Apostolicity—the Present Position of Studies," *One in Christ* 6 (1970): 243–73.

7. Rengstorf, "*apostellō (pempō), exapostellō, apostolos, pseudapostolos, apostolē,*" 407–45.

8. Walter Schmithals, *The Office of Apostle in the Early Church* (Nashville: Abingdon, 1969).

9. Agnew, "Origin of the NT Apostle-Concept," 88, 92.

10. Robert W. Herron Jr., "The Origin of the New Testament Apostolate," *Westminster Theological Journal* 45 (1983): 101–31, here 130. P. W. Barnett also notes the

Agnew sees a "growing consensus on the connection of apostleship with the OT sending convention expressed by use of the word group [*shalakh-apostellein*]."[11]

Sending

While scholarship debates the origin of the term, the concept of *apostolos* is frequently connected with the notion of being sent for a specific purpose.[12] The LXX uses *apostellō* and *exapostellō* approximately 700 times to translate *shalakh* (send / stretch out), thus involving the idea of an authorized messenger, with emphasis on the sender.[13] The New Testament uses these two expressions 132 and 13 times, respectively. Another frequently related word is *pempō*, used 79 times.[14] A comparison of several definitions reveals the emphasis on one party sending another with a specific message to share or task to accomplish:

- An apostle in the New Testament is an envoy, an ambassador, or a missionary. In the New Testament, the term *apostle* is applied to one who carries the message of the gospel.[15]

- An apostle is properly one sent on a definite mission, in which he acts with full authority on behalf of the sender and is accountable to him.[16]

New Testament "phenomenon of the apostle must be sought within the ministry of Jesus." P. W. Barnett, "Apostle," in *Dictionary of Paul and His Letters*, ed. Gerald F. Hawthorne, Ralph P. Martin, and Daniel G. Reid (Downers Grove, IL: InterVarsity, 1993), 45–51, here 47.

11. Agnew, "Origin of the NT Apostle-Concept," 96.

12. Of course, such purposes are debated among scholars as well.

13. R. David Rightmire, "Apostle," in *Evangelical Dictionary of Biblical Theology*, ed. Walter A. Elwell (Grand Rapids: Baker, 1996), 33–35, here 33.

14. See https://www.billmounce.com/greek-dictionary. Translations include: *apostellō* = to send forth a messenger, agent, message, or command; to put into action; to liberate, rid; to dismiss, send away; *exapostellō* = to send out, forth, away, dismiss; to dispatch on a service or agency; to send as an influence; *pempō* = to send, dispatch on any message, embassy, business; to transmit; to dismiss, permit to go; to send in; to put forth.

15. Hans Dieter Betz, "Apostle," in *The Anchor Bible Dictionary*, ed. David Noel Freedman (New York: Doubleday, 1992), 1:309.

16. E. F. Harrison, "Apostle, Apostleship," in *Evangelical Dictionary of Theology*, ed. Walter A. Elwell (Grand Rapids: Baker, 1984), 71.

- The term *apostle* (*apostolos*) is used in the Gospels to designate the twelve disciples called and sent out by Jesus to preach the gospel of the kingdom and demonstrate its presence by performing signs and wonders (Matt. 10:2; Mark 3:14; Luke 6:13).[17]
- A special messenger of Jesus Christ; a person to whom Jesus delegated authority for certain tasks.[18]
- Envoy, ambassador, or messenger commissioned to carry out the instructions of the commissioning agent.[19]
- Someone, or something, sent. Derived from the verb "to send out." In the New Testament, usually refers to someone sent as an authorized agent by Jesus or the Christian community.[20]

With the notion of sending intimately connected with *apostolos*, it is necessary to ask, What did the sent ones do after they were sent? This is the question addressed in the next chapter. But before a discussion into function can occur, it is necessary to ask who the apostles were in the New Testament. Surprisingly, scholarship lacks a consensus about the answer.

Who Were the Apostles?

As with the divergent views on the origins of *apostolos*, perspectives differ on the count of those who were included in this category. There is much disagreement among scholars regarding who comprised this role in the New Testament. Some argue that the apostles were limited to a few believers in the first century; others recognize a wider usage of the term *apostolos* with implications for the ongoing role of apostles throughout Church history. For example, Robert Duncan

17. C. G. Kruse, "Apostle," in *Dictionary of Jesus and the Gospels*, ed. Joel B. Green, Scot McKnight, and I. Howard Marshall (Downers Grove, IL: InterVarsity, 1992), 27–33, here 27.

18. "Apostle," in *Nelson's New Illustrated Bible Dictionary*, ed. Ronald F. Youngblood (Nashville: Nelson, 1995), 91–92, here 91.

19. Rightmire, "Apostle," 33.

20. Dan Nässelqvist, "Apostle," in *The Lexham Bible Dictionary*, ed. John D. Barry et al. (Bellingham, WA: Lexham, 2016), in Logos Bible Software.

Culver writes, "There is thus no strong evidence that any New Testament persons except the original Twelve, Matthias, Paul, and possibly James the Lord's brother, were ever esteemed in the New Testament times to be apostles of Jesus Christ."[21] H. P. Owen argues that the successor to the apostles is the whole Church.[22] Linda L. Belleville claims "narrow" and "broad" applications of the term.[23] David J. Hesselgrave observes two categories of "special" and "general" apostles.[24] Johannes Munck acknowledges a wider circle of apostles but prefers to call them missionaries sent by Christ.[25] According to Kirk, the general consensus is that three categories exist (the Twelve, Paul, and church delegates).[26] Don Dent provides four categories (the Twelve, other commissioned eyewitnesses, missionary apostles, and envoys of the churches).[27] Larry W. Caldwell's taxonomy begins with the universal element of apostleship for all believers; then he categorizes apostles into those who held the office "once-for-all-time" and the others, who are divided into "missionary apostles" and "task apostles."[28] C. K. Barrett seems to recognize the most possibilities, listing eight categories that include individuals and groups.[29] The fol-

21. Robert Duncan Culver, "Apostles and the Apostolate in the New Testament," *Bibliotheca Sacra* 134 (April–June 1977): 131–43, here 143.

22. Owen writes, "We must assert also that the essentially apostolic call to be a 'witness to the resurrection' was, within history, transferred to the whole Church; that it is for this reason that we call the Church 'apostolic.'" H. P. Owen, "Resurrection and Apostolate in St. Paul," *Expository Times* 65, no. 11 (August 1954): 324–28, here 328.

23. Linda L. Belleville, *2 Corinthians* (Downers Grove, IL: IVP Academic, 1996), 229.

24. Including Jesus (Heb. 3:1), Hesselgrave labels "special apostles" as the Twelve; "general apostles" include those who preached, planted churches, or assisted in such work. David J. Hesselgrave, *Paradigms in Conflict: 15 Key Questions in Christian Missions Today*, ed. Keith E. Eitel, 2nd ed. (Grand Rapids: Kregel Academic, 2018), 194–97.

25. Johannes Munck, "Paul, the Apostles, and the Twelve," *Studia Theologica* 3, no. 1 (1949): 96–110, here 101.

26. Kirk, "Apostleship since Rengstorf," 262.

27. Dent, "Ongoing Role of Apostles," 45.

28. Larry W. Caldwell, *Sent Out! Reclaiming the Spiritual Gift of Apostleship for Missionaries and Churches Today* (Pasadena, CA: William Carey Library, 1992), 71.

29. See C. K. Barrett, *The Signs of an Apostle* (Philadelphia: Fortress, 1972), 71–73, listing the following with little explanation for some: (1) Jesus's original group; (2) Supreme Apostles, who led the Jerusalem church; (3) Apostleship of the circumcision; (4) John in Ephesus; (5) Apostles of the Jerusalem leaders; (6) Paul;

lowing categorizes *apostolos* into four categories: Jesus, the Twelve, Paul, and others.

Jesus

In the high Christology of Hebrews, the author exhorts readers to "consider Jesus, the apostle and high priest of our confession" (Heb. 3:1). He is the one sent from the Father, greater than the angels (and Moses), yet made a little lower than the angels "so that by the grace of God he might taste death for everyone" (2:9). Through the incarnation, Jesus was sent to become "like his brothers" and as the "high priest" who made "propitiation for the sins" of all (2:17). F. F. Bruce states that this dual designation draws attention to Jesus being sent from the Father to represent God before people and to represent people before God: "The faithfulness of an envoy consists in his loyal discharging of the commission with which he has been entrusted; and such faithfulness was manifested preeminently in the Sent One of God."[30] It has not gone without notice that this is the only New Testament passage where *apostolos* is applied to the Son. Donald Guthrie observes that readers should not be surprised at this limitation: "It is striking that the same term used of the men whom Jesus had chosen is used of Jesus himself. It is not, however, so unexpected when Jesus' own words are considered: 'As thou didst send me into the world, so I have sent them into the world' (John 17:18); indeed, it is worth noting that the idea of Jesus being sent is frequent in the New Testament. In other words, they became apostles because he was an apostle. He is the perfect fulfiller of the office. All others are pale reflections."[31]

Calvin Mercer agrees that one should not be surprised with such a designation being applied to Jesus. In the Fourth Gospel, he claims, the evidence "strongly suggests" that it is appropriate to refer to Jesus as the "apostle" of the Gospel. "He was sent from God. His authority

---

(7) Subordinates within Paul's circle; and (8) Delegates and messengers of local churches.

30. F. F. Bruce, *The Epistle to the Hebrews*, rev. ed. (Grand Rapids: Eerdmans, 1990), 91.

31. Donald Guthrie, *Hebrews: An Introduction and Commentary*, Tyndale New Testament Commentaries 15 (Downers Grove, IL: InterVarsity, 1983), 102.

was derived from the Father with whom he was identified and who acted through him. The sending of Jesus was for the revelation of God so that the world might believe."[32]

The Son was sent into the world (John 3:16–17, 34; 5:36–38; 6:29, 57; 7:29; 10:36; 11:42; 17:3, 8, 18–25; 20:21). In the sending of the Son, according to John, the Son's subordination is expressed in relation to the Father (6:57; 13:16). The Son comes to do the will of the Father (5:30) and represents the Father in his teaching (7:16).

The Twelve

Jesus's first followers came from the Baptist's disciples (John 1:35–37). However, those Twelve were called and appointed as apostles by Jesus (Matt. 10:2; Mark 3:14; Luke 6:13; cf. John 15:16). In the Synoptics, the Twelve are called to be with Jesus, sent to preach, manifest power to heal, and cast out demons (Matt. 10:5–15; Mark 3:14–15; Luke 9:1–6). He commissioned them again following the resurrection (Matt. 28:18–20; Luke 24:33–49; cf. Acts 1:8).

The title *apostles* was given to Jesus's twelve disciples. Matthew and Mark scarcely use the word in relation to the Twelve (Matt. 10:2; Mark 3:14; 6:30), but Luke uses it frequently (e.g., Luke 6:13; 9:10; 17:5; 24:10; Acts 1:26; 2:43; 4:35; 8:1).[33] Following the death of Judas, a replacement was necessary (Acts 1:20; cf. Ps. 109:8). Another representative was needed who had been with the apostles from the beginning and was "a witness to [Jesus's] resurrection" (Acts 1:22). Both Joseph and Matthias were selected as candidates, but the lot fell to the latter.

Discussions abound regarding the place of the Twelve in the first century. Some scholars argue that they represented a unique, irreplaceable office that corresponded to the twelve tribes of Israel, thus

32. Calvin Mercer, "Jesus the Apostle: 'Sending' and the Theology of John," *Journal of the Evangelical Theological Society* 35, no. 4 (December 1992): 457–62, here 460. Mercer argues that given John's high Christology, it was appropriate to use *apostellein* in reference to Jesus's divine sending as opposed to granting the title *apostolos*, which could be understood as demoting Jesus to the level of a man (460–61).

33. It has been argued that Matthew and Mark may have only applied the term to the disciples when Jesus sent them on their first mission. See J. C. Lambert, "Apostle," in *The International Standard Bible Encyclopedia*, ed. James Orr et al. (Chicago: Howard-Severance, 1915), 202.

reflecting the foundation of the new Israel (Luke 22:28–30; Eph. 2:20; Rev. 21:14).[34] Others make the case that the title *apostle* does not refer to a restricted office but to the function of missionary service, even when applied to the Twelve.[35] Is it possible that the twelve apostles actually represent a fixed office without succession? For example, no replacement was made when James was killed (Acts 12:2). Yet, could the New Testament writers also apply the title *apostle* to different individuals in different circumstances? As already noted, differences are found among the evangelists and, as explained below, Paul seems to apply the title differently as well. Given the limited appearance of the term prior to the New Testament writings, one should not be surprised if a degree of fluidity existed in the first century.

Paul

Along with Luke, Paul makes the most use of *apostolos*. Unlike the Twelve, his apostleship was not related to having been with Jesus from his baptism to the ascension.[36] He frequently identified himself as an apostle by referencing his call according to God's will for the proclamation of the gospel (Rom. 1:1; 1 Cor. 1:1; Gal. 1:1; Col. 1:1; Eph. 1:1; 1 Tim. 1:1; 2 Tim. 1:1; Titus 1:1). James D. G. Dunn writes, "It can even be argued that Paul's theology as a whole was simply an unfolding of the significance of the initial christophany."[37] John B.

---

34. John B. Polhill, *Acts* (Nashville: Broadman, 1993), 93.

35. Lambert, "Apostle," 202. Lambert also takes Rev. 21:14 as symbolic and not a reference to twelve men.

36. Some argue that since Paul's understanding of apostleship differed from Luke-Acts, the apostle simply changed the criteria. See Betz, "Apostle," 310. Since Paul's writings preceded the Gospels and Acts, Morris Ashcraft argues that the restricted use of limiting apostles to the Twelve had not become widespread. "After the term developed its technical meaning, . . . Paul would have been eliminated by the stated requirements (Acts 1:21, 22)." Morris Ashcraft, "Paul Defends His Apostleship Galatians 1 and 2," *Review and Expositor* 69 (Fall 1972): 459–69, here 461. Kirk, however, writes, "We can affirm that Luke maintained exactly the same continuity/discontinuity in the concept of apostle as Paul. The continuity is rooted in the nature of the call and the specific task of the apostle. The discontinuity is rooted in the nature of the different historical circumstances and mediation of the call." Kirk, "Apostleship since Rengstorf," 264.

37. James D. G. Dunn, *The Theology of Paul the Apostle* (Grand Rapids: Eerdmans, 1998), 22.

Polhill notes, "Conversion and call to the Gentile mission became inseparable for him."[38] Morris Ashcraft also sees the relationship between his conversion and calling. He writes, "Paul's distinctive concept of apostleship is summed up in his term 'called to be an apostle.'"[39] Paul's claim to have been called by Christ denies any human instrumentality in the process. He understood himself to be in line with Old Testament prophets, whom God called for his mission in the world (Gal. 1:16; Jer. 1:5; Amos 7:14–15; Isa. 6:1–6).

If seeing the risen Lord was a prerequisite for apostleship, then he was qualified (Gal.1:16; 1 Cor. 9:1–5; 15:1–10). When questioned about his role, Paul was quick to claim that his calling and commissioning to the Gentiles came from Christ (1 Cor. 9:1; 15:8; 2 Cor. 10–11; 12:11–13; Gal. 1:11–17). Leaders in Jerusalem accepted his calling and role (Acts 15; Gal. 2:9). These two elements were significant in his understanding of identity and functions. He described apostles as "servants of Christ and stewards of the mystery of God" (1 Cor. 4:1), on display for all to see, and viewed as "fools for Christ's sake" as they labor and suffer for God's glory (1 Cor. 4:10–13; 2 Cor. 11:16–12:10). He identifies himself as the apostle to the Corinthians; as a faith community, they serve as the identifying seal confirming his apostolic calling (1 Cor. 9:1–2).[40]

Others

The textual evidence appears to be in favor of the perspective that *apostolos* was applied to a wider group than Jesus, the Twelve, and Paul. Some have asserted that the seventy-two sent on mission (Luke 10:1–3) represented a wider number of apostles. Peter J. Scaer states that Hippolytus may have been correct to refer to them as apostles.

38. John B. Polhill, "Paul: Theology Born of Mission," *Review and Expositor* 78 (1981): 233–47, here 237.

39. Ashcraft, "Paul Defends His Apostleship," 460.

40. Schnabel notes that several passages are specifically related to Paul's self-understanding as a "pioneer missionary": 1 Cor. 3:5–15; 9:19–23; 15:1–11; 2 Cor. 2:14–16; 4:7–15; 5:20; Rom. 1:14; 10:14–21; 15:15–21; Col. 1:24–29. Eckhard J. Schnabel, *Early Christian Mission*, vol. 2, *Paul and the Early Church* (Downers Grove, IL: Inter-Varsity, 2004), 945–82.

He writes, "At the very least, we can say that Christ himself appointed others besides the apostles whom he sent to carry on the very same tasks as the apostles themselves."[41] While Robert H. Stein describes the work of the seventy-two as an "'apostolic' mission" that foreshadows Luke 24:46–48 and Acts 1:8, he stops short of referring to them as apostles.[42] The following include several passages in Acts, the Pauline Epistles, and Revelation related to the possibility of others being identified as apostles.

Acts 14:4, 14. Luke uses the word extensively with application to the Twelve. However, he makes two applications to Paul while including Barnabas as well.[43] Describing their journey to Iconium and Lystra, Luke writes: "The people of the city were divided; some sided with the Jews and some with the apostles" (14:4). "When the apostles Barnabas and Paul heard of it, they tore their garments and rushed out into the crowd" (14:14).

Although Polhill counts this as a noteworthy use of *apostolos*, he is hesitant to make any certain claims: "In Acts, Luke used the term in a restricted sense, which denotes only the Twelve who were eyewitnesses to Jesus' entire ministry. Acts 14:4, 14 are the exceptions to the rule. Perhaps Luke indicated here that Paul and Barnabas were delegates of the Antioch church, commissioned by them for their mission. Perhaps it indicates Luke's awareness of the wider application of the word and that he here slipped into the more customary and less specialized usage."[44]

I. Howard Marshall acknowledges this interpretation as well but adds a more definitive statement:

> It is possible that Luke uses the word here in a very general sense to mean "the missionaries sent out by the church at Antioch." . . . More

41. Peter J. Scaer, "Luke and the Foundations of the Church," *Concordia Theological Quarterly* 76, nos. 1–2 (January–April 2012): 57–72, here 70.

42. Robert H. Stein, *Luke* (Nashville: Broadman & Holman, 1992), 305.

43. Barnabas, while in Jerusalem, was not referred to as an apostle (Acts 4:32–37; 9:27) though he was "sent" to Antioch (11:22).

44. Polhill, *Acts*, 311. On the same page in his commentary, Polhill also notes that Paul "applied the term to others as well; James, the Lord's brother (Gal 1:19; 1 Cor 15:7), Andronicus and Junias (Rom 16:7), and an unnamed group whom he distinguished from the Twelve (1 Cor 15:7; cf. 15:5)."

probably, however, the explanation lies in the fact that by apostles
Luke thinks *primarily* of the Twelve appointed by Jesus during his
earthly life (Lk. 6:13; 9:1f.; 22:28–30) with a particular mission to the
Jews. But Luke was well aware of Paul's apostleship, as is seen in the
present passage and in the use of the cognate verb "to send" (Greek
apostellō) in [Acts] 22:21 and 26:16f. Thus he recognizes that there was
a group of apostles, commissioned by Jesus, wider than the Twelve,
and he does not deny that Paul and Barnabas belong to this group.[45]

First Corinthians 9:1–6. As an apostle, Paul maintains, he has certain rights that he has abdicated. In this passage he equates Barnabas
with himself as choosing to give up freedoms that belong to apostles.
Leon Morris's statement on this text is worth mentioning because
he offers little explanation regarding Paul's wording, assuming that
the context reveals the obvious: Paul and Barnabas are "two apostles
who did not refrain from earning their own living while preaching."[46]
Marshall leans in this direction as well, stating, "1 Cor. 9:6 strongly
suggests that Paul regarded Barnabas as an apostle."[47] However, Robert W. Herron Jr. declares that it would have been "inconceivable" for
Paul to assign the title *apostle* to someone due to merit or missionary
work. An apostle must be "a specially called messenger of God so
designated by an appearance of the resurrected Lord."[48]

First Corinthians 15:5–9 and Galatians 1:19. Some have argued that
Paul's description of the post-resurrection appearances of Jesus reveals a wider circle of first-century apostles. "He appeared to Cephas,
then to the twelve. Then he appeared to more than five hundred
brothers at one time, most of whom are still alive, though some have
fallen asleep. Then he appeared to James, then to all the apostles.
Last of all, as to one untimely born, he appeared also to me. For I
am the least of the apostles" (1 Cor. 15:5–9).

Arguments are made that Paul distinguishes Cephas (i.e., Peter) and
the Twelve from others called apostles. Kirk believes Paul's reference

45. I. Howard Marshall, *The Acts of the Apostles: An Introduction and Commentary* (Grand Rapids: Eerdmans, 1980), 234.

46. Leon Morris, *The First Epistle of Paul to the Corinthians* (Grand Rapids:
Eerdmans, 1975), 133.

47. Marshall, *Acts of the Apostles*, 234n1.

48. Herron, "Origin of the New Testament Apostolate," 123.

to the Twelve is unique and reveals a pre-Pauline understanding of a well-defined group of special disciples.[49] After mentioning James, Paul notes Jesus's appearance also "to all the apostles." When this passage is taken into consideration with Paul's Galatian correspondence, a case can be made that James was labeled an apostle. While visiting Peter in Jerusalem for fifteen days, Paul "saw none of the other apostles except James the Lord's brother" (Gal. 1:19). Johannes Munck, however, doubts James's apostleship, claiming that the text can be read, "but I saw no other apostle, but I saw alone of all the great names in Jerusalem James, the Lord's brother."[50] Hans Dieter Betz declares that the evidence is ambiguous.[51] Others conclude that the translation depends on whether or not Paul believed James to be an apostle.[52]

First Thessalonians 2:6 and 1 Corinthians 16:10. In 1 Thessalonians, Paul reminds the church that his team came to them with the gospel and in the power of the Holy Spirit (1:5). Following their conversions, they became imitators of the team, and the gospel rang forth from Thessalonica with the church serving as an example to other churches in Macedonia and Achaia (1:6–10). As Paul recalls additional details of their ministry in the city, he states, "We could have made demands as apostles of Christ," but instead we were like a "gentle . . . nursing mother" (2:6–7). An examination of the salutation reveals that he is possibly referring to Silvanus and Timothy when he shifts to the first-person plural in this passage. Though not as clear, it is argued that when 1 Corinthians 16:10 is taken into consideration with this passage, Paul is acknowledging Timothy's apostolic work: "He is doing the work of the Lord, as I am." On the other hand, Lightfoot makes the point that while the term applies to a wider circle than the Twelve and Paul, it is probable that Paul understands Silvanus with *apostolos*, however, not Timothy. Lightfoot's evidence to support his view is that Paul never assigns this title to Timothy when it would have been easy to do so in his 2 Corinthians and Colossians' salutations (2 Cor. 1:1; Col. 1:1).[53] Mosbech explains that it is

49. Kirk, "Apostleship since Rengstorf," 256.
50. Munck, "Paul, the Apostles, and the Twelve," 107.
51. Betz, "Apostle," 311.
52. R. Alan Cole, *Galatians* (Grand Rapids: Eerdmans, 1989), 94–95.
53. Lightfoot, *Epistle to the Galatians*, 96n3.

unclear whether or not Paul in 1 Thessalonians 2:6 is simply using the authorial plural to refer to himself or indeed including Silvanus and Timothy. Regardless, the context reveals that "the aim is not especially at 'the twelve,' but at the missionaries in general."[54]

Epaphroditus, our brothers, Titus, Apollos, Andronicus, and Junias. The singular and plural forms of *apostle* are found in Philippians 2:25 and 2 Corinthians 8:23. Though most English translations use the words "messenger" (Phil. 2:25; cf. John 13:16) and "messengers" (2 Cor. 8:23), Epaphroditus is called "your *apostle*" (Phil. 2:25, Greek), and other brothers "are *apostles* of the churches" (2 Cor. 8:23, footnote). These designations lend support to the notion that a category of apostles existed as representatives sent from churches for a particular purpose.

In a complex set of arguments, scholars debate whether or not Paul considered Apollos an apostle. These differing views find support in 1 Corinthians 1–4; 9:1–3. It is beyond the scope of this chapter to address these views. According to Andrew Wilson, they tend to conclude that (1) Paul did not view Apollos as an apostle; (2) Paul was convinced that Apollos had seen the resurrected Jesus; or (3) Paul did not believe every apostle had to have seen the resurrected Jesus. Most conservative scholars have subscribed to the first perspective. However, Wilson makes the case for the third, arguing that Paul uses 9:1–3 as support for his own apostleship and *not* a requirement for all apostles.[55]

The grammar of Romans 16:7 has led some scholars to ask whether Andronicus and Junias were apostles. Were they outstanding "among" the apostles or "to" the apostles? Both views are well represented. While C. E. B. Cranfield grants that the interpretative possibility could go either way grammatically, he is convinced that the couple was outstanding in the group designated as apostles, thus representing the wider circle of "itinerant missionaries who were recognized by the churches as constituting a distinct group among the participants in

54. Holger Mosbech, "Apostolos in the New Testament," *Studia Theologica* 2 (1948): 166–200, here 174.

55. Andrew Wilson argues for Apollos being an apostle, outlining these views in his article "Apostle Apollos?," *Journal of the Evangelical Theological Society* 56, no. 2 (2013): 325–35.

the work of spreading the gospel."[56] The evidence for either perspective appears strong. Perhaps a definitive interpretation is impossible.[57] Regardless, the couple must have been coworkers with Paul at some time since this would explain their imprisonment with him.[58]

False apostles. The New Testament support for a wider application of *apostolos* is also found in passages that warn against false apostles. As Paul defends his ministry, he pits himself against those whom he describes as "super-apostles" (2 Cor. 11:5, 13).[59] These individuals are actually "false apostles, deceitful workmen, disguising themselves as apostles of Christ" (2 Cor. 11:13). Such evildoers were hindering Paul's work in the mid-50s; by the time Revelation is composed, their reputation has spread throughout Asia Minor. Nearly a half century later than Paul, the members of the church in Ephesus are commended for their works, particularly because they "have tested those who call themselves apostles and are not, and found them to be false" (Rev. 2:2).

The reality of false apostles in the first century reveals that some travelers were claiming to be true apostles. These passages imply that a broader usage of the term *apostolos* was in existence. If the list of apostles was limited to the Twelve and Paul, then the need for discernment and testing was irrelevant. The warning was only necessary if the number of apostles was claimed to extend beyond a few.[60]

56. C. E. B. Cranfield, *A Critical and Exegetical Commentary on the Epistle to the Romans*, 6th ed. (Edinburgh: T&T Clark, 1979), 2:789. Others argue for *apostle* being applied to this couple: see Yii-Jan Lin, "Junia: An Apostle before Paul," *Journal of Biblical Literature* 139, no. 1 (2020): 191–209; Craig Blomberg, *1 Corinthians* (Grand Rapids: Zondervan, 1994), 247; Polhill, *Acts*, 311.

57. David Huttar seems to come to this conclusion at the end of his extensive article: "We hope at least to have shown that the playing field on which the two interpretations compete is much more even than modern scholarship has allowed." He believes "the probability has shifted in favor of the non-inclusive interpretation." David Huttar, "Did Paul Call Andronicus an Apostle in Romans 16:7?," *Journal of the Evangelical Theological Society* 52, no. 4 (December 2009): 747–78, here 778.

58. Schnabel, *Early Christian Mission*, 2:1433.

59. For a study on the identity of these interlopers, see Doyle Kee, "Who Were the 'Super–Apostles' of 2 Corinthians 10–13?," *Restoration Quarterly* 25 (1980): 65–76. Mosbech takes Paul's defense to signify his acceptance of a wider circle of apostles (Mosbech, "Apostolos in the New Testament," 175).

60. One may try to argue that only the New Testament writers knew the title was limited to a few individuals and that the churches simply did not know this

Jesus was clearly the ultimate apostle and established a ministry that modeled evangelism, disciple making, care, collaboration, and leadership development. Much of what his apostles continued after the ascension reflected the actions found in his life and teachings. There was no apostolic succession beyond the Twelve (see below). However, it appears that the label *apostolos* was assigned to a wider group of individuals, beyond Paul and possibly James (the Lord's brother). Those in this category seemed to be engaged in apostolic acts but without evidence that they saw the resurrected Christ or provided special revelation as did the New Testament writers. These general apostles appear to have been sent from churches to engage at least in disciple-making activities of evangelism, church planting, leadership development, and to assist special apostles such as Paul. Although they clearly represented the churches from which they were sent, they ultimately represented the Christ of the churches.

Before concluding this examination of apostolic identity in the New Testament, additional matters of related concern must be acknowledged. The following topics are often raised in discussions related to *apostolos*. All these are not necessarily relevant to each of the aforementioned four categories. They are more significant to the apostolic identity of some than others.

Office of Apostle

The calling and actions of the Twelve were specific, unique, and unrepeatable. First Corinthians 15:5 seems to reveal that an early distinction was known between the Twelve and other apostles. Luke reports that Jesus called twelve disciples to himself and designated them *apostles* (Luke 6:13). Jesus taught them with his words and actions and gave them hands-on experience (Mark 3:14–15; Matt. 10:5–15; Luke 9:1–6). He expected them to continue his ministry of proclamation and disciple making throughout the world following the ascension (Matt. 28:18–20; Mark 13:10; 14:9; Luke 24:45–49;

---

information and believed there were many apostles. However, this argument appears to be tenuous.

John 20:21; Acts 1:8). They would be the foundation for the Church in general (Eph. 2:20) and leaders in the Jerusalem expression of the Church in particular (Acts 2:42; 4:35–37; 6:2; 8:1, 14, 18; 9:27; 15:1–6, 22–23; 16:4).[61] The office of the Twelve was partially responsible for penning Holy Scripture (Eph. 3:5; 2 Pet. 3:15–16).[62] With the death of the first-century apostles and their associates, the New Testament canon was closed, and no additional special revelation was provided.

Jesus promised that the Twelve would sit on thrones and judge the tribes of Israel (Luke 22:28–30). The new Jerusalem rests on foundations, on which were the names of the twelve apostles (Rev. 21:14). Following the ascension, the disciples recognized the prophecy of the demise of Judas and the need for his replacement (Acts 1:15–20; cf. Pss. 69:25; 109:8). Given the typology of the twelve tribes of Israel, Jaroslav Jan Pelikan understands this move to reflect the need to restore the integrity of the Twelve.[63] The candidate for the position had to reflect at least two qualifications. First, the person had to be one of the men who accompanied the other disciples from the time of Jesus's baptism until his ascension. Second, he had to have witnessed Jesus's resurrected body. Though two candidates were eligible, Matthias was selected (Acts 1:21–26).[64]

61. Discussing the gift of apostle (1 Cor. 12:28), Rengstorf describes the apostles as "officers of Christ by whom the Church is built. In this respect they may be compared with the prophets of the OT (Eph. 2:20; 3:5), whose office, on the basis of their commission, was to prepare the way for the One who was to come." Rengstorf, "*apostellō (pempō), exapostellō, apostolos, pseudapostolos, apostolē*," 423.

62. Authorship was one of the qualifications the Church used to determine what writings would be included in the New Testament. The writers had to be apostles or associates of apostles.

63. Jaroslav Jan Pelikan, *Acts* (Grand Rapids: Brazos, 2005), 46.

64. Though the Lord's decision was made known through the lots (Acts 1:24), Matthias's calling was different from the Eleven and from Paul, whereby the visible Jesus was present and spoke directly to the one called. Another variation on calling may be found in Acts 13:1–3, in which the Spirit tells the leaders (church?) to set apart Barnabas and Paul. Though Paul's calling (Acts 9) happened before this event at Antioch, does this represent Barnabas's calling as an apostle, or did that occur when the Jerusalem church sent him to Antioch (11:22)? Likely those in disagreement with Barnabas being an apostle (contra Acts 14:4, 14) see no calling related to Acts 13:1–3 except for the team simply being designated to serve as messengers of the Church.

Witness to the Resurrection

Luke's general understanding of apostle required someone who had been a witness to the resurrection and had been present from John's baptism to the ascension (Acts 1:21–22). The Twelve, which included Matthias, met these criteria. Paul's understanding of his apostleship was intimately connected to the post-Easter encounter with the Lord (1 Cor. 9:1–2) and differed from Luke's emphasis. The Christ had to suffer and rise, after which repentance and forgiveness were to be preached to all nations. Witnesses to this magnificent truth were needed to speak of what they experienced with the Lord (Luke 22:46–48; John 1:14; Acts 1:8; 1 John 1:1–4). It seems that after Jesus's appearance to Paul (1 Cor. 15:8), such post-Easter encounters ceased, thereby ending this special category of apostle. As noted in the "Others" category above, apostles as messengers or representatives sent from churches likely were not held to the expectation that they had to be eyewitnesses to the resurrected Lord.

Suffering for Christ

Dunn writes, "The true mark of apostolic ministry is the shared experience of Christ's sufferings, of divine strength in human weakness. . . . As the gospel is the gospel of the crucified, so the ministry of the gospel involves living out a *theologia crucis* rather than a *theologia gloriae*."[65] The life of the apostle contains suffering for the expansion of the gospel (Luke 21:10–19). Prior to sending the Twelve, Jesus stated that they were being sent as sheep among wolves (Matt. 10:16). Persecution comes to all who desire to live a godly life, but especially to those who are sent to preach (2 Tim. 3:12). Since Jesus was persecuted, they would also be persecuted (John 15:20). Luke records numerous examples of persecution as the gospel was spreading, both within and outside of Jerusalem.

God informed Ananias of Paul's future hardships (Acts 9:16). Paul frequently addressed suffering throughout his letters (1 Cor. 4:8–13; 15:30–32; 2 Cor. 4:8–12; 6:4–10; 11:22–29). Sometimes such occurred

65. Dunn, *Theology of Paul*, 580.

at the hands of persecutors (2 Cor. 11:24–25), and other times it was related to life as an apostle (Phil. 4:10–13; 1 Cor. 4:9; 2 Tim. 1:11–12). He confessed to bearing "the stigmata of Jesus" (Gal. 6:17, Greek). The past scars and present chains were to be endured "for the sake of the elect, that they also may obtain the salvation that is in Christ Jesus, with eternal glory" (2 Tim. 2:8–10). Suffering allowed God to manifest his power in the life of the believer. Such reality gave Paul the encouragement and ability to boast in what God was doing through him. In his weakness, he received great strength (2 Cor. 12:9–11). Thomas R. Schreiner explains the connection between such difficulty and Paul's task:

> It is significant that suffering was the means by which Paul extended the message to Gentiles. Such suffering highlighted the weakness of the messenger and pointed hearers to God as the all-sufficient one. God's work in and through weak messengers indicates that the power comes from God rather than ministers. The age to come has invaded this present evil age since God reveals his life in earthen vessels. Suffering also validates the integrity of Paul as a messenger since his willingness to undergo pain indicated that he did not proclaim the gospel as a way to get rich or to promote his reputation. Paul's sufferings were a corollary to the sufferings of Christ inasmuch as they were the means by which the message was brought to the Gentiles. It is not the case that God desired Paul to bring the message to the Gentiles and afflictions got in the way. Suffering was the intended means from the beginning.[66]

Signs and Wonders

The New Testament contains much information regarding signs and wonders in the ministries of Jesus and the apostles. According to the Gospel of John, Jesus performed so many signs pointing to the good news that he was incapable of recording them (John 20:30; cf. 21:25). Luke observed the regularity of the signs and wonders being done in conjunction with the apostles' evangelism (Acts 2:43; 5:12, 15–16; 8:6–8; 9:32–42; 15:12). Paul experienced the same working

---

66. Thomas R. Schreiner, *Paul, Apostle of God's Glory in Christ: A Pauline Theology*, 2nd ed. (Downers Grove, IL: IVP Academic, 2020), 100.

of God through his ministry.[67] Linda L. Belleville writes, "Miracles were performed in virtually every city that Paul visited (Paphos [Acts 13:6–12]; Iconium [14:3]; Lystra [14:8–10]; Philippi [16:16–18]; Thessalonica [1 Thess. 1:5]; Corinth [1 Cor. 2:4]; Ephesus [Acts 19:11–12]; Troas [20:9–12]; Malta [28:1–10])."[68]

The Corinthians called Paul's apostleship into question because of the work of the false apostles. While defending his calling, Paul declared that he was not inferior to those "super-apostles." He reminded the church there that the "signs of an apostle" were revealed to the people, for Paul and his associates came "with utmost patience, with signs and wonders and mighty works" (2 Cor. 12:11–12). Though nothing of the sort is mentioned in Luke's summary in Acts 18:1–17, such must have occurred during Paul's eighteen months in the city. This experience parallels Paul's description of his work elsewhere among the Gentiles by "word and deed, by the power of signs and wonders, by the power of the Spirit of God" (Rom. 15:18–19; cf. 1 Thess. 1:5).

The Corinthians were attracted to the power in the person. However, as Mark A. Seifrid explains, Paul reoriented their perspective to the Christ behind the signs. The signs were related to one who bears the sign of the cross. Seifrid notes that the apostle does not produce signs, but "is only the vehicle for them. Furthermore, it is Christ *crucified* and risen who works the signs of an apostle. Just as this Christ lives by the power of God, his deeds of power take place only in the apostle's weakness."[69]

Fruit of Confirmation

The apostolic imagination is pragmatic in orientation.[70] It leads to practical ministry. Jesus told his disciples to abide in him and bear

67. Andrew D. Clarke claims that signs were not a prerequisite for all the apostles. See Andrew D. Clarke, "The Source and Scope of Paul's Apostolic Authority," *Criswell Theological Review* 12, no. 2 (Spring 2015): 3–22, here 7.

68. Belleville, *2 Corinthians*, 314.

69. Mark A. Seifrid, *The Second Letter to the Corinthians*, Pillar New Testament Commentary (Grand Rapids: Eerdmans, 2014), 458.

70. This is not to be confused with the ungodly philosophy of pragmatism, whereby the end justifies the means.

fruit (John 15:1–5). After declaring the breadth of his authority, he promised to be with them as they go into the world and make disciples (Matt. 28:18–20). The christological expectation is that disciples will go and experience results in their ministries. While such outcomes cannot be predicted with certainty, the sovereign Lord works through different variables in contexts to build his Church.

The result of Gentiles coming to faith was confirmation of the Church's faithfulness to God's mission in the world (Acts 10:44–48; 15:12–19). Paul recognized that new believers and churches planted were a sign of his apostleship. Rather than needing an endorsement for his calling, Paul wrote that the Corinthians themselves were his team's letter of recommendation (2 Cor. 3:1–3).

Use of Authority

Apostolic authority in the New Testament is much different from what it has come to mean over the centuries.[71] In the New Testament, apostolic authority was related to "the faith that was . . . delivered to the saints" (Jude 3). The apostles (and their associates) who wrote the documents now called the New Testament were transmitting divine revelation (and interpretation) to first-century believers (2 Tim. 3:16–17; 2 Pet. 3:2, 15–16). These apostles had direct knowledge of Jesus and were authorized to go and teach as his ambassadors (Mark 6:7; Rom. 1:1, 5; 2 Cor. 5:20; Heb. 1:1–2; 1 John 1:1–4). Inspired by the Holy Spirit, they spoke and wrote God's living and active Word, which communicates the truth of Christ and how his followers are to live the kingdom ethic in the world. Their teachings and practices became normative and were to be imitated (Acts 2:42; 1 Cor. 4:16; 7:17; 11:1–2). Their apostolic authority was no longer needed once the Church was founded and the Scriptures were completed.[72]

Apostolic authority was used to build up local churches (1 Cor. 12:28; 2 Cor. 10:8; 13:10; Eph. 4:11–12). When it came to matters of church conflict and discipline, the apostles were engaged but with

71. John Howard Schütz, *Paul and the Anatomy of Apostolic Authority* (Louisville: Westminster John Knox, 2007), 7.
72. George Eldon Ladd, *A Theology of the New Testament*, rev. ed. (Grand Rapids: Eerdmans, 1993), 390.

a gracious approach. One senses the tension in Paul's Letters as he reminds the young churches of his apostleship but exhorts them to be self-governing and resolve the problems at hand. Sometimes he is explicit in expectation (1 Cor. 5:13) but does not desire to be severe (2 Cor. 13:10). Sometimes he appeals to their calling in Christ to live like a family (2 Cor. 10:7–18; Philem. 14–17). Paul's authority was rooted in the Word of God, and when he did not have such knowledge, he was quick to distinguish his judgment from divine command (1 Cor. 7:10, 12, 25, 40).[73]

No one may claim the original apostolic office and authority. The apostolic imagination applied today is different from the first-century apostles in this area. Authority is found in God's Word as it is rightly communicated. The Church today may declare, "The Lord says," because he has spoken in the Scriptures. It is by texts that local churches (and individuals) are to be held accountable and will be judged. The apostles' authority came from their relationship with Christ and his Word, which was being revealed through them. Authority today comes from one's relationship with Christ and his Word *already* revealed.

Apostolic Succession

The historical notion of apostolic succession being passed from the first-century apostles to subsequent generations has no biblical warrant. There is no passage where any of the apostles transfers his apostleship to someone else. George W. Peters's reminder is helpful: "The apostles of Jesus Christ did not deposit their authority and witness in an office to be perpetuated, but in a *scriptura* which is to become the objective guide and authority of the church of Jesus Christ. This *scriptura* constitutes our New Testament, our apostolic witness, and our authority in doctrine and practice."[74] There was an expectation for the replication of teachers and leaders (2 Tim. 2:2),

73. Ernest Best, "Paul's Apostolic Authority?," *Journal for the Study of the New Testament* 27 (1986): 3–25. For a perspective that Paul's authority is only granted to him by the churches, that he is unable to force it upon them, and that signs were not a prerequisite for all the apostles, see Clarke, "Paul's Apostolic Authority."

74. George W. Peters, *A Biblical Theology of Missions* (Chicago: Moody, 1972), 255.

and Paul wanted them to imitate him, but such is a far cry from apostolic succession.

Continuity or Discontinuity

While there is no biblical warrant for apostolic succession, a related matter must be mentioned. If the Others category is determined to be a valid category of apostles in the first century, then scholars are more in favor of acknowledging an ongoing *role*, or (more likely) *function*, of the *apostolos* throughout history. This view is not the same as advocating the continuation of the apostle as categorized by Jesus, the Twelve, Paul, and possibly James. Though the language of *apostle* is frequently not used, historical substitutes have been provided, such as *missionary* and *church planter*. Some scholars believe that these are not substitutes and such arguments are unhelpful; others advocate their use or consideration.[75]

QUESTIONS TO CONSIDER

1. Before reading this chapter, what was your understanding of those who were considered apostles in the New Testament?
2. Do you agree or disagree that the Others category of apostles existed in the New Testament? Why?
3. Did the Others category of apostles end in the first century, or does this category continue to the present? Explain.

---

75. Wayne Grudem argues against equating evangelists and church planters with apostles; see his *Systematic Theology: An Introduction to Biblical Doctrine* (Grand Rapids: Zondervan, 1994), 911. Donald T. Dent is among a growing number of conservative evangelicals who advocate for the ongoing role of apostles as found in their trans-historical functions. See Dent, "Ongoing Role of Apostles in Missions."

CHAPTER 4

Apostolic Function in the New Testament

here is much debate regarding matters related to apostolic identity, as explained in the previous chapter; yet we find more agreement among scholars regarding apostolic functions. With the notion of sending intimately connected with the *apostolos* concept, it is necessary to ask, What did the sent ones do? Are there certain activities that stand out in the biblical evidence? Assuming that actions are often the result of thoughts, it should be possible to gain a better perspective on the apostolic imagination by considering the primary acts of the apostles.

Evangelism

If anything may be stated regarding apostolic work, it is that gospel proclamation is the primary task. In the New Testament, disciple making began with evangelism. Jesus announced the good news that redemption had arrived, and the recreation of all things was coming. The kingdom of God was already present, but not yet complete. Now was the day of salvation, for "whoever believes in the Son has eternal life; whoever does not obey the Son shall not see life, but the wrath of God remains on him" (John 3:36).

The work of the Old Testament prophets was a ministry of proclamation, calling Israel to covenantal faithfulness and warning the nations of God's judgment to come (Jon. 1:1–2). The ministry of the Baptist was focused on proclamation (Mark 1:4). Jesus's ministry began with evangelism and was saturated with evangelism, calling people to repentance and faith (Mark 1:15). His reading from Isaiah to inaugurate his ministry is filled with the language of proclamation. Jesus was anointed "to proclaim good news," sent "to proclaim liberty," and authorized "to proclaim the year of the Lord's favor" (Luke 4:18–19; cf. Isa. 61:1, 2).

After healing many people and casting out demons, Jesus told his disciples, "Let us go on to the next towns, that I may preach there also, for that is why I came out" (Mark 1:38). Though people were still looking for him to meet their physical needs, he departed to other communities. His primary concern was to seek out and save the lost (Luke 19:9; cf. 1 Tim. 1:15).

Mark revealed that the immediate reason for appointing the apostles was "that they might be with him and he might send them out to preach and . . . cast out demons" (Mark 3:14–15). The instructions given to the Twelve began with "Go . . . and proclaim" (Matt. 10:6–7; cf. Luke 9:2). Gentiles and Samaritans who received the good news returned to their social networks, proclaiming what they had experienced with Jesus (Mark 5:19–20; John 4:28–29). The evangelists anticipated the global evangelistic work of the Church (Matt. 26:13; 28:18–20; Mark 13:10; 14:9; Luke 24:46–49; John 17:20–23; 20:21).

The opening verses of Acts offer a general explanation of what occurred following the ascension as the believers were witnesses in Jerusalem, Judea, Samaria, and throughout the world (Acts 1:8). The overwhelming evidence within this book makes it clear that of the apostolic acts, evangelism was of foremost importance. Evangelism follows the fulfillment of Joel's prophecy (Acts 2:16; cf. Joel 2:28–32). It results in disciples being made in Jerusalem (Acts 2:37–41) and Samaria (8:5), among God-fearers (8:35; 10:34–43) and Gentiles (11:19–21). Peter declares, "[Jesus] commanded us to preach to the people and to testify that he is the one appointed by God to be judge of the living and the dead. To him all the prophets bear witness that everyone who believes in him receives forgiveness of sins through his name" (10:42–43).

Paul summarizes his proclamation as "testifying both to Jews and to Greeks of repentance toward God and of faith in our Lord Jesus Christ" (Acts 20:21). F. F. Bruce writes that Paul's "energy was the fruit of his conviction that he was a figure of eschatological significance, a key agent in the progress of salvation history, a chosen instrument in the Lord's hands to bring Gentiles into the obedience of faith as a necessary preparation for the ultimate salvation of all Israel and the consummation of God's redeeming purpose in the world."[1] Acts begins with the anticipation of gospel expansion and concludes with Paul "proclaiming the kingdom of God and teaching about the Lord Jesus Christ with all boldness and without hindrance" (Acts 28:31).

The apostle begins his treatise to the Romans with a salutation stating that he has been "set apart for the gospel of God" (1:1) and that his apostleship is "to bring about the obedience of faith for the sake of his name among all nations" (1:5). This message leads to obedience and is God's power for salvation to any Jew or Gentile who believes (1:16; 10:12). Salvation comes only through an explicit calling to Christ; therefore, someone must do the work of an evangelist (10:13–17). Following an Old Testament example in Isaiah, Paul writes, "I make it my ambition to preach the gospel, not where Christ has already been named" (Rom. 15:20; cf. Isa. 52:15).

Paul reminds others that Christ sent him to preach the gospel (1 Cor. 1:17; 2 Cor. 10:14), a message of Christ crucified that saves those who believe (1 Cor. 1:21–25; 15:1–11). The gospel message is constant and unchanging (Gal. 1:8–10). He concludes his Letters to the Ephesians and Colossians by requesting prayer that he may exhibit boldness and use the correct words to proclaim the gospel (Eph. 6:18–20; Col. 4:3–4). Paul takes encouragement that his imprisonment has emboldened some to share the gospel (Phil. 1:12–18). He encourages the Thessalonians by acknowledging that "the word of the Lord" rang from them throughout Macedonia and Achaia

---

1. F. F. Bruce, *Paul: Apostle of the Heart Set Free* (Grand Rapids: Eerdmans, 1977), 146.

(1 Thess. 1:8). In a similar fashion with the Ephesians and Colossians, he concludes his writing to them by asking for prayer "that the word of the Lord may speed ahead and be honored" (2 Thess. 3:1). In his last words to Timothy, Paul exhorts him to "preach the word" and "do the work of an evangelist" (2 Tim. 4:2, 5).

Teaching Obedience

The taught gospel is the message that the Spirit uses to bring about regeneration (John 3:3). However, the message of good news is also a message the Spirit uses to sanctify the Church. Paul writes to the believers in Rome that he is "eager to preach the gospel to you also" (Rom. 1:15). The apostolic work involves much more than evangelism, for Paul desires people's obedience and maturity in Christ (Rom. 1:5; 10:14–21; 15:18; Col. 1:28–29). The Great Commission is not to make converts but to "make disciples" (Matt. 28:19). These *students*, or *followers*, of Jesus were to spend the rest of their earthly lives living out the kingdom ethic.

Jesus taught as one with authority (Matt. 7:29). He warned that not everyone who calls him "Lord, Lord" will enter heaven, but "the one who does the will of my Father" (Matt. 7:21–23). Nominal faith is false and unacceptable. It results in death (Acts 5:1–11) and excommunication (1 Cor. 5:13). At great cost to Christ, God provided salvation and entrance into the kingdom of God; similarly, a great cost was expected for one to walk as a disciple (Luke 14:25–33). Making disciples began with evangelism, but it was to be immediately followed by baptizing believers and teaching them obedience to the Lord's commands (Matt. 28:19–20).

Acts reveals a paradigm continued throughout the New Testament. Following the birth of the Church, the believers "devoted themselves to the apostles' teaching" in the fellowship of community with other believers (2:42). This teaching placed the apostles at odds with the authorities (4:18). Following the evangelistic work in Antioch by unnamed disciples, Barnabas was sent from Jerusalem to investigate and encourage the new church to remain faithful. He brought Paul to the city, and for a year "they met with the church and taught a great many people" (Acts 11:19–26). Near the end of Paul and Barnabas's first missionary journey, they returned to the newly planted churches to encourage and strengthen them (14:21–23). Paul remained in Corinth for eighteen months and taught the Word of God (18:11). He reminded the Ephesian elders that for three years he taught them the "whole counsel of God" (20:20, 27). The book of Acts concludes with the apostle teaching about the Christ (28:31).

Paul self-identified as a "teacher of the Gentiles" (1 Tim. 2:7). He replicated a pattern of teaching in every church (1 Cor. 4:17). False teaching was a significant problem, so an elder had to be able to teach correctly (1 Tim. 1:3; 3:2; 6:3–5; Titus 1:9; cf. 2 Pet. 2:1). The apostle had to equip others who would serve as teachers. Paul reminded Timothy, "What you have heard from me, . . . entrust to faithful men who will be able to teach others also" (2 Tim. 2:2). Peter's writings contain his teachings to those scattered throughout "Pontus, Galatia, Cappadocia, Asia, and Bithynia" (1 Pet. 1:1). These letters reflect his thoughts on a variety of topics and are designed to instruct those facing difficult times (1 Pet. 1:6; 4:12), wives married to unbelievers (3:1), elders (5:1), and others.

Church Planting

Jesus promised to build his Church (Matt. 16:18). As people made the great kingdom confession that he is Messiah (Matt. 16:16; cf. Rom. 10:9), they were transferred from the kingdom of darkness into the kingdom of light (Col. 1:13). The physical manifestation of Jesus's universal body, "built on the foundation of the apostles and prophets" (Eph. 2:20), came into existence whenever local churches were planted.[2] Jesus never commanded the apostles to plant churches. It was out of a disciple-making movement that churches came into existence. Biblical church planting was *evangelism* that resulted in new churches. Church planting in the New Testament began in the harvest fields, not by gathering long-term kingdom citizens to start a church in a community.

2. I address church planting at length in my books: J. D. Payne, *Discovering Church Planting: An Introduction to the Whats, Whys, and Hows of Global Church Planting* (Downers Grove, IL: IVP, 2009); Payne, *Apostolic Church Planting: Birthing New Churches from New Believers* (Downers Grove, IL: InterVarsity, 2015).

After Jesus called his disciples to faith, he left behind the nascent Jerusalem church of about 120 followers (Acts 1:15) with eleven leaders. The coming of the Holy Spirit not only marked the fulfillment of Joel's prophecy, but also brought the local ecclesial expression into fullness. This marked a significant turning point in the life of the community regarding how they would relate to God, to one another, and to those outside their fellowship.

Jesus's model in Jerusalem was reflected in the practices found throughout Acts and Paul's writings. The apostolic team began with evangelism. Once disciples were made, they were gathered to be the local expressions of the Church in their locales. These kingdom communities were then taught to live out the kingdom ethic. Elders were appointed to provide oversight and shepherd the churches as the team began labors elsewhere.

Paul and Barnabas's initial journey followed this pattern (Acts 13–14). They entered a city and began their evangelistic work in a synagogue. Some people believed; others did not. They were often expelled from the community only to repeat this process elsewhere. Following their evangelistic work in Derbe, they returned to the communities through which they had come (14:21). Luke records that this return trip included strengthening and encouraging the new disciples and appointing elders in every church that had been planted (14:21–23). The presence of each local assembly of Jews and Gentiles served as a sign of God's end-time activity to redeem and restore all things through Christ.[3]

Leadership Development

Jesus taught, empowered, and equipped his apostles for ministry.[4] He modeled before them what was to be repeated and provided the opportunity for them to apply his teaching and example (Matt. 10:5–8; Luke 9:2; 10:9). They would eventually do even greater works than

3. Walter F. Taylor, *Paul, Apostle to the Nations: An Introduction* (Minneapolis: Fortress, 2012), 92.

4. For a classic practical text on this topic, see Robert E. Coleman, *The Master Plan of Evangelism* (1964; repr., Old Tappan, NJ: Revell, 1972).

Jesus did (John 14:12). This concern for healthy leadership was replicated in the apostolic labors that followed the ascension.

As noted, prior to returning to Antioch, Paul and Barnabas appointed elders from among the disciples to oversee the newly planted churches (Acts 14:23). Paul recognized the significance of healthy pastoral leaders: they were gifts to the Church, "to equip the saints for the work of ministry, for building up the body of Christ" (Eph. 4:11–12). Luke recorded Paul's special effort to meet with the Ephesian elders. In his last words to them, he reminded them of his model of life and teaching and warned them of the problems to come (Acts 20:17–38). His exhortation was to "pay careful attention to yourselves and to all the flock, in which the Holy Spirit has made you overseers, to care for the church of God" (Acts 20:28). In the Pastorals, he delineated to both Timothy and Titus the characteristics of an overseer (1 Tim. 3:1–7; Titus 1:6–9). Though elders were already in place in Ephesus (Acts 20:17), it appears that Titus's context lacked their presence. Paul wrote, "This is why I left you in Crete, so that you might put what remained into order, and appoint elders in every town as I directed you" (Titus 1:5). While writing to scattered believers, Peter shared his concern for elders. His concluding words, found in his first epistle, provided instruction and encouragement to them during most unpleasant circumstances (1 Pet. 5:1–5).

Care for the Churches

The apostolic imagination was deeply concerned with the welfare of the churches (2 Cor. 11:2, 11). It was not sufficient that churches were started; those new kingdom communities were to mature in the faith. Just as Jesus did not abandon his Church, the functions of apostles involved care as well.

Such concern was found in the general oversight, teaching, and leadership provided by the apostles (Acts 4:34–35; 6:1–7; 15:6, 22–23; 16:4). Sometimes this meant involvement in corrective church discipline (Acts 5:3–9; 1 Cor. 5:3–5). Care for the churches also included care for the impoverished saints. After hearing of Paul and Barnabas's labors among the Gentiles, the apostles in Jerusalem encouraged them to continue such work, yet with the request that they "remember the poor." Paul acknowledged he was eager to fulfill this desire (Gal. 2:7–10). Later, Paul informed the Romans that he had been delayed in coming to them because of his care for the poor saints in Jerusalem. The Churches of Macedonia and Achaia were sending aid to the believers in Jerusalem, and Paul was engaged in the transportation of the contributions. He planned, as soon as that task was complete, to depart for Rome and then to Spain (Rom. 15:25–28).

Examples of care may be found as Paul returned and visited churches or elders, a team member (e.g., Timothy, Titus, or Epaphras) spent time with the churches, or letters were written to the fellowships. Paul's language to a church he had yet to visit reflects this concern for their maturity in Christ:

> Him we proclaim, warning everyone and teaching everyone with all wisdom, that we may present everyone mature in Christ. For this I toil, struggling with all his energy that he powerfully works within me. For I want you to know how great a struggle I have for you and for those at Laodicea and for all who have not seen me face to face, that their hearts may be encouraged, being knit together in love, to reach all the riches of full assurance of understanding and the knowledge of God's mystery, which is Christ, in whom are hidden all the treasures of wisdom and knowledge. I say this in order that no one may delude you with plausible arguments. For though I am absent in body, yet I am with you in spirit, rejoicing to see your good order and the firmness of your faith in Christ. (Col. 1:28–2:5)

To the Thessalonians, Paul noted that the team could have arrived and made demands of them, but they were gentle with them, like a mother with a new child, sharing both the gospel and their very lives (1 Thess. 2:5–8). He revealed to the Corinthians that he suffered greatly due to his apostolic ministry, which included daily pressure that caused him anxiety as he thought of the churches (2 Cor. 11:28). His function as an apostle, and the elders he appointed, was to equip the church so that maturity in Christ and love and unity in the fellowship would be present (Eph. 4:11–16; cf. Phil. 2:15). Even a casual reading of the Pastoral Epistles reveals the apostolic heart as Timothy and Titus were exhorted to provide faithful service among the churches.

A great deal of the content found in the General Epistles and Revelation reveals the authors' concerns for the churches. False teaching and persecution were on the rise, and churches needed to be warned and challenged to take a stand amid such troubles. Warnings, calls for perseverance, and remaining in the truth are found throughout these latter writings of the New Testament. The writer of 3 John reflects this desire found in the apostolic imagination when he declares, "I have no greater joy than to hear that my children are walking in the truth" (4).

Partnerships

The apostolic functions reflected an imagination that recognized the kingdom value and potential when believers collaborated for the Church's global work. Partnership, not paternalism, was necessary for the task. More could be accomplished by working together than separated in ministry silos. Jesus extended to his apostles an earthly ministry that was intimately connected to heaven (Matt. 16:19; 18:18). He sent the Spirit and empowered and released them to participate in God's mission. Jesus promised that as they engaged in the global task, he would always be with them (Matt. 20:20). His Church was and is his representative on earth. His partnership with his people was so intimate that persecution of the Church was tantamount to persecuting Jesus himself (Acts 9:4). Barnabas was sent from the Jerusalem church to assist with the development of the Antioch church (Acts 11:22). It was from Antioch that Barnabas and Paul were sent on the first missionary journey (Acts 13:1–3). Paul and his teams operated with the value of partnership as well. An examination of the Scriptures quickly diffuses the romantic notion that Paul was a lone ranger for Jesus. At the conclusion of the first trip, he and Barnabas returned to Antioch with a report of God's grace among the peoples (Acts 14:27–28). Paul's Letters were to be shared among the churches (Col. 4:16). Churches were exhorted to partner with one another during difficult times (2 Cor. 8:13–15). Some members of Paul's apostolic teams came from the younger churches. Developing churches partnered with Paul through their resources to assist with gospel advancement to new locations (Rom. 15:24–29; Phil. 2:25; 4:14–15; Philem. 22).

QUESTIONS TO CONSIDER

1. What is the significance of apostolic functions being represented in the life and work of Jesus, rather than initially represented in the Church?

2. What are your thoughts regarding the claim that evangelism is primary among the apostolic functions?

3. Are there other significant apostolic functions related to the Church's global task that were not included in this chapter? If so, what should be added?

PART 2

REIMAGINING CONTEMPORARY MISSIONS

CHAPTER 5

Reimagining Language

The Church should always be cautious when using language. The terms and phrases used reflect belief, theology, and practice. If Jesus is defined as less than divine, then theological problems arise. If the local church is understood as a building and not the people of God, then many ecclesiastical problems develop over time. Stephen A. Grunlan and Marvin K. Mayers write, "Language communicates what members of a society need to know. It is a major tool of the social group, effecting loyalties based on past, present, or future events and relationships."[1]

Through language the abstract concepts such as *mission* and *missions* are shared and understood across time. Michael W. Stroope is correct in declaring that discussion of language is not a useless exercise. We must recognize that "mission language forms particular ideals and notions that shape identity and purpose, that determines why and how we act."[2] A failure to communicate clearly and biblically, when it comes to the apostolic work of the Church, reveals a

---

1. Stephen A. Grunlan and Marvin K. Mayers, *Cultural Anthropology: A Christian Perspective*, 2nd ed. (Grand Rapids: Zondervan, 1988), 88.
2. Michael W. Stroope, *Transcending Mission: The Eclipse of a Modern Tradition* (Downers Grove, IL: IVP Academic, 2017), xiii.

significant problem in stewarding well the Lord's commission. Kevin DeYoung and Greg Gilbert summarize the problem at hand: "Because *mission* is not a biblical word like *covenant* or *justification* or *gospel*, determining its meaning for believers is particularly difficult. We could do a study of the word *gospel* and come to some pretty firm biblical conclusions about 'What is the Gospel?'. . . But *mission* is a bit trickier."[3]

As a pastor, I never gave my people the following challenge, but I can imagine their frustration and surprise if I had asked them to find every Bible verse that uses the words *mission, missions*, and *missionary*. Many would assume that several verses surely exist, given their unquestioned widespread use.

If the Lord has assigned a task to the Church, then it is necessary to have a clear understanding regarding the task and the Lord's expectations. Imagine the servants telling the master that they were not certain what he meant by putting his "money on deposit" or what was the proper understanding of investing his money with "bankers" (cf. Matt. 25:14–30). The apostolic imagination strives for a clarity of understanding, for much is at stake before his return.

The Problem with the Language of Mission

In 1961, Gerald H. Anderson edited possibly the first comprehensive work on the topic of mission theology. In his introduction he made a statement that still echoes into this century. The "fundamental task of the missionary enterprise today," he wrote, "is to clarify the nature and meaning of its being. This must be done in the realm of theological thought, not only to increase effectiveness in presenting the Gospel to the world, but also to give Christians a deeper understanding of what their task *is* in the world."[4] It was no wonder that Anderson made this claim. Two years earlier, Stephen Neill published

3. Kevin DeYoung and Greg Gilbert, *What Is the Mission of the Church? Making Sense of Social Justice, Shalom, and the Great Commission* (Wheaton: Crossway, 2011), 17.

4. Gerald H. Anderson, "The Theology of Mission among Protestants in the Twentieth Century," in *The Theology of the Christian Mission*, ed. Gerald H. Anderson (Nashville: Abingdon, 1961), 3–16, here 4.

Creative Tension, in which he made the infamous statement: "When everything is mission, nothing is mission."[5] His point was that once the Church believes that everything the Church does is mission, then the apostolic work of the Church is neglected.

Same terms, different dictionaries. When terms are extrabiblical, it is difficult to assign them an agreed-upon meaning.[6] This becomes even more problematic whenever a robust exegetical theology is not attached to such terminology. The result is that the definitions for *mission, missions*, and *missionaries* will not remain constant but will change based on contemporary realities and readers' perspectives. Everything becomes mission—or missions—because the language lacks a biblical origin and justification. Missions becomes evangelism and fighting for social justice. Missions becomes church planting among an unreached people and helping a village dig a well. Since the Scriptures do not contain the word *missions* and since the Scriptures are clear that the Church *is* to be involved in evangelism, social justice, planting churches, and caring for the poor, then each of these may be labeled *missions* and reflect God's mission in the world. What was missions yesterday is not missions today and may be radically different tomorrow.

Instead of asking what *mission, missions*, or *missionaries* mean, the Church should be asking: Is there a biblical terminology and emphasis when it comes to the Church's identity and ongoing actions in the world? What did those actions look like in the first century? These questions force the Church to return to the text to develop an exegetical approach to understanding terms, purpose, and priority in the world. Such a task leads researchers to a variety of ecclesial activities, but not all carry the same gravity based on the narrative descriptions. All service done for the Lord is good, but not all service is equivalent to the apostolic work of the Church. When the Church fails to define and explain Great Commission activities in apostolic terms and descriptions, then disciple-making activities become just one more set of actions, equivalent with everything else the Church does in the world.

5. Stephen Neill, *Creative Tension* (London: Edinburgh House, 1959), 81.
6. Even with biblical words, scholars frequently disagree over definitions.

The language of mission is universal. The Church uses accepted terminology, but members reference different dictionaries. Bosch observed this problem in the early 1980s: "It is a commonplace that we are today experiencing a crisis in the church's understanding of mission. And it is ironic that this crisis is developing in a period when the word 'mission' is being used more than ever before—albeit with many different meanings. We have reached a state at which almost anybody using the concept of mission has to explain how it is understood if serious confusion is to be avoided."[7]

Lest we believe that such confusion was overcome by the end of the twentieth century, Denny Spitters and Matthew Ellison say this challenge is present today: "We are concerned that an uncritical use of words, and in particular a lack of shared definition for the words mission, missions, missionary, and missional, has led to a distortion of Jesus' biblical mandate, ushered in an everything-is-missions paradigm, and moved missions from the initiation and oversight of local churches to make it the domain of individual believers responding to individualized callings."[8]

Eckhard J. Schnabel has challenged the academic community regarding unclear discussions related to this topic: "Many exegetical studies on missions fail to indicate which notion of mission is used or presupposed."[9] If there is a lack of clarity in the academy, then confusion will exist in local churches and on the field. Consider that even the most traditional and conservative evangelical pastors will announce on Sunday that the youth choir's "missions trip" will take place next year as they go to Appalachia to sing in the worship services of another church, and the "men on mission" will be doing "missions" in Honduras this summer by installing a roof on a school. But today they are praying for the missionaries planting churches in the Middle East among an unreached people. The Church is involved in many tasks that reflect the kingdom ethic, but apostolic labors

---

7. David J. Bosch, "Theological Education in Missionary Perspective," *Missiology* 10, no. 1 (January 1982): 13–34, here 13.

8. Denny Spitters and Matthew Ellison, *When Everything Is Missions* (n.p.: BottomLine Media, 2017), 22–23, https://pioneers.org/wp-content/uploads/2019/05/When-Everything-Is-Missions.pdf.

9. Eckhard J. Schnabel, *Early Christian Mission*, vol. 1, *Jesus and the Twelve* (Downers Grove, IL: InterVarsity, 2004), 1:11.

have been relegated to a corner of a room and are surrounded with a multitude of good and noble activities.

Here is a sample of definitions of mission, revealing the understandings of several influential Protestant (mostly evangelical) scholars. While there are similarities, there are significant differences and sometimes a lack of clarity. Mission is said to be one or more of these:

Everything the church is sent into the world to do. (John R. W. Stott)[10]

Carrying the gospel across cultural boundaries to those who own no allegiance to Jesus Christ, and encouraging them to accept Him as Lord and Savior and to become responsible members of His church, working, as the Holy Spirit leads, at both evangelism and justice, at making God's will done on earth as it is done in heaven. (Arthur F. Glasser and Donald McGavran)[11]

An extension of the mission of Jesus. It is the manifestation (though not yet complete) of the Kingdom of God, through proclamation as well as through social service and action. (C. René Padilla)[12]

What the Christian community is sent to do, beginning right where it is located. (J. Andrew Kirk)[13]

The activity of a community of faith that distinguishes itself from its environment in terms of both religious belief (theology) and social behavior (ethics), that is convinced of the truth claims of its faith, and that actively works to win other people to the content of faith and

10. John R. W. Stott, *Christian Mission in the Modern World* (Downers Grove, IL: InterVarsity, 1975), 30. With a confusing turn of words, Stott adds, "'Mission,' then, is not a word for everything the church does. . . . Nor, as we have seen, does 'mission' cover everything God does in the world" (30).

11. Arthur F. Glasser and Donald A. McGavran, *Contemporary Theologies of Mission* (Grand Rapids: Baker, 1983), 26.

12. C. René Padilla, *Mission between the Times: Essays on the Kingdom* (Grand Rapids: Eerdmans, 1985), 192.

13. J. Andrew Kirk, *What Is Mission? Theological Explorations* (Minneapolis: Fortress, 2000), 24.

to the way of life of whose truth and necessity the members of that community are convinced. (Eckhard J. Schnabel)[14]

Our committed participation as God's people, at God's invitation and command, in God's own mission within the history of God's world for the redemption of God's creation. (Christopher J. H. Wright)[15]

The sending activity of God with the purpose of reconciling to himself and bringing into his kingdom fallen men and women from every people, nation, and tongue. (Craig Ott, Stephen J. Strauss, and Timothy C. Tennent)[16]

God's comprehensive purpose for the whole of creation and all that God has called and sent the church to do in connection with that purpose. (Dean Flemming)[17]

The overarching term describing God's mission in the world . . . to bring about redemption of the world, or human participation in this mission. (Scott W. Sunquist)[18]

The whole task of the church to witness to the whole gospel in the whole world. (Michael W. Goheen)[19]

Language of sending. Francis M. DuBose recognizes the limitations of the word *mission* and attempts to determine meaning by appealing to the *consensus* of sending. As noted in a previous

14. Schnabel, *Early Christian Mission*, 1:11; he assigns this definition to both mission and missions.

15. Christopher J. H. Wright, *The Mission of God: Unlocking the Bible's Grand Narrative* (Downers Grove, IL: IVP Academic, 2006), 23.

16. Craig Ott, Stephen J. Strauss, with Timothy C. Tennent, *Encountering Theology of Mission: Biblical Foundations, Historical Developments, and Contemporary Issues* (Grand Rapids: Baker Academic, 2010), xv, xvii.

17. Dean Flemming, *Recovering the Full Mission of God: A Biblical Perspective on Being, Doing and Telling* (Downers Grove, IL: IVP Academic, 2013), 17.

18. Scott W. Sunquist, *Understanding Christian Mission: Participating in Suffering and Glory* (Grand Rapids: Baker Academic, 2013), 7. Sunquist uses the term *missions* to refer to organizations, societies, and agencies used to carry out God's mission in the world (7).

19. Michael W. Goheen, *Introducing Christian Mission Today: Scripture, History, and Issues* (Downers Grove, IL: IVP Academic, 2014), 402.

chapter, the sending concept was related to the nature of the apostolic functions and is found in the apostolic imagination. DuBose writes:

> Is there a biblical concept of mission? Or is it something we impose on Scripture from our history and experience (or even our prejudice)? The first point in this serious hermeneutical question is: what language in Scripture is to guide us in our quest for the biblical meaning of mission? One legitimate and significant approach is to begin with a rather universal consensus: *mission* means sending. This is one point on which most everyone seems to agree. What better beginning point could we have than this kind of consensus? And since references to the word *missions* are negligible in our English Bible and since there is a rich language of the sending in the Scriptures, it would appear to be a high agenda item to look carefully at what that language conveys in the way of theological content. An immediate survey of the term *sending* in its various forms in Scripture suggests that it is more than a simple descriptive word. It seems both appropriate and safe, therefore, at least to begin with the hypothesis that in the sense of "the sending," there is a biblical idea of mission.[20]

Charles Van Engen also argues that when it comes to mission, the Bible regularly emphasizes "the concept of being sent" and "the authority and purpose of the sender."[21] However, others warn of the limitations when too much attention is on the sending concept.

Though referring to *missions,* J. H. Bavinck's point is clear in explaining missions as "more than the sending out of missionaries." He goes on to say, "With the Scriptures in hand we ought to give a broader interpretation to the concept of missions and pay more attention to its diverse aspects."[22] Although he distinguishes between missionaries sent out and the "nonofficial" evangelism done by all believers, he notes that missions is a broad concept. Missionary

20. Francis M. DuBose, *God Who Sends: A Fresh Quest for Biblical Mission* (Nashville: Broadman, 1983), 24.

21. Charles Van Engen, "Essay 1: 'Mission' Defined and Described," in *MissionShift: Global Mission Issues in the Third Millennium*, ed. David J. Hesselgrave and Ed Stetzer (Nashville: B&H Academic, 2010), 10.

22. J. H. Bavinck, *An Introduction to the Science of Missions*, trans. David Hugh Freeman (Philadelphia: Presbyterian and Reformed, 1960), 67.

activity takes place in all of life, "including both the organized and the unorganized activity of believers."[23] Christopher Wright is even more precise in his language. Defining mission in terms of the Latin verb *mitto* (to send) is reductionistic. "If we define *mission* only in 'sending' terms we necessarily exclude from our inventory of relevant resources many other aspects of biblical teaching that directly or indirectly affect our understanding of God's mission and the practice of our own."[24]

These four scholars, including the various definitions presented above, reflect some of the tensions found today. Such differing views represent what has developed in the last one hundred years. The same terms are used, but definitions differ. How did this lack of agreement happen?

Brief History of the Language of Mission

Though the Church had a variety of terms for the expansion of the faith and the individuals sent since apostolic times, the modern understanding of the all-encompassing *mission* draws from the sixteenth-century work of Ignatius of Loyola (1491–1556): he appropriated the word (from the Spanish *misión*, Latin *missio*, Portuguese *missão*, and French *mission*) and developed it for his context.[25] This novelty reframed the Roman Catholic, and eventually Protestant, understanding of service in the world. By the time the Society of Jesus was established in 1538, it was unique among the orders, particularly for the "Fourth Vow" taken by its members: *votum de missionibus*, the mission vow. This aspect of the new society greatly facilitated the expansion of the Catholic Church. The Latin verb *mitto* (I send) and *missio* (mission) were ancient words and had been used by Irenaeus, Tertullian, Augustine, and Aquinas to describe the inner workings of the Godhead. Prior to Ignatius,

23. Bavinck, *Science of Missions*, 68.
24. C. Wright, *Mission of God*, 23.
25. Stroope, *Transcending Mission*, 238. I am indebted to Stroope for his research on early years of the Jesuits. I have adapted portions of his historical study in these paragraphs related to Ignatius and Xavier. For more details, see Stroope, *Transcending Mission*, 238–87.

the Spanish and Portuguese governments used *mission* to describe political and military actions in foreign contexts, and the French used it as a legal term to reveal indebtedness and obligations between differing parties.

The Catholic Church developed a partnership with the state whereby the Catholic Church would support commercial and political advancements as long as the state reciprocated with protection and assistance with the Christianization of new territories. Though not all Catholic missionaries were in favor of European development being attached to their efforts, over time a close relationship developed between colonial expansion and the Church's work. Military, merchants, and missionaries were often in proximity. The government's mission became both a political and ecclesial mission. Horst Gründer writes, "As much as evangelization promised to further the expansion of the empire, so did imperial expansion promise to further the spreading of the Gospel."[26] For Ignatius, mission was related to any location where the pope might send the Jesuits. Mission was comprised of a wide array of activities. It could involve evangelistic work but also included going to serve Christians in need.

Francis Xavier (1506–52) was the first member of the order to be sent outside of Europe. In his correspondence from the field, Xavier did not prefer to use the language of *mission*. Years after arriving in India, however, he began referring to those sent from the order to reach unbelievers as *missionaries*, who participated in *mission*. Yet it was during the seventeenth-century work of the Franciscans in the Americas that the word *mission* became more commonplace but described an established station in pioneer territories. Reflecting on these initial developments in modern missions, Stroope writes, "The endeavor launched by Ignatius and the band of like-minded men differed in meaning and classification because of how they identified and structured the church's task. Mission, and all this uniquely Ignatian term entailed, was the difference. In the Jesuits' introduction and use of *mission*, a monumental

---

26. Horst Gründer, "Christian Mission and Colonial Expansion: Historical and Structural Connections," *Mission Studies* 12, no. 1 (January 1995): 18–29, here 18.

shift occurred in the language and meaning of the church's reach beyond Christendom."[27]

While Catholics maintained the monastic structures for sending missionaries, Protestants avoided such structures and gave attention to other matters. Bosch explains, "It would take centuries before anything remotely as competent and effective as the monastic missionary movement would develop in Protestantism."[28] However, the pre-Reformation history would have great influence on such developments. Gründer notes that after the political decline of Portugal and Spain in the late sixteenth century, "Protestant" nations such as Holland, England, and Denmark rose to power. "Their entrance into colonial history marks the general beginning of Protestant missionary expansion. As had their Catholic predecessors, the Protestants regarded European secular colonialism and imperialism as means of fulfilling Providence. Christian missionaries of all creeds and denominations were united in the common belief that European expansionism was a manifestation of God's decree to spread *His* kingdom in the world."[29]

Protestants were not only slow to come to the mission table but also slow in adopting the modern language of mission. Stroope attributes this hesitation to four reasons: *mission* terminology was an innovation of the Catholic Church; *mission* meant human works and was believed to interfere with God's activity; *mission* meant traveling to a foreign territory, and Protestant witness was understood to be within one's local geography; *mission* was not normative Church language. Various forces eventually resulted in a Protestant shift. Stroope notes that Protestants embraced such rhetoric less out of conviction and more from convenience as their countries dominated the seas in search for colonies.[30] While there were a few exceptions, with the Moravians and William Carey, a great deal of Protestant work was state sponsored. However, by the turn of the twentieth century, the majority of Protestant mission

27. Stroope, *Transcending Mission*, 287.
28. David J. Bosch, *Transforming Mission: Paradigm Shifts in Theology of Mission*, 20th anniversary ed. (Maryknoll, NY: Orbis, 2011), 250.
29. Gründer, "Christian Mission and Colonial Expansion," 19.
30. Stroope, *Transcending Mission*, 303–4, 306–7.

workers were serving in lands in which their governments had no jurisdictions.

During the seventeenth century, Adrianus Saravia (1532–1613), Justus Heurnius (1587–1651), and Justinian von Welz (1621–68) attempted to draw attention to reaching the nations. Anabaptists such as Balthasar Hübmaier (1480–1528) and Menno Simons (1496–1561) were also concerned about the Great Commission. The development and growth of the Pietist movement, however, brought changes that turned attentions toward the nations. German Protestant educator August Hermann Francke (1663–1727) was influenced by this movement through his friendship with Philipp Jakob Spener (1635–1705). Francke's teaching at the University of Halle provided an opportunity to influence others toward the nations. During this time, Frederick IV of Denmark desired missionaries for the Danish colonies. Students at the University of Halle initially filled this request. In 1705, the Danish-Halle Mission was launched with Bartholomäus Ziegenbalg (1682–1719) and Heinrich Plütschau (1678–1747) as the first missionaries to India. Within a few years, Count Nikolaus Ludwig von Zinzendorf (1700–1760) and the Moravians, having been also influenced by the work of Spener (and David Brainerd in the North American colonies) sent many people to some of the remotest places on the planet. Through the leadership of Zinzendorf, the language of mission developed within the Church. Stroope writes, "Just as Ignatius innovated mission language for the Roman Catholic orders, Zinzendorf and the Moravians introduced mission as ecclesial language for Protestants."[31] Between the seventeenth and nineteenth centuries, Protestants developed many societies that used the language of mission in their titles.

Twentieth-Century Shift

Pietism that developed in the seventeenth century had little concern with producing a theology of mission. Jesus had given the mandate. The Church was to go into all the world and preach the gospel, not ponder the idea of preaching. Carl E. Braaten writes, "Orthodoxy

31. Stroope, *Transcending Mission*, 313.

had no heart for mission and the Enlightenment could not square it with reason, so it was left to Pietism to assume a near monopoly on the propagating of the faith."[32] Terminology and language were insignificant. While there were a few exceptions, theologians had little to say about a theology of mission until after the Great Century of missions (1792–1910).[33] However, it was the lack of a robust theological foundation for biblical language and apostolic labors that contributed to much confusion in the last century and to date.

Multiple large ecumenical and evangelical gatherings took place during the twentieth and twenty-first centuries to address the Church and mission.[34] Theologians were forced to respond to the volume and success of the Church's global activity. Some—such as Ernst Troeltsch, with his evolutionary-historical view of religion—argued that the Bible and Jesus were simply a stage in God's work in all religions. Mission was to result in the Church having *dialogue* with other religions. Christianity was not superior, but a Western expression of God's universal work. In 1932, Karl Barth spoke during a conference on the theme "Theology and Mission Today." He

32. Carl E. Braaten, *The Flaming Center: A Theology of the Christian Mission* (Philadelphia: Fortress, 1977), 14.

33. Some of the exceptions include Adrianus Saravia (1532–1613), a Protestant theologian whose work *De diversis ministorum evangelii gradibus* [On the various levels of ministers of the gospel as they have been instituted by the Lord] influenced what would become the discipline of missiology. He influenced Justus Heurnius (1587–1651), Gisbertus Voetius (1589–1676), the Danish-Halle Mission, and English Puritans such as John Eliot (1604–90). Erasmus (1469?–1536) was known for making a mission appeal, but no one accepted the challenge.

34. Some of the gatherings include the 1910 Edinburgh Missionary Conference. Next came meetings of the International Missionary Council (IMC, established at London in 1921): 1928 Jerusalem; 1938 Tambaram, near Madras, India; 1947 Whitby, Ontario, Canada; 1952 Willingen, Germany; 1958 Accra, Ghana; 1961 New Delhi, when and where the IMC was incorporated into the World Council of Churches (WCC) Commission on World Mission and Evangelism, which met: 1963 Mexico City; 1973 Bangkok; 1980 Melbourne. WCC meetings: 1968 Uppsala; 1972 New Delhi; 1975 Nairobi. Also note the Lausanne Congress on World Evangelization meetings: 1974 Lausanne; 1989 Manila; 2010 Cape Town. In addition to 2010 Cape Town, Christians throughout the world recognized the 100th anniversary of the 1910 Edinburgh Conference with gatherings at Tokyo, Edinburgh, and Boston. For an assessment of these 2010 gatherings, see Allen Yeh, *Polycentric Missiology: Twenty-First Century Mission from Everyone to Everywhere* (Downers Grove, IL: IVP Academic, 2016).

decried that missions had become too secular, with its emphasis on humanitarianism, which had been influenced by Gottfried Wilhelm Leibniz and passed on during the Enlightenment. Barth defined mission as the Church's work of proclaiming the gospel to those who had never heard. This witness to the Word of God was the task of mission.[35]

As colonialism was coming to an end, global cultural shifts began to influence the expansion of the Church. Gerald H. Anderson wrote in 1961, "The underlying principles and theological presuppositions for the Christian mission have been called into question and Christians are challenged to rethink the motives, message, methods, and goals of their mission."[36] In what was an accurate assessment in retrospect, Anderson noted that the theology of mission needed and being developed was "leading toward a *theocentric* point of view in thoroughgoing trinitarian perspective." He believed that confusion in missions was present and widespread because of inadequate theology. "There have been attempts from the culture-centered, man-centered, Bible-centered, Church-centered and Christ-centered points of view. While all of these attempts have stressed various aspects of Christian doctrine that are essential for the missionary enterprise, it seems that when any one of them has been made the central point of focus and orientation for the theology of mission, it has proven inadequate for the task, tending to narrow the scope of the mission and causing it to go astray."[37]

Theologians in the twentieth century began to address the concept of mission with much attention.[38] As they turned toward the Scriptures with the modern language of mission in hand, they argued that

35. Braaten, *The Flaming Center*, 29.
36. Anderson, "Theology of Mission," 3.
37. Anderson, "Theology of Mission," 15.
38. Wilbert R. Shenk writes, "The International Missionary Council (IMC) played an indispensable role in the development of mission theology through a series of international assemblies between 1928 and 1958." Wilbert R. Shenk, "Introduction," in *Theology of Mission: A Believers Church Perspective*, by John Howard Yoder, ed. Gayle Gerber Koontz and Andy Alexis-Baker (Downers Grove, IL: IVP Academic, 2014), 13–33, here 18. For a survey of theological developments in 1910–52, see Wilhelm Andersen, *Towards a Theology of Mission: A Study of the Encounter between the Missionary Enterprise and the Church and Its Theology*, International Missionary Council Research Pamphlet No. 2 (London: SCM, 1955).

God's actions were much broader than the redemption of the elect.[39] Traditional terminology was co-opted with an expanded definition that reflected the multiple actions of God throughout the Scriptures. Of course, not all these revisionists allowed the Bible to establish their mission theology. Some assigned great value to speculative theology, comparative religious studies, social science, and liberal theology. William Ernest Hocking's widely influential work *Re-thinking Missions: A Laymen's Inquiry after One Hundred Years* was a revisionist perspective far removed from a biblical understanding of mission.[40]

Mission came to be understood as originating with and belonging to God. Yet the *missio Dei* arguments during this time were not in agreement. Diversity existed among academics and mission leaders. In general, however, a theocentric approach to mission, rather than an anthropocentric or ecclesiocentric approach, was determined to be the starting point. Neither the world nor the Church were to set the agenda for mission. God determined everything, as manifested in the Scriptures. The *missio Dei* involved a wide range of divine acts to bring about the redemption and restoration of all things. By implication, the Church's activities (i.e., missions) needed to become more diverse and multifaceted. Mission belongs to God and is to be reflected in the Church's actions.

Theologians and missiologists failed to temper this breadth with theological urgency and kingdom stewardship.[41] How was the Church to make disciples of the billions who had never heard the gospel if *mission* was broad and included a wide range of activities? Were there

---

39. Anderson's desire for a "radical trinitarian theocentrism" ("Theology of Mission," 15) manifested itself in numerous publications throughout the latter twentieth and early twenty-first centuries. A few examples include Georg F. Vicedom, *The Mission of God: An Introduction to a Theology of Mission* (St. Louis: Concordia, 1965); DuBose, *God Who Sends*; Lesslie Newbigin, *The Open Secret: An Introduction to the Theology of Mission*, rev. ed. (Grand Rapids: Eerdmans, 1995); Bosch, *Transforming Mission*; Timothy C. Tennent, *Invitation to World Missions: A Trinitarian Missiology for the Twenty-First Century* (Grand Rapids: Kregel, 2010); and Sunquist, *Understanding Christian Mission*.

40. William Ernest Hocking, ed., *Re-thinking Missions: A Laymen's Inquiry after One Hundred Years* (New York: Harper & Brothers, 1932).

41. Such was part of the concern of McGavran, who accused the WCC of betraying the billions of unreached peoples. See Donald McGavran, "Yes, Uppsala Betrayed the Two Billion: Now What?," *Christianity Today* 16, no. 19 (June 23, 1972): 16–18.

more important questions to ask, given the breadth of God's mission? The demise of colonialism and the rapid growth of the Church in the Majority World led many to ask multiple questions regarding the role of the Church in the traditionally Western countries. With such global expansion, and with mission now being from everywhere to everywhere, should the Church in the West become more pastoral and less apostolic? Was it possible that the day of sending missionaries to other nations was over? Could it be that those from the West should not engage in church-planting activities? Had the time arrived for traditional societies and agencies to consider shifting to developing established churches that had been around for years? The shift to a theocentric approach to mission, grounded on Scriptures, quickly resulted in conflict between two parties: the traditionalists and revisionists.

Traditionalists and Revisionists

The traditionalists[42] had a long heritage of defining mission (and missions) primarily in terms of evangelism, church planting, and leadership development. Zeal, love for the Lord, sacrifice, and a commitment to the Great Commission that developed from Pietism led many to the nations. They were the ones in the trenches sharing the gospel. Over the centuries, multitudes were sent, preached the gospel, planted churches, trained leaders, and gave their lives for the cause of Christ and his kingdom. If anything, they earned the right to define the terms.

However, if *mission* is of God, then they incorrectly limited missions (stemming from God's mission) as being primarily evangelism and church planting. The Scriptures reveal God being engaged in more than personal redemption. Jesus manifested multiple actions to point to his messiahship and the kingdom. The Church engaged in

---

42. At the risk of being reductionistic, I am developing these two typologies for heuristic purposes, recognizing that variations of perspectives were found in the twentieth century and to date. Traditionalists disagreed with other traditionalists, and the same was true among the revisionists. Stroope even describes a group with the title "Revisionists" (*Transcending Mission*, 344), but differences likely exist among our understandings of the group.

numerous tasks in the world to display the glory of God among the community of saints. As Bosch and others have explained, the traditionalist understanding of mission and missions was reductionistic. The revisionists revealed that such had been the case and offered a different perspective. Dependence on modern language and the lack of a robust theology for identity and practice limited the traditionalists' perspective and resulted in a heavy dependence on tradition and zeal.

Though the work of the revisionists revealed the shortcomings of the traditionalist view, they also made two significant mistakes: The apostolic work of the church became one equivalent function among many, and the urgency to communicate the gospel to the lost was diminished. Just because God's activity is broad does not lead to the conclusion that the Church's multiple actions are equivalent. It is true the Church was involved in many activities throughout the New Testament, but the apostolic functions received special attention, a matter often overlooked by revisionists. When everything became equal, the urgency of evangelism and disciple making faded. If God was just as concerned about restoring a polluted environment as he was with saving an unbeliever, then why prioritize?

A Way Forward—Watch Our Language

The revisionists won the debate. But in the end, both sides fell short of providing a more excellent way to the nations. Both failed to discern a biblical nomenclature and clung to modern terminology in need of biblical definition. While the revisionists had a more comprehensive understanding of God's work in the cosmos and the need for many Church actions, they lacked the biblical priority and urgency given to the apostolic work. Though the traditionalists emphasized the specific function of the Church's apostolic labors, they overlooked a great deal of what the Church was to do once established within a context.

In the introduction to this chapter, I referenced Neill's famous statement. But what is the solution to the problem when everything is considered mission and all missions are equivalent? His response: Change the language. "If everything that the Church does is to be classed as 'mission,'" he writes, "we shall have to find another term for the Church's particular responsibility for 'the heathen,' those who have never heard the Name of Christ."[43]

Timothy C. Tennent states that mission needs a "reclaiming of something closer to the original meaning of the word."[44] Keith Ferdinando comes to a similar conclusion. If it may be said that everything God does in the world is his mission, then, he notes, "a new terminology is required to categorise his specifically redemptive activity."[45]

Stroope takes a more radical approach and advocates the removal of the traditional terms and concepts from the Church's rhetoric. He believes the heart of the problem is that our language is reflective of the colonial legacy and of Christendom. Mission is no longer "over there," meaning in other countries. Since mission and modernity developed together, as the latter declines, so does the former. Traditional language communicates that one expression of Christianity is to dominate other expressions throughout Majority World contexts. New language is needed for mutual exchange and respect, and such language is found in the Scriptures.[46]

According to Stroope, the solution is found in the use of kingdom language. For an "orientation to and formation in the kingdom of God readies us for engagement with the world by transforming us into *witnesses to* the kingdom and *pilgrims of* the kingdom. *As pilgrim witnesses we participate in the coming reign of God.*"[47] This language would include all believers, with none being called *missionaries*. They witness to the coming reign of God, which results in more witnesses and pilgrims. Kingdom language gives priority to the formation and mobilization of people for kingdom work. It gives attention to the place of the Church and does not try to remove people from their witnessing communities and place them in mission organizations. Such language liberates the Church from the Christendom view that mission means crossing boundaries related to land, language, religion, and sociocultural matters to reach the lost. Pilgrims are led by

43. Neill, *Creative Tension*, 81.
44. Tennent, *Invitation to World Missions*, 54.
45. Keith Ferdinando, "Mission: A Problem of Definition," *Themelios* 33, no. 1 (2008): 46–59, here 50.
46. Stroope, *Transcending Mission*, 347–53.
47. Stroope, *Transcending Mission*, 370.

the Spirit for power and witness, not in the use of business or military strategies for witness.[48]

Stroope is to be commended for his extensive study and for calling the Church to a more biblically specific vocabulary. His attention to widespread witness, personal formation, and the emphasis on the local church is critical for a more excellent way. Though he is correct in the importance of kingdom language, his solution is reductionistic. Most important, he comes very close to making every believer a missionary without using the language of mission. If everyone is a pilgrim, a witness, and filled with the Spirit, where are the apostolic teams? What becomes of the apostolic functions? Or have they been subsumed under the function of witness? Has the apostolic, once again, been consumed by the Church's general ministry?

The centuries-old language of mission is here to stay. *Mission* is an umbrella term that encompasses a diverse array of actions. Although it is easy to state that the way forward is to stop using such language, such is easier said than done. Some will venture down this path while using biblical terminology, which is the best route to travel. Most groups will try to continue squeezing biblical definitions into modern terminology. If such is the case, a language of apostolic priority is still needed. For those continuing with modern terms attached to their definitions, then explanations must always be provided when communicating with those outside their local church, denomination, agency, or network, a wordy endeavor and yet absolutely necessary.

Another way forward is a possible hybrid approach. The language of mission is to be understood in at least two categories: apostolic categories (e.g., the sending nature of the Church, preaching, teaching, witnessing, disciple making, church planting) and other important kingdom-related activities. Rethinking language with an apostolic imagination may mean drawing from both the modern terminology and biblical language and concepts.

The language of kingdom and *apostolic* is used frequently throughout this book. This not only reflects the language of Scripture (cf. Gal. 2:8 ESV; 2 Cor. 13:6 NLT; Acts 1:25 NIV, CSB) but also offers a

48. Stroope, *Transcending Mission*, 376–81.

degree of clarity related to Church activities. For years, I have used the expressions *apostolic missionaries* and *apostolic teams* and *apostolic church planting* to communicate a specificity and urgency lost in the classic terms of *missions, missionaries,* and *church planting*.[49] Given that many people have significant misunderstandings and reservations with the word and concept of *apostle*, the use of the adjective makes the neologisms more palatable while making a point. Other scholars follow a similar direction. For example, Ferdinando suggests *apostolic mission* as a possible expression instead of *mission*.[50] Caldwell and Dent take a similar approach and use *missionary apostle*.[51] Peters collapses *apostle* into *evangelist* and states that they are "fully responsible for the apostolic function minus the apostolic office and original authority."[52] Robertson McQuilkin's wordy descriptions include *pioneer church-starting evangelists* and *pioneer apostolic church-starting evangelists*.[53] Others—such as Daniel Sinclair, Alan R. Johnson, and Alan Hirsch—advocate for the usage of *apostle*.[54]

Regardless of tradition and theological perspectives, the Church must speak in terms that clearly prioritize and distinguish apostolic labors from other global activities. The apostolic imagination will not allow the Church to remain content with the status quo. A linguistic shift to kingdom language that includes use of *apostolic* is needed, a shift that will be easier for some than for others. But change is desperately needed for all.

---

49. J. D. Payne, *Discovering Church Planting: An Introduction to the Whats, Whys, and Hows of Global Church Planting* (Downers Grove, IL: IVP, 2009), 383–84; Payne, *Apostolic Church Planting: Birthing Churches from New Believers* (Downers Grove, IL: InterVarsity, 2015).

50. Ferdinando, "Mission: A Problem of Definition," 59.

51. Larry W. Caldwell also makes use of this term in *Send Out! Reclaiming the Spiritual Gift of Apostleship for Missionaries and Churches Today* (Pasadena, CA: William Carey Library, 1992), 104. Donald T. Dent, "The Ongoing Role of Apostles in Missions," DMiss diss., Malaysia Baptist Theological Seminary (November 2009), 173.

52. George W. Peters, *A Biblical Theology of Missions* (Chicago: Moody, 1972), 247.

53. Robertson McQuilkin, "The Missionary Task," in *Evangelical Dictionary of World Missions*, ed. A. Scott Moreau (Grand Rapids: Baker Academic, 2000), 648–50, here 648–49.

54. Daniel Sinclair, *A Vision of the Possible: Pioneer Church Planting in Teams* (Waynesboro, GA: Authentic Media, 2005), 4; Alan R. Johnson, *Apostolic Function: In 21st Century Missions* (Pasadena, CA: William Carey Library, 2009); Alan Hirsch, *The Forgotten Ways: Reactivating the Missional Church* (Grand Rapids: Brazos, 2009).

QUESTIONS TO CONSIDER

1. Were you surprised to learn that the language of mission is a modern development? If so, why? If not, do you think most Christians would be surprised by this reality?

2. What language will you use to communicate the specific apostolic work of the Church within your tradition?

3. Does your language reflect biblical terms, functions, and the present global urgency for the gospel to reach the unreached?

CHAPTER 6

Reimagining Identity

One Sunday morning I was scrolling through my social media feed when a challenge caught my attention. Someone posted the following: "Look around your worship areas this morning. If you see someone sitting alone, go and talk to them! Today, we are all missionaries!"

I have heard preachers declare, "Every believer is a missionary! Now, go and share the gospel this week in your workplace, school, and neighborhoods!" Usually this exhortation is followed by a large collective "Amen!" that comes from everyone present, . . . except for the "missionaries" in the room who have come from other countries to share about their ministries. Students attend conferences and are told that they are missionaries on their campuses. Parents are told that they are to be missionaries in their homes by raising their children in the fear of the Lord.

An uncertainty of language has extended to identity. Is everyone a missionary? If so, then how should the Church identify those who relocate to remote regions to share the gospel? If a teacher moves to the Middle East to teach in a Christian school, does that make him a missionary? If a certified public accountant takes a job in Asia and serves with a church-planting team, is she a missionary, a CPA, or both? What does she tell others when asked, "What do you do?" Is it correct to refer to the short-term team of adults sent from their church as missionaries? Or what about a person in the home country who is serving among an unreached people there?

Is Everyone a Missionary?

I often hear the question, Are all Christians missionaries?[1] Of course, the grammar used in this question is reflective of the modern language of mission. Just as confusion abounds with terms such as *mission* and *missions*, *missionary* is no exception. The answer to this question is unclear because it depends on the definition of mission.[2] Consider the following confusing situations:

- If one holds to the revisionist perspective (broad view) that everything is mission, then it is likely the answer will be yes, for all Christians are to engage in God's mission.
- If one holds to the traditionalist perspective (narrow view) that mission is restricted to acts of evangelism and church planting, then the answer is no, for all Christians are not involved in such labors. Some may disagree, limiting *mission only* to evangelism and therefore assigning every Christian the title *missionary* because all Christians should share the gospel.
- If one holds to the traditionalist perspective (narrow view) that *mission* is primarily understood as crossing significant cultural gaps (often meaning traveling "overseas") to minister to others, then the answer is no, for not all Christians cross significant cultural gaps in their ministries.
- Regardless of perspective, others reserve the title *missionary* for those who have been formally commissioned or sent by a church or agency.

1. David Platt, "We Are Not All Missionaries, but We Are All on Mission," interview in *Conversations on When Everything Is Missions: Recovering the Mission of the Church*, by Denny Spitters and Matthew Ellison (n.p.: BottomLine Media, 2020), 97–105.

2. Here is another practical example of communication breakdown: If the parties involved in the dialogue hold to different perspectives and do not recognize this matter, then they will misunderstand one another in the conversation.

Identity Crisis

Robertson McQuilkin notes that referring to every believer as a missionary "may have the appearance of elevating their significance but in historic perspective it only serves to blur and diminish the original missionary task of the church."[3] As noted in the previous chapter, the modern language of mission has become distorted. The related term, *missionary*, has been affected as well. Dana L. Robert is correct: "'Rethinking mission' requires 'rethinking missionaries.'"[4] *Missionary* has become a term that represents a few believers or all believers. Often now, the term *missionary* is applied to every Christian regardless of calling, gifts, interests, passions, experiences, or ministries. A missionary is someone who travels to Central Asia to plant churches and also a person who travels to that location as a business leader and works with churches to feed the poor. A missionary is someone who takes a one-week trip to help lead worship for a church on a Native American reservation and a person who moves to a remote area of Canada to teach in a Christian school.

Paul's Self-Understanding

One way to approach an understanding of *apostolos* is to examine how the first-century apostles conceptualized their identities through their writings. Although it is challenging to develop a psychology of Paul, a task that extends beyond the realm of this book, it is possible to get a glimpse into his apostolic imagination. From this perspective, the Church is better positioned to rethink what believers have come to call missionary identity. In his significant work *Early Christian Mission*, Eckhard J. Schnabel works with several biblical passages that are related to Paul's self-understanding as a "pioneer missionary." In this section, I adapt portions from Schnabel's outline.[5]

3. Robertson McQuilkin, "The Missionary Task," in *Evangelical Dictionary of World Missions,* ed. A. Scott Moreau (Grand Rapids: Baker Academic, 2000), 648–50, here 649.

4. Dana L. Robert, "'Rethinking Missionaries' from 1910 to Today," *Methodist Review* 4 (2012): 57–75, here 58.

5. Eckhard J. Schnabel, *Early Christian Mission*, vol. 2, *Paul and the Early Church* (Downers Grove, IL: InterVarsity, 2004), 945–82.

Servant (1 Cor. 3:5–15; 9:19–23; Col. 1:24–29)

The Corinthians struggled with divisions within their fellowship (1 Cor. 1:10). Some sided with Paul, others with Apollos or Cephas (1:12; 3:4). Paul writes to help restore order: he begins by declaring that since no division exists in Christ (1:13), his body is not to be divided but unified. The church is not to boast in various spiritual fathers (3:21–23). The jealously and strife within this local church reveal believers' immaturity and need for sanctification. Paul attempts to address the problem by reminding them that he and Apollos are servants and not lords over them (3:5). Then he reveals three additional metaphors of how he understands the nature of such servanthood.

Farmer. The apostolic servant of the Lord plants and waters the gospel seed. Paul's agrarian metaphor would not have been lost on this community. The need for proper cultivation and irrigation of crops was a must for a significant harvest. Although Paul was likely unaware of Jesus's parable of the sower (Matt. 13:1–15 // Mark 4:1–9 // Luke 8:4–10), his use of this language is consistent with other New Testament writers. Paul understood that the servant who had received a commission from the Lord was to herald, warn, and teach others in wisdom so the team could "present everyone mature in Christ" (Col. 1:28).[6]

The result of his evangelistic and discipling work in Corinth was not of his doing. God was the source of the growth (1 Cor. 3:7) and the power that worked within him (Col. 1:29). Lest anyone should claim divine sovereignty and shy away from the apostolic responsibility of creating and cultivating a healthy environment for such divine growth to occur, Paul was quick to note that God would reward the servant "according to his labor" (1 Cor. 3:8).

Coworker. The servant is also described as God's fellow worker. This understanding of being a laborer with God likely brought a sobriety to his identity. Paul was not at liberty to think more highly

---

6. For a discussion of why *oikonomia* (v. 25) should be translated as "commission" rather than "office," see Douglas J. Moo, *The Letters to the Colossians and to Philemon* (Grand Rapids: Eerdmans, 2008), 153–54. Schnabel translates the word as "office" (Schnabel, *Early Christian Mission*, 2:980).

of himself than he should. Rather, his apostolic identity was in partnership with the God of mission, who called and sent him to the nations. Paul's labors were rooted in his identity; his identity as a servant was found in his Lord.

Builder. Paul describes the servant as a "master builder" (1 Cor. 3:10). The apostolic task was to lay the foundation on which another would build. Such thought was consistent with his words to the Romans (Rom. 15:20). N. T. Wright states that Paul's mission to the Gentiles was "energized and shaped by his missional reading of Israel's Scriptures."[7] While not communicated to the Corinthians, Paul's theological rationale for this apostolic paradigm was taken from one of Isaiah's passages on the servant of the Lord: "For that which has not been told them they see, and that which they have not heard they understand" (Isa. 52:15; cf. Rom. 15:21). Paul connects his servanthood with Isaiah's servant. As the apostolic servant, he takes the message of the servant of the Lord to the nations. In conjunction with Corinth, he understood his servant task as a necessary step in "God's building," not Paul's church, being established (1 Cor. 3:9).

Paul develops this servant theme as a means to reveal his willingness to "become all things to all people, that by all means I might save some" (9:22). Apostles are privileged to certain rights (9:4–12). However, Paul and Barnabas at times abstained from those rights if they believed such privileges would "put an obstacle in the way of the gospel of Christ" (9:12). Master builders were not to erect a stumbling block in front of others who were trying to get to the stumbling block of the cross. In Paul's desire to preach the gospel to unbelievers, his contextualization procedures sometimes required him to become like the Jews under the law and Gentiles outside the law (9:19–22).

Preacher of the Gospel (1 Cor. 15:1–11)

Toward the conclusion of his First Letter to the Corinthians, Paul draws attention to his apostleship and Christ's appearance to him

7. N. T. Wright, "Paul and Missional Hermeneutics," in *The Apostle Paul and the Christian Life: Ethical and Missional Implications of the New Perspective*, ed. Scot McKnight and Joseph B. Modica (Grand Rapids: Baker Academic, 2016), 179–94, here 190.

as one "untimely born" among the apostles (1 Cor. 15:8). Some were doubting the bodily resurrection of Jesus, so Paul sets the record straight. He brought them a specific message of good news. Paul had personally experienced a transformation by the resurrected Christ and had to communicate the *evangel* to them. Being an apostle meant that his self-understanding involved embracing and communicating matters of "first importance" (1 Cor. 15:3). The apostle was a preacher. He identified himself as heralding the fulfillment of an ancient prophecy that the Messiah was to die for sins and be resurrected (1 Cor. 15:4). Paul recognized and identified with a long heritage of God's messengers. His priority on preaching also corresponds with his other writings and those of Luke (Acts 6:2, 4; 18:5; 20:20–21; 1 Thess. 1:5; 2:8–9).

Fragrance of Christ (2 Cor. 2:14–16)

While some "peddlers of God's word" attracted a following during Paul's day, he and his team operated from sincerity and in accord with their commission (2 Cor. 2:17). It was through the team that God in Christ "spreads the fragrance of the knowledge of him everywhere" (2:14). Their very presence and proclamation either appealed to or appalled listeners. Among those being saved, the apostles and their message were "the aroma of Christ," and to those perishing, the stench of death (2:15–16).

Clay Jars (2 Cor. 4:7–15)

Rather than the apostles manifesting great and audacious characteristics, Paul described the apostolic identity as being like clay jars. The ordinary, uncomely, and fragile vessels of daily use were nothing in and of themselves. Rather, their worth was derived from the treasure they held (2 Cor. 4:7). While this treasure was of great worth, it often brought challenges and suffering.

Paul reported that his team frequently encountered opposition (by unbelievers and even by some Christians) while they were manifesting the treasure within themselves (4:8–12, 15).

Ambassadors for Christ (2 Cor. 5:20)

The language of diplomacy reveals the significance of Paul's self-awareness. The Christ who confronted him on the Damascus road was the one he represented. His desire was to please him (2 Cor. 5:9). When Paul spoke, his words came with authority since they originated in the throne room of heaven (13:3). Paul's actions were understood to be according to the will of the One on high (1:1, God). Though Paul would tell the Ephesians that he was "an ambassador in chains," he understood that the will of the one he represented was paramount (Eph. 6:20). As ambassadors, the apostolic team appealed to the Corinthians to "be reconciled to God." Only through such action would the righteousness of God be applied to them (2 Cor. 5:20–21).

Debtor to All (Rom. 1:14)

Paul's introductory remarks to the Romans reveal his apostolic identity in terms of the scope of his evangelistic work. The only means by which people could become righteous and live to please God was through faith (1:17). And the only way someone could come to such faith was through the message of the gospel, which was "the power of God for salvation to everyone who believes" (1:16). Paul describes himself as one who is "under obligation" to others to share this good news (1:14). He preached without prejudice to those who would listen. No one was excluded from Paul's list of potential hearers. The sophisticated and wise Greeks, uncouth Gentiles, and Jews (1:14, 16) were all eligible to receive the message from the team.

Sent (Rom. 1:1–6, 10–11)

Paul's apostolic identity included being one sent to preach an end-time message as part of God's salvation-historical mission. His acknowledgment of Joel's exhortation to both Jews and Gentiles (Rom. 10:13; cf. Joel 2:32), Isaiah's words (Rom. 10:15–16; cf. Isa. 52:7; 53:1; 65:1), Psalm 19:4 (Rom. 10:18), and Moses's prophecy (Rom. 10:19;

cf. Deut. 32:21)—all show that Paul believed his identity was related to the last days on God's timetable before the day of the Lord.

A limited and temporal hardening had come upon Israel (Rom. 11:7), due not to a lack of evangelists, but to their lack of faith (10:18). The eschatological ingathering of the Gentiles had arrived. Paul understood his commission to include observing that great train of Gentiles streaming to Mount Zion, which would provoke Israel to jealousy (10:19; 11:11) and lead to repentance (11:14). God constantly held out his hands to a disobedient people, who would not believe, but now another people, previously uninterested in the God of Israel, would believe (10:21).

The apostolic identity of being sent was connected to God's universal mission. The image bearers of God were filling the earth but not glorifying him. They did not know God's salvation and remained his enemies. The centrifugal aspect of the apostolic work required others to go forth and preach to these image bearers. However, if one was not sent to preach the good news (10:14–15), then no one would "believe in him of whom they have never heard" (10:14). The faith that reconciled one to God was communicated by the apostolic team, who was sent to preach "the word of Christ" (10:17).

Priest (Rom. 15:15–21)

Paul's understanding of his calling to the Gentiles was a "priestly service of the gospel" (Rom. 15:16), with the goal that the "offering of the Gentiles may be acceptable." Given Paul's penchant for Isaiah, he quite possibly was drawing from the prophet's words that spoke of the eschatological Gentile ingathering to Jerusalem as "an offering to the LORD" (Isa. 66:20). Addressing this concept, Robert H. Mounce writes, "Using the language of religious ceremony, he pictured his role as that of a priest bringing an offering to God. The offering consisted of believing Gentiles who had been sanctified by the Holy Spirit."[8] This apostolic priestly work was to continue "until the fullness of the Gentiles has come in" (Rom. 11:25), a terminus known only to God.

8. Robert H. Mounce, *Romans* (Nashville: Broadman & Holman, 1995), 266.

Paul's apostolic identity not only clarified his understanding of his life and calling in Christ, but also shaped the kingdom activities in which he and other members of his teams engaged. He knew that any disciples made, churches planted and developed, and elders appointed would come only as God's grace produced such growth (1 Cor. 3:6–7). Paul recognized that his apostolic identity was intimately connected to God's mission, which began before the world was created. However, even though the message was given priority over the messenger, who would suffer and possibly be killed, God's sovereignty was no excuse for inaction. The last days had arrived, and the apostolic teams were to engage with urgency as wise stewards so that both Jews and Gentiles would enter the kingdom and become part of the multiethnic body of Christ.

Rather than uncritically embracing the modern language of *missionary*, the Church would be wise to use these biblical descriptors when considering the identities of apostolic workers. While such do not provide a neat label, they do communicate more accurately to the body of Christ what Paul had in mind as opposed to our contemporary understandings of *missionary*. Without casting everyone as an apostle, many of these characteristics are also to be applied to all believers. This should come as no surprise since Paul challenged others to imitate him as he imitates Christ (1 Cor. 4:16; 11:1; Phil. 3:17). While there is a close connection between identity and function, they are not the same. The apostolic imagination recognizes that such biblical terminology was used to communicate to the household of faith and was not designed as a title on a business card, to be distributed to unbelievers throughout a neighborhood.

Removing this deeply cherished word *missionary* from the Church's vocabulary may provide the liberation many "missionaries" desire. Nearly everyone serving under this modern appellation wonders how they can honestly say "no" when asked by a potentially hostile person, "Are you a missionary?" Missionaries have no problem being recognized as followers of Jesus, but they are appalled at the notion of being misunderstood by nationals because of a label that is usually associated with colonialist ideology and distorted by stereotype and caricature. This term has often erected stumbling blocks before unbelievers, keeping them from getting to the stumbling block of the cross. If no church or organization provides this modern identifying label, then such is a step in the direction of a more excellent way.

QUESTIONS TO CONSIDER

1. Do you prefer the language of missionary? Why or why not? What are the strengths and limitations of using such language?
2. Is everyone a missionary? Explain your answer.
3. Why do you think Paul identified himself with a variety of terms that reflected his apostolic work as opposed to a single word such as *missionary*?

CHAPTER 7

Reimagining Priority

The world is filled with great spiritual and physical needs. These are numerous and overwhelming. At the time of this writing, over five billion people in the world are not followers of Jesus. Approximately three billion have never heard the name of Jesus. Wars shed blood and decimate countries. Racism is everywhere. Injustices exist throughout the world. Illness, disease, and poverty are commonplace. With so many wrongs throughout the world, where should the Church's attention reside? Should the Church work to solve every spiritual and physical problem? Do the Scriptures provide guidance in dealing with these overwhelming issues?

When it comes to the Church's global efforts, the priority among many today is that no priority exists. Bosch represents the majority perspective: "The missionary task is as coherent, broad, and deep as the need and exigencies of human life."[1] The use of modern language and twentieth-century revisions have contributed to an

---

1. David J. Bosch, *Transforming Mission: Paradigm Shifts in Theology of Mission*, 20th anniversary ed. (Maryknoll, NY: Orbis, 2011), 10.

equality of functions. However, when it comes to the apostolic imagination revealed through the Church's first-century actions, the initial disciples did not seem to embrace our contemporary view.

Great Commission Triage Is Needed

There are aspects of the Church's actions in the world that demand a significant level of attention. When it comes to participation in God's mission, all things are not equal, based on the biblical evidence. There is a distinction between general obedience to all of God's commands and the Church's apostolic work. A distinction is also found between the multitude of Church actions done throughout the world and those that are apostolic expressions.

While the local church consists of a diversity of gifts, services, and activities (1 Cor. 12:4–6), the apostolic team is limited in scope and function. The team may *represent* a church but is not a church, which would eventually develop many contextualized ministries. Jesus came and birthed the Jerusalem church. Now a reciprocal relationship is found: churches exist because of apostolic teams; and apostolic teams exist because churches send them into the world.

While local churches are to engage in a variety of ministries at home and abroad, a Great Commission triage should be in place. Mission involves multiple tasks, but the Church's apostolic work is to be given first order. Without teams taking the gospel to those who have never heard, communities of men, women, and children will be lost for eternity. If teams are not sent to bring the good news of hope and plant churches, then the kingdom ethic will not be lived out within that society to bring glory to God and civic transformation. Of all the kingdom activities related to what is called mission, sending such ambassadors to the nations across the street and the world is of the highest action, as reflected in the Trinity.[2]

2. Worship surely should have priority, but this is unhelpful to say on a practical level when referring to the Church's global task. *Everything* the Church does is as worship to God (cf. Rom. 12:1) and not limited to a brief weekly corporate gathering. The Church's apostolic work occurs because the earth is filled with God's image bearers who are not worshiping him.

Apostolic Priority Rooted in God

In the beginning, God establishes time and space and reveals himself as an apostolic God. He is the initial sender and bears his own message. God sends himself into his creation. He comes to Adam and Eve and speaks with them (Gen. 3). God sends himself to walk with them in the garden. After the fall, he sends himself to bring a message of hope in view of judgment. Francis M. DuBose notes the significance of this encounter as a model for what was to come. "The Genesis mission which paves the way for all subsequent missions is the 'incipient sending.' God is the 'source' and 'medium' (agent), and his first redemptive promise to man is the 'purpose.' The *proto-missio* (the 'original mission') precedes the *proto-evangelium* (the 'original gospel') of Genesis 3:15. What flowers ultimately in all Scripture has its roots in this primal mission and the purpose behind it."[3]

Mission begins within God's heart and extends from his nature. He is deeply concerned with his plan from eternity past (Eph. 1:4; cf. Rev. 13:8) and the work of the Son (1 Pet. 1:20). This plan involves a strategy that finds its execution in time. The redemption and restoration of all things would be preceded by God sending himself to the elect, bringing them to himself with good news, and sending them on his mission into the world.

Apostolic Priority Embodied by the Son

The incarnation was the ultimate act of sending. "In the fullness of time, ... God sent ... his Son" to redeem those "born under the law" (Gal. 4:4). Jesus came "to seek and ... save the lost" (Luke 19:10). "For God so loved the world that he" sent his Son (John 3:16). Lesslie Newbigin explains: "The mission of Jesus was not only to proclaim the kingdom of God but also to embody the presence of the kingdom of God in his own person."[4] After spending an evening healing many people and casting out demons in one city, Jesus refused to continue such work the

3. Francis M. DuBose, *God Who Sends: A Fresh Quest for Biblical Mission* (Nashville: Broadman, 1983), 57.

4. Lesslie Newbigin, *The Open Secret: An Introduction to the Theology of Mission*, rev. ed. (Grand Rapids: Eerdmans, 1995), 41.

next day, telling his disciples, "Let us go on to the next towns, that I may preach there also, for that is why I came out" (Mark 1:38).

Apostolic Priority Empowered by the Spirit

The Spirit is the spirit of mission.[5] The Spirit empowered the early apostolic teams to carry out their ministry. They became global witnesses for Jesus through making disciples, *after* the Spirit came upon them (Acts 1:8). The Spirit's arrival marked the last days, and his presence led the Church with urgency to the nations.

Apostolic Priority Continued through the Church

The evangelistic labors of the Church were prioritized on the day of Pentecost (Acts 2). When conflict arose over food distribution, the apostolic priority was hindered until the matter could be resolved (6:1–7). Paul's priority on proclamation was evident in his writing (1 Cor. 9:16). He did not shy away from a priority in his work: "For I delivered to you as of first importance what I also received" (15:3). Ferdinando notes a distinction found in the first-century Church between the apostolic functions and other important actions:

> There is a distinctive apostolic mission taking place in Acts which is an expression of explicit obedience to the great commission. Its focus is on winning people to the faith and to the way of life which that faith produces, and its method is proclamation of the word of Christ. It is also true that Acts portrays believers engaging in social action—caring for widows, for example—but that is a consequence of apostolic mission rather than its substance: it is one of the forms—albeit a vitally important form—which faithful discipleship takes among those who have responded to the gospel. Nevertheless, it does not have the same place as the making of disciples itself, and this relates to the obvious fact that Christian social engagement depends on the existence of Christians, and there would be none if disciples were not made.[6]

5. George W. Peters, *A Biblical Theology of Missions* (Chicago: Moody, 1972), 177.
6. Keith Ferdinando, "Mission: A Problem of Definition," *Themelios* 33, no. 1 (2008): 46–59, here 55.

Goal of Mission

If an apostolic priority exists, then such is to be reflected in the Church's strategy related to the goal of mission. Limited perspectives often lead the Church to engage in actions that fall short. Bosch's historical study of the various paradigms of mission serves as a caution to each generation.[7] Therefore, a missiological humility is needed as every generation maintains a perennial return to the Scriptures and further filling with the Spirit. The Church has redefined the goal of mission several times throughout history. For some, it was the conversion of souls. Individual salvations were paramount. While conversion is a significant part of the apostolic and evangelistic work of the Church, it must not be divorced from teaching new believers to obey the commands of Christ. For others, it was church planting (*plantatio ecclesiae*) as a means to extend colonialism and Christianize civilizations with Western cultural expressions.[8] The goal of planting churches that were self-governing, self-supporting, and self-propagating, an objective developed more fully in the nineteenth century, was an excellent move away from church planting as a Christianization tool. At times, however, churches planted with this three-self formula still reflected Western expressions. Others set the goal of mission as forming a Christian society or as social justice. Disciples should indeed live out the kingdom ethic in the world and stand for righteousness and justice, yet leaders with such goals often wanted to establish a theocracy or remove reference to personal sin and the need for repentance from the task of mission.

Even with the Church's shortcomings, missiologists are correct to speak of the goal of mission as they return to the Scriptures and reflect on their contexts. As Johannes Verkuyl writes, "[The goal] is an inescapable issue and . . . of great practical importance, for it determines missionary strategy and the choice of means and methods."[9]

7. Bosch, *Transforming Mission*.

8. Flett seems to refer to this as "ecclesiocentrism": "Mission becomes the task of replicating the structures, liturgies and order necessary to the primary witness of the church's culture." John G. Flett, *Apostolicity: The Ecumenical Question in World Christian Perspective* (Downers Grove, IL: IVP Academic, 2016), 202.

9. Johannes Verkuyl, *Contemporary Missiology: An Introduction* (Grand Rapids: Eerdmans, 1978), 176.

Asking about the goal is an exercise in kingdom stewardship. If mission belongs to God, then the Church must inquire about his goal. To understand this, it is necessary to frame the conversation in terms of God's kingdom.

Kingdom Present, Kingdom Come

The kingdom of God is where his rule and reign exist. As sovereign Creator, who holds all things together (Col. 1:15–17), no space extends beyond his domain. However, the Scriptures specifically mention that his kingdom is designed to be populated with people. In the beginning, God desired his image bearers to fill the earth and bring glory to him (Gen. 1:28). This command was given not only to the first couple but also extended to Noah and his family after the flood (9:1). The difference between these two kingdom commands is the time in which they were given. When Noah heard God's words, sin had existed in the world for a long time. Following the fall, sin separated God's image bearers from bringing glory to him and caused creation to groan under its weight (Rom. 8:18–22).

However, the biblical story line that follows reveals God's goal as working toward the redemption of sinners and the restoration of all things through his Messiah-King. Though limited in revelation to Abraham, Moses, and the prophets, God's plan to bless the nations is significantly developed in the New Testament. What began in the garden with image bearers glorifying God will end in the urban garden of the new heaven and new earth, filled with image bearers from all nations, glorifying God (Rev. 21:5). While the people of God are not to be confused with the kingdom, the former is a significant part of the latter and the primary means by which God is working to extend his reign over the hearts of his image bearers throughout the world before the parousia.

Although disciple-making efforts will eventually cease, for now, Jesus is building his Church on the great kingdom confession that he is Messiah (Matt. 16:16–18; cf. Rom. 10:9). Conversion is a significant part of the expansion of the kingdom and the building of his Church. Since the "kingdom of God is at hand," people are to "repent and believe in the gospel" (Mark 1:15). Those who enter into the kingdom, thus becoming part of Christ's body, are expected to live according to his commands (Matt. 28:20; John 14:15). The practical expectation by which God's people are to display his kingdom in the present and point to the kingdom to come (Matt. 6:10) is participation in local expressions of his Church. These local assemblies of the called-out ones are to manifest love toward God, other kingdom citizens, and those outside the kingdom in their communities and beyond. As salt and light, they are to display the glory of God before others as they call them to make the kingdom confession and experience the blessings and mission of the King (1 Chron. 16:24 // Ps. 96:3).

Verkuyl's reflections are helpful at this point: "This is the work of God alone—the Father, Son, and Holy Spirit. At the same time, it would be a sign of sinful sloth and indolence if we were not to attempt in faith, together with the children of the kingdom throughout the world, to erect in the midst of the wide range of human burdens and evils signs and signals of that which is coming. He who prays 'Thy kingdom come, Thy will be done' is thereby called to aid in spreading the kingdom of God over the length and breadth of the earth."[10] What is critical for the Church in relation to God's goal of redemption and restoration of all things is the *means* by which he works to extend his kingdom. Although there are different ways in which he acts, some known and others unknown (Isa. 55:8–9; Rom. 11:33–36), the Scriptures reveal a priority given to God's work in and through his Church, particularly the manifestation of his local churches in specific geographical locations.

God's attention is given to the preaching of the good news (1 Cor. 1:17; 2 Tim. 4:2), the conversion of unbelievers (Luke 15:7), and the sanctification of his people (1 Thess. 4:3), with the latter designed to produce good works (John 15:5; James 2:26) within the household of faith and in the community at large. While local churches give attention to these matters in their contexts, an expectation exists for apostolic workers to be sent to contexts where God's image bearers are not bringing glory to him. It is this apostolic means that receives a priority in kingdom labors in the heart of God and is to be manifested in and through local kingdom communities.

10. Verkuyl, *Contemporary Missiology*, 204.

Hindrances to Apostolic Priority

Chapter 2 addressed several challenges to the development of the apostolic imagination. Although these have some bearing on apostolic priority, especially two issues keep the Church from making claim to such priority. Ironically, the first is apostolic success in the field. The second is the perennial holism-prioritism debate.

Success in the field. Jesus's words that his disciples would do "greater works" than he does (John 14:12) have been and are being fulfilled since the ascension and the coming of the Spirit. For two thousand years the Church has sent laborers, across the street and the world, to be his witnesses (Acts 1:8). They have gone to preach the gospel to all nations (Mark 14:9) and make disciples (Matt. 28:18–20). Along highways and hedges, the good news of the serpent-crushing Messiah has been shared. People have heard the message of repentance toward God and faith in Jesus (Acts 20:21) and have believed. Churches have been planted; elders have been appointed. Sanctification happened and continues. The Church has gone into all the world and accomplished much for the kingdom.

Accomplishment brings change, sometimes fundamental shifts in purpose. As social organizations grow, they generally develop into complex institutions. What begins at an elementary and simple level, given enough time, becomes more formal and structured. Contexts that used to be labeled as pioneer areas now are locations with multiple churches serving their communities. The apostolic purpose of those initial pioneering laborers diminished in significance once the

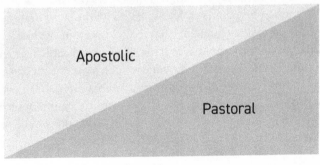

Figure 7.1. Apostolic-pastoral transition

churches were well established and the pastoral leadership began to develop (see figure 7.1).

This shift is an expected part of apostolic work, yet the result was a change in the ministry descriptions to fit within the established church context. Rather than *apostolic* teams phasing out in a location and entering new territories, the language of *missionary* was kept for that context, with a new definition applied. Alan R. Johnson recalled this shift among the Assemblies of God:

> Virtually anyone going out before 1970 went somewhere where the church movement was relatively small, and probably, by a rigorous definition of indigeneity, not yet fully capable of functioning without outside help to evangelize their sociocultural setting. . . . On the other hand, missionaries going out after 1970 were confronted with a new situation: national church movements that were increasingly large, robust and powerful. No longer needed in evangelism, church plant-ing, and even first-tier Bible training, missionaries became advanced education specialists, managed (and helped finance) various institu-tions, became conduits to connect short-term teams from the west, supervised various construction efforts, and worked in various forms of media and communications.[11]

What began with pioneer labors then developed into a complex organization in need of Western managers. According to Johnson, "Success creates a machinery of mission."[12] Of course, this story is not limited to the Assemblies of God but is repeated among de-nominations and nondenominational groups throughout the world. Missionaries, agencies, and churches become so invested among the people that, in order to remain a permanent fixture, they must rede-fine the purpose in the context.[13]

Whenever the global task becomes filtered through the lens of established church ministries, the apostolic is often collapsed into

11. Alan R. Johnson, *Apostolic Function: In 21st Century Missions* (Pasadena, CA: William Carey Library 2009), 24.

12. Johnson, *Apostolic Function*, 25.

13. Notice a difference between remaining a permanent fixture and partnership. The former often results in a codependency and carries aspects of paternalism; the latter is about fostering long-term relationships, with nationals developed, empow-ered, and released as primary leaders within their own contexts.

developed ministries designed for church members. This frequently means that the apostolic is now conceptualized and defined as pastoral. The context is considered "reached," and church development is now the focus. Whenever the apostolic permanently shifts into the pastoral, then attention is given to evangelism among people of the same culture as the church and to the development of church members. Although the established church must engage in evangelism and social transformation in the local context and work for the sanctification of the believers, such must not be done at the expense of apostolic labors, which are to continue elsewhere. While the New Testament teams seemed to function in pastoral roles (e.g., Timothy and Titus), elders were tasked with the primary function of permanently shepherding churches (Acts 20:28; Titus 1:5; 1 Pet. 5:2). It is only fair to note that Peter referred to himself as an elder and apostle (1 Pet. 1:1; 5:1); he, James, and John were pillars in the Jerusalem church. However, it seems that apostles generally were not pastors and that pastors were not apostles.

Part of the rationale for redefining purpose and remaining in place is related to the needs of the new churches. The apostolic drive to continue disciple making where a foundation does not exist (Rom. 15:20) becomes stalled—and possibly thwarted—because there are other lost people in the church's community, or because the churches need workers, or because success comes faster when working with Christians. Are we to believe that the apostle Paul never knew of such circumstances? Though he never abandoned the churches, he was able to commit them to God and the word and depart, even knowing that "fierce wolves" would attack the church at future times (Acts 20:28–32). There will always be unbelievers in the area; that is why the churches have been planted. There will always be the need for workers; that is why churches must multiply leaders by raising them up from the fellowship. There will always be injustices that need to be overcome; that is why the new churches are to live out the kingdom ethic in their communities. There will always be a desire to send reports home showing quick and glorious statistics; but the "success" of the apostolic team should not be evaluated by that standard.

Those who go to the nations usually love their work and the people they serve. New believers are their sons and daughters in the faith

(Gal. 4:19). This passion is part of the apostolic heart. Paul was greatly concerned for the new believers and mentioned the "daily pressure" of "anxiety" on his mind "for all the churches" (2 Cor. 11:28). He wrote to the Thessalonians, reminding them that his apostolic team came "like a nursing mother taking care of her own children." They were "affectionately desirous" of them and shared life with them because they "had become very dear" to the team (1 Thess. 2:7–8). The apostolic affection was also revealed in his Letter to the Philippians:

> I thank my God in all my remembrance of you, always in every prayer of mine for you all making my prayer with joy, because of your partnership in the gospel from the first day until now. And I am sure of this, that he who began a good work in you will bring it to completion at the day of Jesus Christ. It is right for me to feel this way about you all, because I hold you in my heart, for you are all partakers with me of grace, both in my imprisonment and in the defense and confirmation of the gospel. For God is my witness, how I yearn for you all with the affection of Christ Jesus. (Phil. 1:3–8; cf. 1 Cor. 1:4; 1 Thess. 1:2)

Yet Paul did not allow such deep affection to hinder his apostolic labors elsewhere. His love coincided with his calling. Paul's love for the churches required that they continue what was begun in them. The churches had been planted with everything they needed to be the local expressions of the body of Christ in their communities and beyond. Great challenges and needs were present and would arise in the future, but the apostolic priority included proclaiming the good news elsewhere. Paul's loving apostolic arms were big enough to embrace both the successes he observed among the new churches and future churches yet to be planted.

Holism versus prioritism. Any discussion among evangelicals regarding a prioritization of acts in the Commission of the Church will soon become a heated debate. Those who give emphasis to evangelism in the mission of the Church are now in the minority even among evangelicals.[14] While evangelicals do have a long history of being

14. Christopher R. Little, "The Case for Prioritism: Part 1," *Great Commission Research Journal* 7, no. 2 (Winter 2016): 139–62, here 140.

engaged in social action, over time the gospel proclamation has diminished to the point of receiving merely equal attention when it
comes to the Church's mission in the world.[15] This is not a recent
debate but has a detailed history; I shall attempt to be brief to save
space.

The late nineteenth-century work of Dwight L. Moody and A. T.
Pierson exhorted college students to work toward the evangelization
of the world in their generation. By 1910, the World Missionary Conference embraced this concept and stressed it among participants.
However, the Commission on World Mission and Evangelism held
in New Delhi in 1961 described the work of the Church as taking the
whole gospel to the whole world, with evangelism redefined as witness related to the transformation of the physical, social, economic,
and spiritual aspects of life.[16] The Church was to give attention to
the engagement of social justice issues while letting the gospel light
shine before the world. No longer was priority given to calling people
to repentance and faith; instead, if practiced at all, evangelism was
simply another action to be done in the world among a multitude
of ecclesial activities.[17]

Evangelicals quickly grew in their distrust of those connected
to the World Council of Churches and began organizing their own
global meetings to address this aspect of apostolic work. In 1974,
the Lausanne Movement was born with the Lausanne Congress for
World Evangelization taking place there in Switzerland. Both Billy
Graham and John Stott were significantly committed to this gathering. However, the partnership between these two men involved tension over the place of evangelism in the mission of the Church. Stott
became known as a leading advocate for what is described as the
holistic perspective.[18] Graham stressed the priority of evangelism in

---

15. For two perspectives addressing this matter at the end of the last century, see
Arthur P. Johnston, *The Battle for World Evangelism* (Wheaton: Tyndale, 1978); and
Harvey T. Hoekstra, *The World Council of Churches and the Demise of Evangelism*
(Wheaton: Tyndale, 1979).

16. The International Missionary Council was incorporated into the WCC in 1961
and rebranded as the Commission on World Mission and Evangelism.

17. Little, "Case for Prioritism: Part 1," 149.

18. A great deal of tension on the priority of evangelism existed between John
Stott and Billy Graham during and soon after this gathering. Roger Steer has described

the work of the Church's mission (prioritist perspective). By the end of the Congress, the Lausanne Covenant declared that although the Church is to give attention to social action, evangelism is the priority. This outcome did not sit well with some evangelicals, who spoke out against such a distinction.

One year later, Stott published the influential book *Christian Mission in the Modern World*. He confessed how his views on the Great Commission had shifted and how the mission of the Church was to include a much tighter connection between evangelism and social action. Reflecting on the Great Commission, he wrote: "It is not just that the commission includes a duty to teach converts everything Jesus had previously commanded (Matthew 28:20), and that social responsibility is among the things which Jesus commanded. I now see more clearly that not only the consequences of the commission but the actual commission itself must be understood to include social as well as evangelistic responsibility, unless we are to be guilty of distorting the words of Jesus."[19] Stott thus represents the view that David Hesselgrave categorizes as "restrained holism," whereby one attempts to preserve the priority of evangelism while "elevating social action."[20] For Stott, the "crucial form" of Jesus's Commission was found in the Fourth Gospel (John 17:18; 20:21). As Jesus had been sent into the world by the Father and was sending his disciples, Stott wrote, "Our understanding of the church's mission must be deduced from our understanding of the Son's."[21] He advocated that the service and proclamation rendered by Jesus to the world is the model that should be followed. Jesus's purpose involves presence and proclamation; therefore, Jesus sent his disciples to do likewise.

Stott takes the notion of Jesus's model to a degree that John's Gospel fails to represent. John portrays the unique nature of Jesus's incarnation (John 1:1, 14, 18; 3:14, 16, 18) and atonement as being unrepeatable and never needing repetition. Although Stott would never

this matter in his book *Basic Christian: The Inside Story of John Stott* (Downers Grove, IL: IVP, 2009), 159–67.

19. John R. W. Stott, *Christian Mission in the Modern World* (Downers Grove, IL: InterVarsity, 1975), 23.

20. David J. Hesselgrave, *Paradigms in Conflict: 15 Key Questions in Christian Missions Today*, ed. Keith E. Eitel, 2nd ed. (Grand Rapids: Kregel Academic, 2018), 109.

21. Stott, *Christian Mission*, 23.

claim that the Church is to repeat Jesus's atonement, he is unclear as to his basis for how he determines what is to be repeated and what is not to be repeated by the Church.[22] He seems to pick and choose what is to constitute an incarnational model. Köstenberger declares that Stott's view "appears to jeopardize Jesus' salvation-historical uniqueness" and that John's Gospel "does therefore not appear to teach the kind of 'incarnational model' advocated by Stott."[23] Kevin DeYoung and Greg Gilbert are even more poignant: "We cannot re-embody Christ's incarnational ministry any more than we can repeat his atonement. Our role is to *bear witness* to what Christ has already done. We are not new incarnations of Christ but his *representatives* offering life in his name, proclaiming his gospel, imploring others to be reconciled to God (2 Cor. 5:20)."[24]

Stott's incarnational model readily embraces the cultural mandate. The Church's purpose is to serve and establish shalom throughout a broken world. Creating and manifesting a counterculture in accord with God's kingdom is considered the task at hand. Helping others in need is considered part of mission. According to Stott, mission is not everything God does in the world, but "everything the church is sent into the world to do."[25]

In his 1974 book, *The Church and Its Mission: A Shattering Critique from the Third World*, Orlando E. Costas challenges the Church to be more holistic in viewing mission: "The question is no longer what is the church's 'primary' task, but what is [the church's] *total* task. The issue today is not whether or not people are being converted to Christ but whether this is happening as part of a total process:

22. Andreas J. Köstenberger, *The Missions of Jesus and the Disciples according to the Fourth Gospel: With Implications for the Fourth Gospel's Purpose and the Mission of the Contemporary Church* (Grand Rapids: Eerdmans, 1998), 216.

23. Köstenberger, *Missions of Jesus and the Disciples*, 216–17.

24. Kevin DeYoung and Greg Gilbert, *What Is the Mission of the Church? Making Sense of Social Justice, Shalom, and the Great Commission* (Wheaton: Crossway, 2011), 57.

25. Stott, *Christian Mission*, 30. Stott restricts God's involvement in mission while broadening the church's involvement. He writes, "The word 'mission' cannot properly be used to cover everything God is doing in the world. In providence and common grace he is indeed active in all men and all societies, whether they acknowledge him or not. But this is not his 'mission.' 'Mission' concerns his redeemed people, and what he sends *them* into the world to do." Stott, *Christian Mission*, 19.

is the church a community totally committed to and involved in the fulfillment of the gospel in the context of the concrete historical situations in which men and women find themselves?"[26]

According to Christopher Little, by the time of the Third Lausanne Congress, held in Cape Town in 2010, a holistic understanding of mission had "become a mainstay within the Lausanne Movement," and evangelical perspective "paralleled the trajectory of the WCC in the twentieth century."[27] Little is not alone in his observations regarding the similarities between the World Council of Churches and evangelicals by the twenty-first century. Charles Van Engen writes, "Given these new emphases in Evangelical mission activism, it behooves us to consider carefully how Evangelical views of mission today may be tempted to repeat the same errors made when mission was redefined and eventually lost in the World Council of Churches between the 1960s and the 1990s."[28] A. Scott Moreau states, "Many evangelicals have moved toward positions closer to conciliar thinking than earlier evangelicals would have dreamed."[29] While authors such as Stott and Costas have done well to draw attention to the holistic work of the Church, their elevation of social matters to the level of disciple making shifted attention away from emphasis upon the need for and functions of apostolic teams. Purpose and priority morphed over the past several decades to the point that gospel proclamation is now relegated to a room

26. Orlando E. Costas, *The Church and Its Mission: A Shattering Critique from the Third World* (Wheaton: Tyndale, 1974), 11.

27. Little, "Case for Prioritism: Part 1," 151–52. On October 13, 2010, prior to the Cape Town meeting (on October 16–25), I wrote a post for my blog titled "Cape Town 2010—Will be Known For . . ." In it I explained my concern over the lack of attention given to evangelism in some of the promotional events prior to the Congress. It created such a stir that the executive director of the Lausanne Movement contacted me to clarify that Lausanne had not abandoned evangelism. I was thankful for his response yet also surprised and led to assume that I was not the only one sensing a move away from the spirit of 1974. See https://www.jdpayne.org/2010/10/cape-town -2010-will-be-known-for/.

28. Charles Van Engen, "Essay 1: 'Mission' Defined and Described," in *MissionShift: Global Mission Issues in the Third Millennium*, ed. David J. Hesselgrave and Ed Stetzer (Nashville: B&H Academic, 2010), 7–29, here 20.

29. A. Scott Moreau, *Contextualization in World Missions: Mapping and Assessing Evangelical Models* (Grand Rapids: Kregel Academic, 2012), 319.

filled with a multitude of good works that the Church is to carry out in the world.

These two contrasting perspectives represented by Stott and Graham have been labeled as holism and prioritism. David J. Hesselgrave has written extensively on these views.[30] Although both of these have variations, holism may generally be understood as the blending of social action with evangelism. Holism emphasizes the transformation of societies and ministering to the whole person: body, spirit, and mind. Holism may be separated into two categories: revisionist and restrained. Revisionist holism makes evangelism and social action *equal partners*. Restrained holism maintains the traditional view of an evangelistic priority but *elevates* social action to a new height.

Traditional prioritism distinguishes between primary mission activities and secondary activities. Evangelism takes priority over social action, yet while not neglecting social action. The primary understanding of mission is to make disciples; other ministries are important, though secondary and supportive. Little, who argues that restrained holism and prioritism should be combined, summarizes the general distinction between holism and prioritism: "What distinguishes prioritism from holism is a qualitative difference between word and deed, evangelism and social action, and proclamation and demonstration. . . . What is being stipulated here is not that there is a *dichotomy* between word and deed, but also that there is not an *equity* between them either. Rather, there exists a *hierarchy* of word over deed."[31]

Donald McGavran wrote extensively regarding God's desire and mission. Asking if God has assigned priorities to the Church's global actions, he responds, "We believe that God, indeed, has assigned priorities. His will in these matters can be learned from his revelation and is mandatory for Christians." Acknowledging that the Church is placed within contexts whereby "Christian mission must certainly engage in many labors," McGavran warns that it is easy to lose focus and view all of those actions as equivalent. "In doing the good," he writes, the Church "can fall short of the best." Although he defines

---

30. A couple of these paragraphs summarize some of Hesselgrave's thoughts in *Paradigms in Conflict*, 106–23.

31. Christopher R. Little, "Update Reflection on Holism and Prioritism," in Hesselgrave, *Paradigms in Conflict*, 124–28, here 126.

mission narrowly as "*an enterprise devoted to proclaiming the good news of Jesus Christ, and to persuading men and women to become his disciples and responsible members of his church,*" he stresses that working toward justice issues is very important but not primary. He writes, "Social service pleases God, but it must never be substituted for finding the lost." For McGavran, as well as many other prioritists, the "Christianizing of the social order" is the "fruit of new life in Christ and of church multiplication," following the redemption of peoples as they live out the kingdom ethic in their communities.[32]

Christopher Wright makes an extensive and passionate argument for holistic mission. By asking "How then can it be suggested that evangelistic proclamation is the only essential mission of the church?" Wright continues by declaring that it is "impossible" for someone "to justify such reductionism" when it comes to an honest examination of the Bible. He seems to redefine evangelism as the proclamation of the good news *and* providing righteous actions when asking, "Why should we imagine that doing evangelism in obedience to the New Testament excludes doing justice in obedience to the Old?"[33] Such behavior is required of the kingdom citizen and is part of teaching new believers to obey all that Christ has commanded.

However, evangelism is restricted to heralding the gospel. An examination of the New Testament models represented by both Jesus and the Church reveals this. These evangelists most definitely let their lights shine before others, but most of their encounters were with complete strangers, and no time was allowed for their lives to be examined by their audiences. While their service in the world involved many actions, the gravity of their work was found in the verbal communication of the Messiah and his expectations.

Although Christopher Wright is correct to acknowledge the breadth of God's mission and the fact that Israel and the Church were to be living models by foreshadowing the kingdom to come, he

32. Donald A. McGavran, *Understanding Church Growth*, 3rd ed. (Grand Rapids: Eerdmans, 1990), 21–22, 24.

33. Christopher J. H. Wright, *The Mission of God: Unlocking the Bible's Grand Narrative* (Downers Grove, IL: IVP Academic, 2006), 304. He argues that the Old Testament notion of Jubilee is where the Church should find a paradigm for evangelistic work (300, 306, 312, 414).

refuses to assign priority to the proclamation of the gospel among the nations. Making an extensive argument on the limitations of the language of priority and the flaws in the belief that evangelism alone results in social transformation, he prefers the term "ultimacy."[34] He believes "the language of priority and primacy quickly tends to imply singularity and exclusion. . . . We are back to so exalting the New Testament evangelistic mandate that we think it absolves us from all other dimensions of God's mission."[35] He correctly notes that the Church's global work does not always begin with evangelism, but "mission that does not ultimately *include* declaring the Word and the name of Christ, the call to repentance, and faith and obedience has not completed its task."[36] Yet he disagrees with the argument that "the best way to achieve social change and all the good objectives we have for society on the basis of what we know God wants (justice, integrity, compassion, care for his creation, etc.) is by vigorous evangelism."[37] His rationale is that those who want to make this case divorce evangelism from teaching new believers to obey all that Christ commanded. His argument appears to be a straw man. I am unaware of anyone who would make the case for redemption and societal lift while advocating evangelism as all that needs to occur.[38]

Wright reveals his view that there are no priorities. The result is a relativism in practice. Since every member of the Church cannot do everything, what is important is that each believer focuses on what is primary *for oneself*. The different callings, gifts, and expressions of ministry are necessary for carrying out the mission of God in the world. Everyone is to be a witness, but no actions are elevated above other actions. He writes,

34. C. Wright, *Mission of God*, 316–23.
35. C. Wright, *Mission of God*, 317.
36. C. Wright, *Mission of God*, 319.
37. C. Wright, *Mission of God*, 319.
38. A significant piece of evidence for Wright's claim is the corrupt behavior found in Nagaland, one of the most Christianized regions on the planet. For him, this shows that evangelism does not produce social change (*Mission of God*, 320–21). However, just because missionaries failed to teach radical obedience to Christ in that state of northeast India is no reason to write off the primacy of evangelism and its significance in leading to social transformation. The Great Commission demands both reaching and teaching. The teaching must be present, but *first* the reaching needs to occur!

> The apostles in Acts recognized their own personal priority had to be the ministry of the Word and prayer. But they did not see that as the only priority for the church as a whole. Caring for the needs of the poor was another essential priority of the community and its evangelistic attractiveness. So they appointed people who would have as *their* priority the practical administration of food distribution to the needy. That did not limit their ministry to such work . . . but it does show that the overall work of the church requires different people to have different gifts and priorities.[39]

Such claims overlook the example and language of priority in the New Testament. While Acts 6:1–7 clearly reveals the importance and value of food distribution, there is no evidence in the text that the apostles understood such service as equivalent to evangelism and prayer. In fact, the opposite is the case. One only need to look at the attention given to the spread of the gospel. Luke chooses to focus on the result of the word spreading and the priests coming to faith, rather than the harmony achieved after the discrepancy was resolved. Again, if the model of Jesus and the apostles is to have any gravitas, then their emphasis was squarely to preach the good news. Paul's correspondence with the Corinthians also carries a certain weight of emphasis. In the text on the unity of the body and the need for diversity of gifts, activities, and service, Paul includes his exhortation that the Corinthians should "earnestly desire the higher gifts" (1 Cor. 12:31). He wants them to prophesy rather than speak in tongues (1 Cor. 14:5, 39) and declares that God has appointed within the Church "first apostles, . . . third teachers" (1 Cor. 12:28).

God's mission in the world is broad and multifaceted, but both the Trinity and New Testament Church reveal an apostolic priority related to God's goal of redemption and restoration of all things. Though the Church's actions in the world are also numerous, they are not equivalent to one another. Life in the kingdom through local expressions of the Church is to be represented by gospel proclamation and social transformation. Believers are to be salt and light with both word and action. Confusion has often resulted when the Church has overlooked the apostolic role and concentrated on the

39. C. Wright, *Mission of God*, 322, on Acts 6.

established-church role. While apostolic teams were part of the Church, their function was narrow in scope. This laser focus was meant to be manifested through the Church, with a prioritization among the kingdom activities.

QUESTIONS TO CONSIDER

1. Do you agree or disagree that an apostolic priority exists? Explain.
2. How would you describe prioritism and holism in your own words?
3. How could apostolic teams avoid the problem that comes with success on the field?

CHAPTER 8

Reimagining Function

Apostolic language helps provide a clearer identity and priority for teams, but what are the primary activities in which teams participate? What is the function of the apostolic worker? Could someone be a physician and serve in an apostolic manner? What does it mean for the social worker sent to Nigeria to practice social work and apostolic labors? This chapter addresses the primary tasks of such teams.

Christianize and Civilize

The notions of Christianization and civilization, which had been part of missionary functions before William Carey (1761–1834), continued to influence actions throughout the Great Century of missions. Reflecting on the Edinburgh World Missionary Conference of 1910, Dana L. Robert writes: "Missionaries saw themselves largely as evangelistic westerners embedded in colonial-era structures such as mission stations, medical and educational institutions, and the emerging nation-state. The missionary was both to make converts and to establish Christian churches and civilizations. In other words, the major role of the colonial-era missionary was to create leaders for both emerging churches and emerging nations."[1]

1. Dana L. Robert, "'Rethinking Missionaries' from 1910 to Today," *Methodist Review* 4 (2012): 57–75, here 59.

She reports that, among Methodist missionaries of the mid-twentieth century, was the belief that "educating people about racism and other aspects of colonial injustice was a major part of their calling as missionaries."[2] Part of such practices was due to the historical link between the Church and the state.[3] While standing against racism and for the betterment of society must be reflected among kingdom citizens, a great deal of the Protestant missions movement has been an unhealthy blurring of the emphases of local churches and those of apostolic teams. What existed in microcosm in the team was to become magnified in the church's actions in society.

Observing the shift in priority, evangelicals in the late twentieth century turned their attentions toward "hidden peoples" in pioneer regions.[4] Their reorientation toward the frontiers allowed them to function in the traditional missionary paradigm of evangelization, church planting, and leadership development while retaining the language of missions and missionaries.[5] However, it was not long before evangelicals turned to what they had tried to avoid, thus discarding the notion of the apostolic altogether or expecting missionaries to function in the same ways as established churches.

The Great Distinction

Much of the confusion regarding mission function is due to misplaced expectations. An apostolic team and a local church are not the same. One gives birth to local churches; the other commissions and sends teams. One establishes communities to live out the kingdom ethic;

2. Robert, "'Rethinking Missionaries,'" 64.

3. The interactions of merchants, military, and missionaries had been together throughout centuries in the minds of many people. Though an overstatement, Wati Longchar's point is worth pondering: "Even if the missionaries did not consider themselves agents of colonial powers, they participated, wittingly or not, in advancing the colonial project." Wati Longchar, "Rethinking Mission in Asia: Looking from Indigenous People's Experience," *Theologies and Cultures* 6, no. 2 (December 2009): 188–202, here 192.

4. The language of "hidden peoples" was soon replaced with the expression "unreached people groups."

5. Dana L. Robert, "Mission Frontiers from 1910 to 2020," *Missiology* 39, no. 2 (April 2011 Electronic Issue): 5e–16e. This helpful article shows how the language of "frontier" and its various definitions relate to twentieth-century missions.

the other lives out the ethic in ways unavailable to the team. The expectation that teams are to engage in mission as broadly as churches is a gross misunderstanding of the primary activities of the apostolic role. In addition to prioritizing disciple making, local churches are to engage in a variety of ministries, which include worship gatherings, standing for social justice in their contexts, counseling, and caring for widows and orphans. Local churches have the necessary gifts and structures for equipping their members to sustain many functions while communicating the gospel.

Broad is the way of the church, but narrow is the way of the apostolic teams. When the Church speaks of mission, it is necessary to distinguish between the two. Herein lies a great failure in contemporary conversations: *Little distinction is often made between the local church and the apostolic team.* Many of the functions frequently described by writers today are to be applied to the local church's ministry and fail to recognize the narrow set of parameters out of which apostolic teams primarily operate. For example, Daniel Topf writes: "In the twenty-first century, however, missionaries will need technological skills in order to make a difference, ideally paired with an entrepreneurial spirit, so that they can engage in job creation. If having a stable and well-paying job is the most reliable way for people to step out of poverty, then missionaries of the twenty-first century need not only to contribute to job creation but also help people to upgrade their qualifications so that they will be able to compete on the labor market."[6]

While such actions are noble and may be very effective in ministering in certain contexts, is this a reflection of apostolic labors or of gifts that could be developed through local churches? Paul and his team were eager to "remember the poor" (Gal. 2:10), but was job creation to raise people from poverty anywhere near the realm of their actions? Paul was so restrictive in his imagination that he wrote, "Christ did not send me

---

6. Daniel Topf, "The Global Crisis of Unemployment in an Age of Automation and Artificial Intelligence," *Occasional Bulletin of the Evangelical Missiological Society* 33, no. 2 (Spring 2020): 13. He continues this thought: "To be missional in the twenty-first century, Christians will need to invest in their own research universities, so that, by participating in the creation of knowledge, they will also provide platforms for the creation of new jobs that can lift people out of poverty." These noble actions reflect the expansion of the kingdom of God; they are not apostolic functions but are actions to be considered by established churches in their contexts.

to baptize but to preach the gospel" (1 Cor. 1:17). While he was clearly engaged in more functions than preaching, his comments represent a laser focus related to his kingdom labors. Before continuing with the discussion of the apostolic functions, it is necessary to consider the ongoing debate surrounding the role of the Bible and practice.

The Bible: A How-To Guide?

Do the Scriptures teach the Church how to do what has historically been labeled missions? According to J. H. Bavinck, the answer is a resounding no. "In consequence, on the basis of the conviction that the Scriptures must be used as a guide book, all sorts of conclusions have been drawn from the missionary activity of the apostles. In practice, however, many of these conclusions have as a rule been proven to be foolish and absurd. In the mission field of Central Africa or somewhere on an island in the South Seas, it is impossible to follow the method chosen by Paul in his day and world, under the circumstances he faced."[7]

However, in what reads as if the author is backpedaling, Bavinck attempts to explain that theology must have the "decisive voice" and that "the principles of the missionary approach must still be derived from Scripture." Using preaching as an example, Bavinck writes, "The content of preaching is not unrelated to the method of preaching, but in one way or another the content supplies the principles which determine the method. There is, of course, a great deal of leeway for all sorts of nuances in approach. . . . The content of preaching, the Word of God, must tell us what we ought in every instance to do and not to do."[8]

Although he is correct here, he appears to lack consistency in his hermeneutic. If the content found in the Scriptures provides the principles behind the method of preaching, then the Scriptures should be able to provide the principles behind other apostolic methods. Clearly, the Bible was not written as an instruction manual for how to do apostolic work. However, the Church learns the principles through

7. J. H. Bavinck, *An Introduction to the Science of Missions*, trans. David Hugh Freeman (Philadelphia: Presbyterian and Reformed, 1960), 80.

8. Bavinck, *Science of Missions*, 81.

imperatives and indicatives and considers their application in light of the descriptions of the first-century believers. For example, while Bavinck is correct that just because Paul was a tentmaker does not mean that all missionaries are to follow suit, he rules out an attempt to understand the principles behind Paul's practice, how Paul applied such principles, and how we may apply those principles today.

At the turn of the twentieth century, Roland Allen had a great deal to say regarding the apostolic approach. In his book *Missionary Methods: St. Paul's or Ours?*, he observes that in just over a decade the apostle Paul established the Church in four Roman provinces. Comparing the work of his day to Paul's, Allen writes:

> This is truly an astonishing fact. That churches should be founded as rapidly, so securely, seems to us today, accustomed to the difficulties, the uncertainties, the failures, the disastrous relapses of our own missionary work, almost incredible. Many missionaries in later days have received a larger number of converts than St. Paul; many have preached over a wider area than he; but none have so established churches. We have forgotten that such things could be. . . . Today if a man ventures to suggest that there may be something in the methods by which St. Paul attained such wonderful results worthy of our careful attention, and perhaps of our imitation, he is in danger of being accused of revolutionary tendencies.[9]

Troubled with the practices of his day, Allen left no room for debate. His conclusion was "Either we must drag down St. Paul from his pedestal as the great missionary, or else we must acknowledge that there is in his work that quality of universality."[10] Assuming the latter, Allen argued for a return to the New Testament to understand the apostolic functions and their application to the Church's work throughout the world.

The widening of missionary functions troubled Allen. He recognized that those sent during his day were engaging in a multitude of good actions, but were they apostolic functions? Based on his biblical studies, he concluded that they were not.

9. Roland Allen, *Missionary Methods: St. Paul's or Ours?* American ed. (1912; Grand Rapids: Eerdmans, 1962), 3–4.
10. Allen, *Missionary Methods*, 5.

That missionaries should set out to inaugurate and conduct social reforms is so familiar to us that we scarcely question it; but if we look at the New Testament account of the work of the Apostles, we see at once how strange it appears. If we try to imagine St. Paul, for instance, setting out to serve the people of Macedonia in the sense in which we set out to serve the peoples of China or Africa, . . . we find that we cannot imagine any such thing. And the reason? . . . It is because there is a great gulf between our idea of direct social service as the work of a missionary of the Gospel and his conception of his work as a missionary of the Gospel.[11]

Allen's provocative challenge to the Church involved a simple question that would manifest itself in a variety of ways throughout his writings: "Are we following the Apostolic way, the most successful way, of extending the Church, or are we employing a method which experience has proved to many people to be a conspicuous failure?"[12] One should not be quick to conclude that there is no place for the social worker, educator, nurse, entrepreneur, artist, or scientist on apostolic teams. On the contrary, the Lord frequently uses marketable skills and careers for his glory among the nations. The utmost concern is whether such people are engaged in apostolic functions as well as their professions.

Apostolic Functions

As addressed in chapters 3 and 4, there is a distinction between the apostolic *office*—restricted to Jesus, the Twelve, Paul, and possibly James—and the Church's apostolic *function* that continues throughout history. While the function was related to the work of those who held the office, it was also related to "the unique ministry of the brethren designated and delegated by the apostles and/or by local churches for ministries outside of the established churches."[13]

11. Allen, *Missionary Methods*, 21–22.
12. Roland Allen, *Discussion on Mission Education* (London: World Dominion, 1931), 14.
13. George W. Peters, *A Biblical Theology of Missions* (Chicago: Moody, 1972), 257–58.

Since I have spent considerable space addressing primary functions of teams in chapter 4, here I summarize the sixfold array of activities.

Preaching the gospel to unbelievers. Paul's desire was that both Jews and Gentiles would be saved (Rom. 10:1, 12–13). The manifestation of God's redemption in the world was revealed through the preaching of the gospel and then the salvation that came to the repentant. After the apostolic teams arrived in a community, they would begin their evangelistic work, often in a synagogue (if one existed) or a location of religious activity (Acts 13:14; 16:13).

Teaching new disciples. Though the apostolic team proclaimed the good news, they were not satisfied with conversions. Paul reported that he toiled and struggled that "we may present everyone mature in Christ" (Col. 1:28–29). God's "whole counsel" needed to be taught to the new believers (Acts 20:27; cf. Matt. 28:20).

Planting churches. Michael W. Goheen writes, "The church's missionary calling is to the ends of the earth. . . . And so if there are places that lack a witnessing community it is the task of the church to create a witness in life, word and deed there until a community is established that will take responsibility for mission there."[14] The apostolic work of those initial teams continued until a local church was started in the community with the new believers. The church was birthed from the harvest fields of lostness and was expected to carry out Christ's commands locally and globally.

Developing elders. While the Scriptures have much silence regarding ecclesial details, it seems that the apostolic teams functioned temporarily as overseers until permanent elders could be established. The teams were involved in appointing elders for the new churches, elders selected from members of those churches (Acts 14:23; Titus 1:5).[15] While no biblical prescription exists as to this duration of time for apostolic teams, it was not necessarily a lengthy period. Paul spent three years in Ephesus, with elders present by the time of

14. Michael W. Goheen, *Introducing Christian Mission Today: Scripture, History and Issues* (Downers Grove, IL: IVP Academic, 2014), 402–3.

15. Understanding that the elders (and deacons) were to come from the churches helps explain how those churches were to identify leadership. Aside from being able to teach, give instruction, and rebuke contradictions, the qualifications listed in 1 Tim. 3:1–13 and Titus 1:6–9 were to be discerned by living in community with others rather than by what could be observed on a résumé.

his Miletus visit (Acts 20:17–18), and eighteen months in Corinth (18:11). Possibly he was in Thessalonica for only three weeks (17:2). Paul returned to visit the churches, write letters, and send emissaries. But the shepherding responsibilities were transferred to the elders (20:28; 1 Pet. 5:1–2). It seems that apostles are not expected to function indefinitely as pastors.[16] There are differences in these roles for a reason. The elders were to increase in local involvement; the apostles were to decrease.

Caring for new churches. The apostolic attitudes, and therefore functions, were imagined in familial terms. As a "nursing mother" (1 Thess. 2:7), the teams displayed great compassion and concern for the new churches. Even after they went into new territories for continued ministry, the welfare of the churches was a constant matter. Letters and visits helped maintain the relationships and provide encouragement, exhortation, and correction.

Partnering with churches. Paul's ministry involved partnerships with churches. At times this revealed itself with the church in Antioch sending and receiving the first team (Acts 13:3; 14:26–28). Other times it was revealed through providing additional team members, financial contributions, prison visits, and lodging (Acts 11:29–30; Rom. 15:24–29; Phil. 2:25; 4:14–15; Philem. 22).

QUESTIONS TO CONSIDER

1. Do you agree with Roland Allen's statement on the universality of Paul? Why or why not?

2. If you were to serve on an apostolic team, how do you envision carrying out apostolic functions while also using your marketable skills or profession?

3. Which of the primary apostolic functions do you anticipate will be the greatest challenge to your ministry? What can you do now to better prepare for future service?

---

16. The reverse is also true. Unfortunately, some church-planting groups place pastors into ministries that should be served by apostolic workers.

CHAPTER 9

Reimagining Location

An overwhelming majority of kingdom labors are being conducted among reached people groups. With an estimated five billion unbelievers in the world, it is safe to claim that the Church's functions are not even close to reflecting a balance between service to Christians and non-Christians. While activities among believers are necessary and important, the apostolic imagination requires not building on another person's foundation (Rom. 15:20) and even rethinking activities in areas where the Church already exists. Jesus commanded the Church to go into all the world, to make disciples of all nations. But what does *all the world* mean? Who are the nations? Another relevant matter to consider related to the location of the Church's work is the modern construct of unreached people groups. How does this recent category relate to the Church's task? This chapter attempts to respond to these and other questions, beginning with a brief examination of Jesus's Great Commission.

Matthew 28:19–20

The most popular expression of Jesus's commission has received its share of critical scholarship over the years, with many questioning its authenticity.[1] Though such debate extends beyond this book, there is nothing in the text that would discredit Matthean authorship. The book's conclusion is in line with the themes of the Gospel, in harmony with the other evangelists, and reveals a paradigm that is reflected in the first century.

Drawing from Old Testament allusions of divine power and authority, especially found in the Davidic covenant and book of Daniel, Matthew writes: "All authority in heaven and on earth has been given to me. Go therefore and make disciples of all nations, baptizing them in the name of the Father and of the Son and of the Holy Spirit, teaching them to observe all that I have commanded you. And behold, I am with you always, to the end of the age" (28:19–20).

God's promise to David included a descendant whose kingdom would be eternally established by God himself (2 Sam. 7:12–13). Daniel's vision revealed the Ancient of Days presenting both authority and eternal reign to the Son of Man, who receives "dominion and glory and a kingdom, that all peoples, nations, and languages should serve him; his dominion is an everlasting dominion, which shall not pass away, and his kingdom one that shall not be destroyed" (Dan. 7:13–14).

No longer are the disciples restricted to "the house of Israel" (Matt. 10:5–6); here Matthew widens the scope of the apostolic work. The disciples are sent into the world to represent Jesus's kingdom claims. He tells them to make disciples of *panta ta ethnē* (all the nations), a phrase surely interpreted to include both Jews and Gentiles (Matt. 24:9, 14; 25:32).[2] The latter twentieth century experienced a surge of exegetes rushing to this text to argue that *ta ethnē* best represented ethnic groups of people as opposed to just Gentiles or nation-states. Jesus was not telling his disciples to enter into Egypt, make one disciple, and then move on to the next bordering country to repeat the process until every nation had at least one believer obeying the claims of Christ. Communities of kingdom citizens were to

1. R. V. G. Tasker responds to a couple of objections in *The Gospel according to St. Matthew: An Introduction and Commentary*, Tyndale New Testament Commentaries (Grand Rapids: Eerdmans, 1961), 274–76. See also D. A. Carson, "Matthew," in *The Expositor's Bible Commentary*, vol. 8, *Matthew, Mark, Luke*, ed. Frank E. Gaebelein (Grand Rapids: Zondervan, 1984), 591–99.

2. Even though Matthew often uses *ta ethnē* to refer to Gentiles (4:15; 6:32; 10:5, 18; 12:18, 21; 20:19, 25).

be established throughout all the groups of Gentiles and Jews. The "blessing of Abraham" (Gen. 12:3) was now fulfilled in Jesus, and this good news was to be taken to all nations so that in him they would find blessing.

Mark 13:10; 14:9

The commission passage assigned to the earliest Gospel is usually referenced in the disputed ending (Mark 16:9–20). However, there is more to Mark's commission than this debated text. Prior to the passion narrative, the Second Evangelist foreshadows the global reach of the gospel. Before the end comes and while persecution increases, Jesus declares, "The gospel must first be proclaimed to all nations" (Mark 13:10 // Matt. 24:14). In rebuke to those who opposed his pre-burial anointing by the woman, he states, "Truly, I say to you, wherever the gospel is proclaimed in the whole world, what she has done will be told in memory of her" (Mark 14:9).

R. Alan Cole takes "all nations" of Mark 13:10 to be understood as "all Gentiles," delivering a blow to Israel's ego, but says nothing regarding the scope of the proclamation in 14:9.[3] However, R. T. France recognizes these two texts as revealing "the most explicit indication in Mark's gospel of the universal scope of the good news and therefore of the Christian mission."[4] Though not as comprehensive as Matthew, Mark's global vision made it clear that the good news was not limited to one people. The Jesus who engaged with Gentiles (Mark 5:1–20; 7:24–8:10) believed that all nations were welcomed in God's presence (Mark 11:17), and the disciples were to have a role to play in the global enterprise to come.

Luke 24:46–49

Luke's concluding commission ties into his introductory declaration that Jesus is a light to the Gentiles and glory for Israel (Luke

3. R. Alan Cole, *Mark* (Grand Rapids: Eerdmans, 1961), 201, 210.
4. R. T. France, *The Gospel of Mark: A Commentary on the Greek Text* (Grand Rapids: Eerdmans, 2002), 516.

2:32). Recording Jesus's words, he writes, "Thus it is written, that the Christ should suffer and on the third day rise from the dead, and that repentance for the forgiveness of sins should be proclaimed in his name to all nations, beginning from Jerusalem. You are witnesses of these things. And behold, I am sending the promise of my Father upon you. But stay in the city until you are clothed with power from on high." Both Jews and Gentiles were included in this evangelistic work. Since the disciples had been witnesses and were soon to be empowered with the Spirit, the work would begin in Jerusalem and expand deeper and deeper into Gentile territory. Those who had not yet heard would hear the declaration of his good news.

Acts 1:7–8

Luke's second volume provides additional commentary on the geographical expanse of the Church's work. After being asked if he was to set up his kingdom, Jesus said to his disciples, "It is not for you to know times or seasons that the Father has fixed by his own authority. But you will receive power when the Holy Spirit has come upon you, and you will be my witnesses in Jerusalem and in all Judea and Samaria, and to the end of the earth." According to Schnabel, "People in the first century were rather well informed about numerous regions between the border of the Roman Empire and the 'ends of the earth.'"[5] The terminal points on the map would have been understood as Gaul, Spain, Germania, and Britannia on the West, the Arctic (e.g., Scythia) in the North, Ethiopia to the South, and India and China on the East.[6]

Schnabel notes that if the disciples understood their assignment in geographical terms, then they would have either embraced a minimal or maximal perspective. The former would limit their assignment in terms of the locations of the Jewish Diaspora. The latter would have embraced the wider Greco-Roman perspective. After extensive research, Schnabel sees sufficient evidence to conclude that the

5. Eckhard J. Schnabel, *Early Christian Mission*, vol. 1, *Jesus and the Twelve* (Downers Grove, IL: InterVarsity, 2004), 445.
6. Schnabel, *Early Christian Mission*, 1:373–74.

first-century disciples embraced the Greco-Roman understanding of the "ends of the earth."[7] This expansion is traced throughout the book of Acts, revealing the conversion of both Jews and Gentiles. Wherever disciples are made through the preaching of repentance and faith (Acts 20:21), churches are planted in their communities and beyond.

John 20:21 (cf. 17:18)

John's Gospel is filled with the language of sending. "The Word became flesh" and came to earth (John 1:14). The Father reveals his love by sending the Son to save the world (3:16–17). In his high-priestly prayer, Jesus anticipates the mission of sending the disciples into the world: "As you sent me into the world, so I have sent them into the world" (17:18; cf. 13:20; 15:26–27). Following his resurrection, Jesus appears to the disciples and says, "As the Father has sent me, even so I am sending you" (20:21). The disciples were to bear witness to what they had seen, heard, and experienced, which involved communicating that the Savior had been sent on behalf of the world. D. A. Carson writes, "Christ's disciples do not take over Jesus' mission; his mission continues and is effective in their ministry (14:12–14)."[8] They go into the world so that others may believe (20:30–31). John's lack of geographical focus in his commission account emphasizes the universal scope of the apostolic task. There is no off-limits place when it comes to God's mission.

Table of Nations

When considering the scope of the Church's labors, it is important to consider the Table of Nations found in Genesis 10. What bearing, if any, did this text, listing seventy nations from Noah's descendants, influence the first-century understanding of locations where the disciples' work was to be accomplished? Did the Table of Nations provide a first-century understanding to *panta ta ethnē*? Scholarship is somewhat divided on this issue.

7. Schnabel, *Early Christian Mission*, 1:498.
8. D. A. Carson, *The Gospel according to John* (Grand Rapids: Eerdmans, 1991), 649.

Schnabel states that Jesus's commission to all nations would have reminded the disciples of this passage.[9] James M. Scott makes a strong argument that this list of nations was what Paul had in mind when he used the word *ethnos*. As the apostle to the nations (Rom. 11:13), Paul clearly recognized that "the blessing of Abraham" was to reach all nations (Gal. 3:8, 14). According to Scott, the "full number of the nations" (Rom. 11:25; cf. CEB) that must come to faith during Israel's hardness of heart probably refers to the list provided in Genesis 10.[10] Other scholars, such as Ksenija Magda, argue that Paul was not only concerned with the sons of Japheth but also those of Ham and Shem and was more influenced by Greco-Roman thought when it came to his understanding of geography and territory of apostolic engagement.[11] Schnabel finds much of Scott's hypothesis plausible from a tradition-historical perspective: "It founders, however, on account of the very diverse geographical identifications in the Jewish (and early Christian patristic) tradition, and also on account of the details of Paul's actual missionary work."[12] A strong case is made that the early apostles were not limited to the Roman Empire.[13]

Paul and Geography

Did Paul maintain a geographical strategy? Scott believes such indeed was the case.[14] After an extensive treatment of Paul's apostolic tactics and communication, however, Schnabel concludes that the evidence is lacking:

> Paul pursued a comprehensive *international* missionary strategy: he wanted to preach the gospel of Jesus Christ in provinces and regions, in cities and towns in which no other missionary had preached before. Paul pursued a comprehensive *social* missionary strategy: he

9. Schnabel, *Early Christian Mission*, 1:365.
10. James M. Scott, *Paul and the Nations* (Tübingen: Mohr Siebeck, 1995), 135.
11. Ksenija Magda, *Paul's Territoriality and Mission Strategy* (Tübingen: Mohr Siebeck, 2009).
12. Eckhard J. Schnabel, *Early Christian Mission*, vol. 2, *Paul and the Early Church* (Downers Grove, IL: InterVarsity, 2004), 1298.
13. Schnabel, *Early Christian Mission*, 1:365.
14. Scott, *Paul and the Nations*, 154.

wanted to reach both Jews and pagans, Greeks and barbarians, the educated and the uneducated. Whether Paul pursued a comprehensive *geographical* missionary strategy is unclear, unless we are content to assert that he moved from Damascus to Jerusalem, from Antioch to Paphos, from Pisidian Antiocheia to Ephesus, and from Corinth via Rome to Spain. . . . Shall we assume, as some scholars suggest, that Paul developed a comprehensive geographical strategy around A.D. 44 during his ministry in Antioch, after missionary work in Arabia, Syria and Cilicia for twelve years? Perhaps, but such a scenario must remain hypothetical.[15]

The apostle was apparently concerned with geography but only as it related to people. His apostolic functions required an audience, not the development of structures and organization in locations where unbelievers did not exist. Paul gave priority to work where a gospel foundation had not been established (e.g., 1 Cor. 3:5–17). He gave particular attention to cities of influence. Paul preferred preaching to receptive peoples, who at times were Gentiles (Acts 13:46–51; 18:6). An examination of his writings reveals his desire to labor in areas where others had not worked. He wanted the Corinthians to develop in the faith so his team's "area of influence" would "be greatly enlarged," so that his team "may preach the gospel in lands beyond you, without boasting of work already done in another's area of influence" (2 Cor. 10:15–16).

This language and motivation appear to be in line with what Paul shares with the Roman Christians. He announces plans to spend time with them and be assisted in his journey to Spain (Rom. 15:24). He describes his labors as having concluded in a particular region: "From Jerusalem and all the way around to Illyricum I have fulfilled the ministry of the gospel of Christ; and thus I make it my ambition to preach the gospel, not where Christ has already been named, lest I build on someone else's foundation, but as it is written, 'Those who have never been told of him will see, and those who have never heard will understand'" (Rom. 15:19–21).

Paul Bowers was correct that the culmination of the apostle's labors in an area involves local churches established in their ministries

---

15. Schnabel, *Early Christian Mission*, 2:1320.

of the gospel. A priority was given to evangelism, but such proclamation was to result in local kingdom communities. "For Paul, however, conversion meant incorporation. Baptism is baptism into the body of Christ. The new believer implicitly becomes a believer-in-community, and Paul is concerned in his mission not only with the emergence of such believers but also with the emergence of such communities, for only in such a setting could that which is offered in the proclamation be properly realized and experienced."[16] C. E. B. Cranfield notes that Paul's statement of completion should not lead to the conclusion that nothing remained to be done in the area. It was Paul's concept of the pioneer worker that influenced this conclusion. His specific apostolic functions had been completed in the region, the task of the ministry had been passed to the new churches, and it was time to serve elsewhere.[17]

Crossing Cultural Gaps, not Oceans

All disciple making involves a conflict of worldviews. A believer who shares the gospel with an unbeliever is engaging in a cultural exchange between the kingdom of God and the kingdom of darkness. This cultural difference exists even if both parties share the same mailing address. The biblical understanding of the apostolic work is primarily about crossing cultural gaps, not oceans.[18] Though geographical dis-

16. Paul Bowers, "Fulfilling the Gospel: The Scope of the Pauline Mission," *Journal of the Evangelical Theological Society* 30, no. 2 (June 1987): 185–98, here 187.

17. C. E. B. Cranfield, *A Critical and Exegetical Commentary on the Epistle to the Romans*, 6th ed. (Edinburgh: T&T Clark, 1979), 2:763. See also Robert H. Mounce, *Romans* (Nashville: Broadman & Holman, 1995), 267; and Leon Morris, *The Epistle to the Romans* (Grand Rapids: Eerdmans, 1988), 514. Paul desired the Roman church's assistance to reach Spain, yet in addition to blessing them through his letter, he wrote of his desire to visit and nurture them by imparting "some spiritual gift to strengthen you" (Rom. 1:11).

18. At first glance it appears that Köstenberger disagrees with this view when he writes, "In contemporary usage, *missions* generally refers to cross-cultural ministry. In biblical terminology, however, it appears that the cross-cultural aspect of Christian ministry is not a necessary part of mission. . . . Rather, mission in the New Testament usually centers around a person's (or group's) commissioning (e.g., Matthew 28:18–20; Luke 24:46–48; John 20:21–23) to a particular task." However, Köstenberger is juxtaposing the widespread modern understanding that "cross-cultural ministry" is done in another country that is radically different from the culture of the person

tances were involved, many of the apostolic labors addressed in the Scriptures did not require the teams to go "overseas" or travel great distances. Much of their work was carried on via land routes. The geographic boundaries outlined in Acts 1:8 have more to do with cultural differences than geographical distances.

The apostolic imagination came to recognize that such kingdom labors would require involvement with people who did not share one's perspective on life and the cosmos. A familiar cultural worldview contrasted with a worldview at some distance; such were the major differences between work among the Jews in Jerusalem and Hellenists in Antioch. The cultural gaps between those preaching the gospel and the hearers receiving the message differed, depending on the preacher and the hearers. The cultural gap between Peter and the Jews in Jerusalem (Acts 2; cf. Gal. 2:7) and the God-fearers in Cornelius's house (Acts 10) was substantial, so much so that it took a divine vision to change Peter's thinking! Philip encountered worldview differences between the Samaritans (Acts 8:4–8) and the Ethiopian (8:26–39) as he shared the gospel with them. Many recognized the significance when the unnamed men of Jerusalem took the gospel to the Greek-speaking Gentiles of Antioch (11:20–26). The cultural gap between Paul and the Athenian Epicureans and Stoics was larger (Acts 17:16–34) than those between Paul and the Jews of many synagogues.

Nations versus Peoples

Exegetical studies of the twentieth century resulted in what became known as people-group thinking. The unit of evangelization was no longer viewed as a country, but the subgroups of people in the

---

sent to that *foreign* land. We apparently agree that the biblical description of mission did not require great geographical travel. I draw attention to this matter because most people conceptualize "cross-cultural" work as entering into a radically different cultural *and* geographical context and do not understand that worldview creates cultural gaps even within one's geographical area. See Andreas J. Köstenberger, "The Place of Mission in New Testament Theology: An Attempt to Determine the Significance of Mission within the Scope of the New Testament's Message as a Whole," *Missiology* 27, no. 3 (July 1999): 347–62, here 348.

population of a given country. Dave Datema and Leonard N. Bartlotti describe this interpretative shift as "arguably the most significant thought innovation in twentieth century missiology."[19] This
understanding of sociocultural diversity was not new. Rather, the
developing global awareness and mission strategy brought a paradigm shift.

Rather than focus on making disciples of Indonesians in Indonesia, Indonesia was understood as one country consisting of a multitude of peoples, groups that held to common ethnic, linguistic,
and cultural connections. A large Christian presence was evident
in Indonesia. However, a multitude of other Indonesian peoples
(e.g., Muslim groups) were unreached with the gospel. They would
remain in this state until Christians, particularly Indonesian Christians, crossed the cultural gaps that separated them from Indonesian
Muslims.

Ralph Winter brought attention to recognizing the highest priority as taking the gospel across these cultural gaps, not necessarily national borders, without which over 30 percent of the world's
population (i.e., hidden peoples) would remain lost.[20] These groups
comprised the "final frontier." Aided with the development of maps
and graphics, evangelicals began developing strategies influenced
by people-group thinking. The world was no longer understood to
consist of a couple hundred countries and territories to be reached
with the gospel, but rather as having thousands of people groups.
Winter was not content to believe one cultural manifestation of the
Church within a country was sufficient to reach the cultural diversity
found there. What came to be called *frontier missiology* was developed primarily from the missiology of Donald A. McGavran and
Ralph Winter. Johnson declares that this field was designed to "take
us beyond a geographic view of mission, reaching individuals, and
planting our preferred style of church. Rather, reminiscent of Paul

19. Dave Datema and Leonard N. Bartlotti, "The People Group Approach: A
Historical Perspective," *Evangelical Missions Quarterly* 56, no. 4 (October–December
2020): 8–11, here 11.
20. Ralph D. Winter, "The Highest Priority: Cross-Cultural Evangelism," *Let the
Earth Hear His Voice: International Congress on World Evangelization, Lausanne,
Switzerland,* ed. J. D. Douglas (Minneapolis: World Wide Publications, 1975), 213–41.

in Romans 15, frontier missions is an 'ambition' and call to relentlessly cross boundaries to penetrate segments of people who have no near-neighbor access to the gospel."[21]

In the late 1970s, the Missions Advanced Research and Communications Center (MARC), a division of World Vision under Ed Dayton's leadership, began publishing annual directories of unreached people groups. Although these early directories were incomplete, they provided lists of various ethnolinguistic groups in great need of the gospel. In his book *Reaching the Unreached: An Introductory Study on Developing an Overall Strategy for World Evangelization* (1974), Ed Pentecost was one of the early scholars who suggested defining unreached peoples as those with 20 percent or less of their population being Christian adherents. This somewhat arbitrary number was chosen because it was "estimated that when 20 percent of a people are Christians, the church within the group no longer needs any help from the outside" to spread the gospel and plant churches.[22] This percentage was soon accepted by the Lausanne Strategy Working Group, which influenced the wider evangelical community. Yet this number was of little value to the strategist since most people groups fell under this definition, making nearly every identified group unreached.[23]

David Barrett's 1982 *World Christian Encyclopedia* was the first comprehensive list of people groups. This initial work greatly influenced the people-group research that followed. Presently, there are three comprehensive people-group databases. Each differs from the others, and each is revised as new data is discovered. The dataset generally lists the people groups of the world by countries in which

21. Alan R. Johnson, "Foundations of Frontier Missiology: Core Understandings and Interrelated Concepts," *Evangelical Missions Quarterly* 56, no. 4 (October–December 2020): 12–15, here 13.

22. Edward R. Dayton, *That Everyone May Hear: Reaching the Unreached* (Monrovia, CA: MARC, 1979), 27. Although the percentages shifted over the years, the early suggestions ranging from 10–20% were connected to the theory of the diffusion of innovation developed by sociologist Everett M. Rogers, as he explained in *Diffusion of Innovations*, 5th ed. (New York: Free Press, 2003).

23. Ralph D. Winter, "Unreached Peoples: The Development of the Concept," in *Reaching the Unreached: The Old-New Challenge*, ed. Harvie M. Conn (Phillipsburg, NJ: Presbyterian and Reformed, 1985), 17–43, here 30–31.

they are found and languages they speak. The World Christian Database was developed in 1982. People groups considered less than 50 percent evangelized were listed as unreached.

Throughout the 1980s and 1990s, the stipulated percentage defining unreached peoples diminished. Among the two other databases at present, a 2 percent threshold has become an accepted standard, with some variation. The Church Planting Progress Indicators, housed with the International Mission Board, was developed in 1991. An unreached people is defined as a group that is less than 2 percent evangelical. The Joshua Project's dataset was started in 1995 and listed an unreached group as being less than or equal to 2 percent evangelical *and* less than or equal to 5 percent Christian Adherent. According to the Joshua Project's definition of unreached, there are an estimated 7,400 people groups that fall into this category, representing over 3 billion people.[24]

The Global Research Department identifies four categories of unreached people groups, with particular attention given to church planting:

- Status 0 = No evangelicals or churches; no access to major evangelical resources
- Status 1 = Less than 2 percent evangelical; some evangelical resources available, no active church planting in past 2 years
- Status 2 = Less than 2 percent evangelical; local church planting in past 2 years
- Status 3 = Less than 2 percent evangelical; widespread church planting in past two years

Global Research Department estimates that seven thousand people groups in the world are considered unreached, representing 4.5 billion people.[25]

R. W. Lewis has provided a more nuanced picture of unreached people groups with the *frontier people groups* subset "where there are no movements to Christ, no breakthroughs of indigenous faith, and

24. See https://joshuaproject.net/global/progress.
25. See https://www.imb.org/research/reports/#gsec.

less than 0.1% of the population is Christian." Frontier work always involves crossing significant cultural divides. Apostolic teams must come from believers who belong to different ethnolinguistic people groups. It is estimated that 72 percent of frontier peoples reside in South Asia, comprising 25 percent of the world's population.[26]

It is an understatement to say that much good came from people-group missiology. The Lord used such work to lead the Church from the days of colonialism into the postcolonial period. Millions of people came to faith and became members of local kingdom communities. While this shift greatly advanced the gospel and resulted in the multiplication of disciples, churches, and leaders among some of the least reached peoples on the planet, missiologists have noticed limitations of this approach, particularly in the areas of terminology and statistics. People groups were conceptualized to assist with global disciple-making strategies. All people-group lists have limitations and are flawed to some degree. But, as Brad Gill notes, they served as a strategic map to assist with the journey.[27] Fifty years of people-group missiology have allowed for a great deal of self-reflection and evaluation. Over the past few years, missiologists, missionaries, and church leaders have raised new challenges to this missiology. While a people-group focus is not going away anytime soon, it is overdue for adjustment. Globalization, urbanization, and migration, as well as somewhat arbitrary and unclear definitions of what constitutes reached and unreached, have brought the conversation to a new level.[28]

26. R. W. Lewis, "Clarifying the Remaining Frontier Mission Task," *International Journal of Frontier Missiology* 35, no. 4 (October–December 2018): 154–68, here 156–57, 160. In this article Lewis makes numerous excellent statements and offers many important tables and charts.

27. Brad Gill, "A Church for Every People: A Retrospect on Mapping Peoples," *Evangelical Missions Quarterly* 56, no. 4 (October–December 2020): 43–45.

28. See Alan McMahan, "Ferment in the Church: Missions in the 4th Era," *Evangelical Missions Quarterly* 56, no. 4 (October–December 2020): 36–38; Minh Ha Nguyen, "Globalization, Urbanization, Migration, and Rethinking the People Groups Concept," *Evangelical Missions Quarterly* 56, no. 4 (October–December 2020): 32–35; Len Bartlotti, "Reimagining and Re-envisioning People Groups," *Evangelical Missions Quarterly* 56, no. 4 (October–December 2020): 46–50; R. W. Lewis, "Fog in the Pews: Factors behind the Fading Vision for Unreached Peoples," *Evangelical Missions Quarterly* 56, no. 4 (October–December 2020): 28–31.

People Everywhere, but Where to Begin?

The Church is to go into all the world and make disciples. The apostolic imagination understands geography in view of the peoples who live there. Christ did not die for the boundaries of villages, towns, cities, and countries. His substitutionary atoning sacrifice was for the world's sins (Rom. 3:25; 1 John 2:2; 4:10; Heb. 2:17). The apostolic imagination recognizes the potential of Spirit-filled believers who follow Christ's commands. As kingdom citizens live out love, justice, mercy, and humility, ungodly systems and structures are transformed.

All are lost without Christ; but all lostness is not the same. Evangelism is needed wherever people are found. Unbelievers exist in Birmingham, Alabama, and in Rabat, Morocco. However, the apostolic imagination is governed by a stewardship related to the lack of a gospel foundation for engaging with global need. Need is everywhere, but all need is not the same. Some locations are home to peoples who are needier than others. Access is critical. How might the apostolic imagination respond to the question, Where should the Church's efforts be focused? Such a question relates to strategy, the topic of the next chapter.

QUESTIONS TO CONSIDER

1. How does the understanding of "nations" affect the interpretation of Matthew 28:18–20 and the apostolic work of the Church?
2. How does the application of Romans 15:20 relate to apostolic work in Birmingham, Alabama, and in Rabat, Morocco?
3. What is meant by the statement, "Need is everywhere, but all need is not the same"?

CHAPTER 10

Reimagining Strategy

A ccording to people-group research, several billion people have no relationship with Christ. Unbelievers are found in Mississippi and Mongolia. Should the Church's global efforts receive the same attention in all locations? Are some places needier than others? Churches often engage the world without regard for stewardship. Given the limited resources and the vast global needs, Spirit-led discernment is critical to the task. This chapter considers how the apostolic imagination influences where the Church should prioritize disciple-making efforts.

Apostolic strategy has been debated for years. Generally, the discussion revolves around the question, Did Paul have a strategy that guided his apostolic labors? Schnabel notices that "Paul planned his missionary initiatives in the context of a general strategy that controlled his tactical decisions."[1] However, Michael Green questions the existence of such an endeavor: "There does not seem to have been anything very remarkable about the strategy and tactics of the early Christian mission. Indeed, it is doubtful if they had one. I do not believe they set out with any blueprint. They had an unquenchable conviction that Jesus was the key to life and death, happiness and

---

1. Eckhard J. Schnabel, *Early Christian Mission*, vol. 2, *Paul and the Early Church* (Downers Grove, IL: InterVarsity, 2004), 1293.

purpose, and they simply could not keep quiet about him. The spirit of Jesus within them drove them into mission."[2]

Making a creative calculation in 1988, David B. Barrett and James W. Reapsome estimated that the Church had developed over 700 strategies for world evangelization.[3] Others estimated that this number swelled to 2,600 plans by 2020.[4] On one hand, it would be easy to state that such a large number of attempts offers strong evidence against the need to develop strategy. After all, if that many plans have not resulted in making disciples of all nations, then strategy is a waste of time. On the other hand, the argument could be made that Christianity is the world's largest religion; therefore, imagine the detriment to Church growth if such attempts had not been applied. McGavran was correct in declaring, "It is better to put an imperfect plan into operation than to carry on splendid church and mission work while waiting for the perfect plan to appear."[5] However, Barrett and Reapsome conclude with an honest, yet blunt, assessment of their findings:

> We Great Commission Christians are in a mess. We have not obeyed the Commission in the past. We are not obeying it in the present. We are not, on present trends, likely to obey it in the future. . . .
>
> Yet we continue to produce grandiose global plans for AD 2000 at the rate of at least one new one per week. In other words, the leadership of the church has convinced itself that all its existing activity actually is fulfilling the commission. Worse, it is telling everybody else that it is succeeding in this way. Worst of all, the 1.3 billion unevangelized remain at roughly the same number week after week, year after year, decade after decade.[6]

2. Michael Green, "Methods and Strategy in the Evangelism of the Early Church," in *Let the Earth Hear His Voice: International Congress on World Evangelization, Lausanne, Switzerland*, ed. J. D. Douglas (Minneapolis: World Wide Publications, 1975), 165–66.

3. David B. Barrett and James W. Reapsome, *Seven Hundred Plans to Evangelize the World: The Rise of a Global Evangelization Movement* (Birmingham, AL: New Hope, 1988).

4. Gina A. Zurlo, Todd M. Johnson, and Peter F. Crossing, "World Christianity and Mission 2020: Ongoing Shift to the Global South," *International Bulletin of Mission Research* 44, no. 1 (2019):, 8–19, here 17.

5. Donald A. McGavran, *Understanding Church Growth* (Grand Rapids: Eerdmans, 1970), 360.

6. Barrett and Reapsome, *Plans to Evangelize the World*, 65.

Decades into the twenty-first century, 4.5 billion people are categorized as unreached,[7] including an unreached and unengaged population of 273 million.[8]

The later twentieth century saw the rise of mission-strategy books.[9] Tensions arise whenever conversations turn toward strategy. This is often the case since a great deal of discussion regarding the topic comes from military or business considerations.[10] Some have refrained from serious consideration of strategy since they fear that it is an attempt to replace God's sovereignty, exclude the Holy Spirit, or allow for pragmatism.[11] The Church, however, is not in the business of waging war on other nations or marketing novel products.[12] Furthermore, the Church does not find obedience to the Lord's Commission related to conquest or competition. Christ's Church absolutely must enter the world while filled with the Spirit, governed by the Scriptures, and owning limited resources.

Understanding Strategy

The apostolic imagination understands strategy as based on God's Word and the historical work of the Spirit. Strategy involves a future

7. See https://grd.imb.org/research-data/.

8. See https://grd.imb.org/research-data/. "Unreached unengaged" is a category whereby a people group is both unreached and there is no active evangelical church planting strategy being executed among them.

9. For example, several were related to the work of Edward Dayton, who provided leadership for the Missions Advanced Research and Communications Center: Edward R. Dayton and David A. Fraser, *Planning Strategies for World Evangelization*, rev. ed. (Grand Rapids: Eerdmans, 1990); Edward R. Dayton and Ted W. Engstrom, *Strategy for Leadership: Planning, Activating, Motivating, Elevating* (Old Tappan, NJ: Revell, 1979); Edward R. Dayton and Ted W. Engstrom, *Strategy for Living: How to Make the Best Use of Your Time and Abilities* (Glendale, CA: Regal, 1976).

10. Strategists of all stripes often cite Sun Tzu, *The Art of War* (Barnsley, UK: Pen & Sword Military, 2013), a 2,600-year-old work on military strategy that is still consulted today.

11. These and other objections are addressed by John Mark Terry and J. D. Payne in *Developing a Strategy for Missions: A Biblical, Historical, and Cultural Introduction* (Grand Rapids: Baker Academic, 2013), 24–33.

12. Since a significant portion of the modern history of mission was connected to business expansion and military conquest, it is no wonder that strategy has often been bedfellows with these as well.

orientation and plans for process. The wise strategist understands that if it is the Lord's will, then plans will come to pass (James 4:13–16). Dayton and Fraser write: "If we are going to get on with the business of world evangelization we need to have a way of thinking about the future. Since we cannot predict it in any detail, we can only consider the future and our actions in it in broad terms. But think of them we must."[13]

Strategy forces the team to have a vision of the possible future. It enables them to concentrate on the future transformation that will occur if the gospel is embraced and a kingdom ethic is lived out in the community. However, strategy is not meant to remain in the theoretical ether but is to be applied to a context. Strategic planning is a process that combines thinking *and* acting.[14] Mission strategy is the overall process describing what a team believes the Lord would have them accomplish to make disciples of all nations.[15] Developing a strategy requires obtaining a vision from the Lord of what the team believes the Lord desires and is followed by setting goals and action steps necessary to achieve that vision. Strategies do not violate biblical principles but are governed by them. Contextually relevant strategies allow teams to be wise stewards with their resources.

Strategic Planning

Strategic planning is a prayerfully discerned, Spirit-guided process of preparation, development, implementation, and evaluation of the necessary steps involved for apostolic endeavors.[16] The development of apostolic strategy is a supernatural act and should never be entered into as if it is simply humanistic work. Teams do not create their strategies and then ask the Lord to bless them. Rather, in consideration of the billions without Christ, they want to know his will for their resources and opportunities. He is the one to whom they look for the establishment of their steps (Prov. 16:9). As Wilbert R. Shenk teaches, "Strategic

13. Dayton and Fraser, *Planning Strategies for World Evangelization*, 24.
14. Aubrey Malphurs, *Advanced Strategic Planning: A New Model for Church and Ministry Leaders*, 2nd ed. (Grand Rapids: Baker Books, 2005), 30.
15. John Mark Terry and I address this definition and strategy in extensive detail in *Developing a Strategy for Missions*.
16. Terry and Payne, *Developing a Strategy for Missions*, 13.

planning ought to begin and end with the prayer 'Your will be done.'"[17] Process denotes movement, for strategy implementation takes the team from where they are to where they believe they need to go. The team needs to understand their own beliefs, values, passions, gifts, talents, abilities, opportunities, and resources. They need to understand the people in their contexts.[18] As the team implements plans on the field, they must aggressively evaluate their labors and adjust accordingly in relation to the Spirit's leading, goals, and vision. The process of strategic planning may be reduced to at least four actions.

Asking good questions. The apostolic imagination wants to know if the team is being faithful to the Lord. This mindset asks questions such as these: Is this method the most Christ-honoring act? What is working well and not so well on the field? What needs to be changed? What needs to be kept? Are we being wise stewards? What should we do first? Second? Third? The apostolic imagination makes inquiries about the health of the team as well as the characteristics of the people in the context. What is the best way to share the gospel? Plant churches? What are our goals? What are we doing to achieve those goals?

Responding with healthy answers. Answers provided to the multitude of questions should be given within biblical parameters and missiological principles that support healthy practices. Inquiring minds attempt to move thoughts and questions toward practical action steps.

Applying wise action steps. Strategy remains theory until it is applied. The team must make decisions on how they are to work toward their goals, which eventually culminate in the accomplishment of the vision. Actions must happen. The execution of the plan is the most difficult part of the strategic planning process.

Evaluating everything. Wise kingdom citizens practice aggressive evaluation. The team should hold their strategy loosely. Adjustments on the field are necessary as the Spirit leads. Evaluation keeps the team

17. Wilbert R. Shenk, *Changing Frontiers of Missions* (Maryknoll, NY: Orbis, 1999), 107.

18. A basic understanding should involve knowing the people geographically, demographically, culturally, spiritually, historically, politically, economically, and linguistically; and understanding their knowledge of the gospel and attitude toward the gospel. See J. D. Payne, *Discovering Church Planting: An Introduction to the Whats, Whys, and Hows of Global Church Planting* (Downers Grove, IL: IVP, 2009), 183–200. See also Terry and Payne, *Developing a Strategy for Missions*, 147–57.

from continuing with their plans to go into Asia Minor or Bithynia when the Spirit wants to take them to Philippi (Acts 16:6–15). Contextual dynamics affect the execution of the strategy. It is a grave mistake for a team to develop a strategy and never allow for adjustments. Such rigidity will result in significant problems on the field. The apostolic imagination recognizes numerous factors affecting the implementation of a strategy and that, therefore, evaluation and adjustment are constants.

Unfortunately, churches and apostolic teams are often so conservative with their strategies that they come to believe they are sacred and untouchable. Since much time, effort, and prayer went into the process to develop the strategy, no one should tamper with it. While there is a sacred element involved in strategy development, strategy is a tool to accomplish a divine task. The strategy and methods that got the team to where they are today are not the same elements that will take them to where they need to go in the future. Evaluation and adjustments are constants.

Apply the Strategic Filter

In light of the global need for the gospel, where should the apostolic team begin its labors? The following strategic filter is a *guide* to assist in the process. As the team considers the use of the filter, they should be fasting, praying, studying the Scriptures, and consulting with other believers, all while looking across the vast multitudes.

Begin with God's calling. The filter challenges the team to consider God's calling in their lives. Though both Peter and Paul engaged Jews and Gentiles with the gospel, there appears to have been a particular emphasis in their work with Peter's "apostolic ministry to the circumcised" and Paul's "to the Gentiles" (Gal. 2:8). While there is one Spirit working in the apostolic teams, there are varieties of service and activities (1 Cor. 12:4–6). The team with an apostolic imagination is set on the call of God and determined to glorify him through obedience, working among the people (in the location) impressed upon them.

Guideline 1: Assume the Great Commission. The team should assume that Jesus's commission is relevant today. The apostolic imagination is concerned primarily with being a witness for Christ in the world as they preach the gospel with the intention of making disciples.

Therefore, wherever disciples do not exist in local kingdom communities (i.e., churches), there is need.

Guideline 2: Ask: Is the call to a resistant people? Although unbelievers are enemies of God and dead in their sins (Rom. 5:10; Eph. 2:1), not everyone responds to the gospel in the same way. Some hear the Word with much delight, others with apathy, still others with hostility (Acts 13:48; 17:32–33). Many teams are called to resistant fields. Many will serve in contexts whereby it will take years (maybe decades) before people come to faith. History is filled with such examples. Although people groups may not be hostile to the good news, their ignorance about the message (along with other social and cultural factors) may require a lengthy time of proclamation and witness. Teams called to resistant peoples are just as important as teams called to receptive peoples. One calling is not better than the other. Multitudes of peoples are very resistant to the gospel. Many of these include unreached people groups. The apostolic imagination is greatly concerned for such groups and celebrates the labors of teams serving among the resistant.

Guideline 3: Determine the neediest and most receptive peoples. If a calling to a resistant people is not present, then the team should consider beginning among the neediest and most receptive peoples. The following Need-Receptivity Guide is a tool to help visualize this matter.

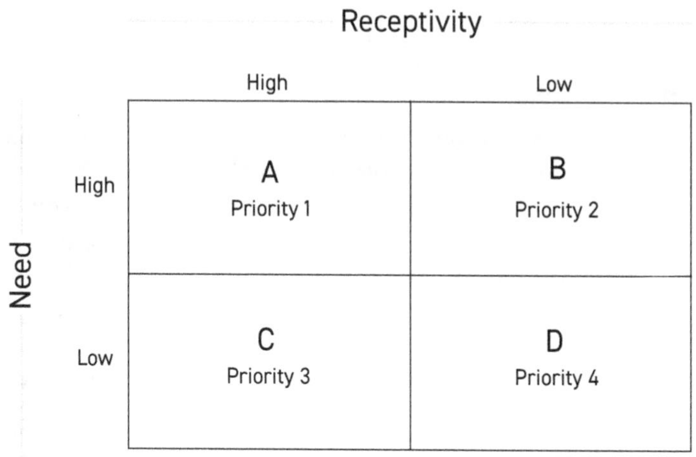
Receptivity
High
Low
Need
High
Low
A
Priority 1
B
Priority 2
C
Priority 3
D
Priority 4

Figure 10.1. Need-receptivity guide

Although the gospel is to be shared with everyone regardless of need and receptivity, the Church should give priority to Fields A and B. Both fields represent peoples who are the neediest of the needy. Among both fields, there is little to no access to gospel-centered churches, Christians, Christian literature, music, videos, broadcasts, and other resources. Peoples in these fields are the unreached people groups. Here is the location of pioneer work and where the frontier peoples and the unreached-unengaged are located. Fields C and D represent people groups where there is much access to evangelical churches and resources.

The distinction between Fields A and B is the element of receptivity. Every individual and all people manifest levels of receptivity to the gospel and the Church and the methods used. Receptivity is never a constant. Various factors affect the waxing and waning of a people's response.[19] If the Spirit has heightened a positive receptivity to the gospel among a group (Field A), then teams should begin there.[20] The only way to understand receptivity is to share the gospel with people and observe their responses over time. Many apostolic teams will be the trailblazers and need to evaluate responses as peoples first encounter the gospel. Even for those working among a resistant people, the team should ask, What individual, segment of society, etc. is the neediest of the needy *and* the most open to what we have to share?

Considering "Success"

The apostolic imagination strives for a definition of success that is not confined to a secular ideology. Though baptisms, churches planted, and leaders developed are desirable and important outcomes that represent goals accomplished, the arbitrary numbers achieved are not the golden standard of success. Success is recognized more as faithfulness to calling and the Lord's leadership and as steward-

19. Donald A. McGavran, *Understanding Church Growth*, 3rd ed. (Grand Rapids: Eerdmans, 1990), 179–92.

20. For more details on the Need-Receptivity Guide, see Payne, *Discovering Church Planting*, 141–82; and on discerning need and receptivity, see Terry and Payne, *Developing a Strategy for Missions*, 175–92.

ship of opportunities and resources in view of the Church's task and global realities.

Success is a somewhat relative issue, based on the Spirit, context, and team dynamics. Bruce Nicholls writes, "Mission Boards would never have approved of the rashness of Philip's leaving the revival in Samaria for the deserts of Gaza, or the foolishness of Paul returning to Jerusalem to certain imprisonment, yet these acts of obedience to the Holy Spirit achieved more for the Kingdom of God than would have any strategy of missions."[21] Paul's team planted the church in Philippi after their strategy was interrupted twice (Acts 16:6–15). A plan in one context may be unthinkable in another situation. The team that is free to evangelize openly without interference should be held to a different standard than the team whose actions are constantly being monitored by authorities. Each team should be accountable for determining the means by which they will evaluate their strategies on the field. Although there is continuity from team to team, a one-size-fits-all scorecard of effectiveness is foolish and does not reflect the apostolic imagination.

QUESTIONS TO CONSIDER

1. If someone stated that strategic planning was an attempt to play God, how would you respond?

2. What are the strengths and limitations of the Need-Receptivity Guide?

3. How do you define success for apostolic teams?

21. Bruce Nicholls, *Missionary Strategy* (London: Evangelical Missionary Alliance, 1962), 1.

CHAPTER 11

Reimagining the West

Lesslie Newbigin did much to bring attention to the shifting contexts of the traditionally Western countries where the Church has maintained a strong presence. He felt so strongly about the changes in the West that he wrote, "There is no higher priority for the research work of missiologists than to ask the question of what would be involved in a genuinely missionary encounter between the gospel and this modern Western culture."[1] Although his work was most helpful, it never resulted in the necessary paradigm shift for apostolic work, at least not in North America.[2] Much of the missiology developed became filtered through a pastoral imagination to be implemented through established church structures. Since the turn of the twenty-first century, the expression "the West as a mission field" has grown in popularity. The language of mission(al) is regularly used, but little apostolic function occurs.

At the same time, the Western Church has many resources, centuries of mission experience, much wisdom, and numerous opportunities for global engagement. Reimagining the West, as discussed in this

1. Lesslie Newbigin, *The Gospel in a Pluralist Society* (Grand Rapids: Eerdmans; Geneva: WCC Publications, 1989), 242.
2. The Gospel and Our Culture Network, which began in the UK, and the Missional Church Movement were greatly influenced by Newbigin and had major influence among churches in the US.

chapter, involves two categories for consideration.[3] On the one hand, it is important to understand and apply the apostolic imagination to the Church's labors within the traditionally Western countries. On the other hand, a challenge is offered for the Church to consider how these numerous resources and opportunities are being used throughout the world.

A Disclaimer

The greatest spiritual and physical needs are located outside the traditionally Western contexts. Although needs are great within the boundaries of Western countries, access to the gospel and resources for assistance are more prevalent here than throughout many Majority World contexts.[4] The highest priority for the apostolic labors of the Church should be given to those contexts.

However, it would be sinful to neglect the Western world. The apostolic imagination has much to contribute to the churches found in these locations. Apostolic teams need to be sent into Western contexts as well. In chapter 10, I argued that a disciple-making priority should be given to the peoples with the highest percentage of lostness and the highest degree of receptivity to the gospel. This is not a guideline only to be considered in Majority World contexts. Rather, this approach is to be used in the West as well. Unfortunately, the Church has often overlooked the need for apostolic work within the local context.

The Pastoral Hegemony

As noted in chapter 2, churches and agencies generally view the West through pastoral lenses. Developed pastoral structures are needed and must complement the numerous well-established churches. This

3. Other than short-term international travels, my ministry has taken place in the US. I recognize the limitation of my perspective and that some concepts and suggestions within this chapter will not translate into other Western countries.

4. To be fair, there are several Majority World countries with evangelical percentages that greatly exceed those in many of the traditionally Western countries. See n. 36 in this chapter.

reality has resulted in many churches viewing the North American context as reached and not in need of apostolic labors. Such a parish mentality often assumes a reached context with the belief that pastoral ministry is sufficient for the needed disciple-making activities. For unbelievers living in environments within sight of the steeple, it is thought that established church ministry is enough to reach them and assimilate them into membership. However, cultural and worldview shifts have been occurring, making such methods and strategies difficult to execute with the same effectiveness as yesteryear. Cultural gaps have been growing between believers and nonbelievers; the greater the gap, the more likely an apostolic approach is necessary for the task. The fact that the United States' evangelical constituency hovers around a quarter of the population should cause the Church to wonder if the predominate approaches to reaching this country have achieved their maximum potential.

Although some churches and denominations use the words "mission field" to rally Christians for locations in the West, generally what is meant is the need for additional churches to be established among *reached* people groups and more pastors to serve those churches, *not* for apostolic teams to be sent to plant churches among unreached people and raise up pastors from among the new churches. Such is the usual understanding of church planting in North America.

Whenever the Church becomes more established in a society and less apostolic, disciple-making activity is filtered through the pastoral lens. The result is methods and strategies that support ongoing pastoral training and established church development with little to no structural support for apostolic labors. Such methods and strategies are absolutely necessary, but not to the exclusion of apostolic ministry. Misapplication of a pastoral missiology to an unreached field results in the satisfaction of starting churches with long-term kingdom citizens and pastoral leadership coming from seminaries, rather than planting churches and raising up leaders from the harvest fields (Acts 13–14).

The Church now is in a time when both mature church structures and apostolic structures are needed. Pastoral paradigms for long-established churches and apostolic teams must operate within the same geography, though among different contexts and people groups, functioning in various ways. This is a great challenge.

Pastoral expressions have a long history and are well established. Over the past several decades, the Church has developed support structures for individuals who desire to plant *and* pastor a church. However, the greatest need is for the Church to embrace the apostolic imagination and develop structures to facilitate identifying, training, funding, caring for, and sending apostolic teams to the unreached peoples in the West. It should not be assumed that apostolic teams be sent only to people groups of an ethnolinguistic group different from that of the team, though such will frequently be the case. In many locations, cultural and worldview gaps are already present to an extent that there is a need for apostolic work among people of the same ethnolinguistic groups as the teams.

The apostolic imagination recognizes the dearth of vision and organization and does not remain content with the status quo. Change is needed. This does not mean that the Church should cease sending pastors to plant and oversee local congregations. It does mean, when it comes to church planting, that what is currently the *expectation* should become the *exception*. And the sending of apostolic teams, which presently is the exception, should become the expectation.

Post-Christianized Contexts

The West is comprised of post-Christianized contexts.[5] While ecclesial strongholds remain in certain locations, the influence of the Church wanes in others. Many Western countries were significantly shaped with a Judeo-Christian worldview, but global and local factors have contributed to a loss of the Church's prestige. Although the United States continues to experience a great deal of Christian influence, such has been declining in recent years.

5. David Lyon, *The Steeple's Shadow: On the Myths and Realities of Secularization* (Grand Rapids: Eerdmans, 1987); Alan Wolfe, *The Transformation of American Religion: How We Actually Live Our Faith* (Chicago: University of Chicago Press, 2005); Stuart Murray, *Post-Christendom: Church and Mission in a Strange New World*, 2nd ed. (Eugene, OR: Cascade, 2018).

Religious shifts. Compared to the other traditionally Western countries, the United States is by far the most evangelical. In 2014, evangelical Protestants in the United States comprised just over 25 percent of the population, a slight decline from 26 percent in 2007.[6] The estimated evangelical populations in select Western countries in 2010 included the following: Canada, 8 percent; Australia, 14 percent; New Zealand, 18 percent; United Kingdom, 9 percent; Denmark, 4 percent; Germany, 2 percent; Spain, 1 percent; and France, 1 percent.[7]

One of the other shifts in the religious landscape of the United States is the increase in the percent of the population who claim no religious preference. While this group is increasing, the numbers of Protestants and Catholics are shrinking.[8] Church attendance is also on the decline in the United States.[9] At the same time, a growing number of people have migrated from predominately Islamic, Buddhist, and Hindu contexts, bringing their faith traditions with them.

Migration of unreached peoples. God is the Divine Maestro orchestrating the movements of some of the worlds least-reached peoples into Western countries (Acts 17:26–27). People from all over the world now work, attend school, and reside in the West. Approximately 1,100 unreached people groups reside in Western countries. *The United States is home to the third largest number of unreached people groups in the world, and Canada is home to the sixth largest number.*[10] How should this affect the way the Church thinks about

6. Pew Research Center, "America's Changing Religious Landscape," May 12, 2015, https://www.pewforum.org/2015/05/12/americas-changing-religious-landscape/.

7. Jason Mandryk, *Operation World: The Definitive Prayer Guide to Every Nation*, 7th ed. (Colorado Springs: Biblica, 2010), 118, 194, 341, 360, 624, 765, 800, 854.

8. Some scholars believe growth is slowing for those subscribing to no religious preference. See Yonat Shimron, "Is the Rise of the Nones Slowing? Scholars Say Maybe," February 20, 2020, Religion News Service, https://religionnews.com/2020/02/11/is-the-decline-in-religious-affiliation-slowing-some-scholars-say-maybe/.

9. Pew Research Center, "In U.S., Decline of Christianity Continues at Rapid Pace," October 17, 2019, https://www.pewforum.org/2019/10/17/in-u-s-decline-of-christianity-continues-at-rapid-pace/.

10. These numbers are based on the research published in J. D. Payne, *Strangers Next Door: Immigration, Migration and Mission* (Downers Grove, IL: IVP, 2012), 60. When this book was written, I estimated the range of unreached people groups

global outreach in the West? Most churches are not only unaware of this reality and opportunity but also have no idea how to respond except through ministries designed for believers and people who share the same cultural expressions. If church members were being sent to the Somali in East Africa, then many churches would have some idea of how to begin this process, usually by partnering with a mission agency. But if Somali are found in Columbus, Ohio, then the contextual reality does not square with the present paradigm for engagement.

At the same time, large numbers of Christians have migrated from Majority World countries to the West. There are numerous opportunities for churches to partner with them to reach people groups in the West and in other countries as well. However, few churches have a vision for these possibilities, and those that do have such a vision often try to approach this opportunity with an inappropriate ministry model.[11]

Where Our Treasure Is

At the 2004 Forum hosted by the Lausanne Committee for World Evangelization in Pattaya, Thailand, a paper was presented with the title "Funding for Evangelism and Mission," addressing several related issues identified at the beginning of the twenty-first century. Charles Roost and E. LeBron Fairbanks (coeditors of the paper)[12] identified the challenge of the day: "God often chooses to use the resources of this world to accomplish His work. Human resources and financial resources seem to be those most significant in the work

---

in the West to be between 1,054 and 1,173. At that time, Canada was home to the fifth largest number of unreached people groups (62).

11. Diaspora missiology is a young and rapidly growing area of study in the field of missiology, with numerous books published on this topic over the past twenty-five years. For more information, see Lausanne Diaspora Leadership Team, *Scattered to Gather: Embracing the Global Trend of Diaspora,* rev. ed. (Vernon Hills, IL: Parivar International, 2017); the Global Diaspora Network's website, https://www.global-diaspora.com/; and Payne, *Strangers Next Door*, 150–58. I have also written several related posts on my blog. See jdpayne.org and search for "diaspora missiology" and "migration."

12. The paper represented the collaborative work of twenty-seven global leaders.

of the church. History proves that funding for evangelism and mission is very important for the work of the kingdom."[13]

They asserted that "money is a God-given tool for catalyzing mission."[14] The apostle Paul recognized there was clearly a need for the use of financial resources in his apostolic work. Whether it was his reminder to the Philippians of their partnership with him in gospel extension (Phil. 4:14–18) or his expectation that the Romans would assist him in traveling to Spain (Rom. 15:24), the Church was to leverage the material goods of the day for the apostolic task. John warned the disciples not to use their resources to show hospitality to false teachers (2 John 9–11). During the first century a culture had developed of using financial resources for apostolic endeavors.

Present reality. It is difficult to conduct research on individual and ecclesial finances.[15] People and churches in the West do not like to share information about income amounts. In their 2001 publication *World Christian Trends, AD 30–AD 2200*, David B. Barrett and Todd M. Johnson report that the Church has an enormous amount of financial wealth. With an annual estimated $270 billion, "Christians have enough money to implement even their wildest dreams of worldwide ministry and global evangelization."[16] However, even in light of this reality, the Joshua Project states that limited resources directed toward the unreached pose one of five contemporary Great Commission challenges.[17] It appears that, on the whole, global disciple making is not part of Christians' wildest dreams.

Barrett and Johnson report that approximately 95 percent of this income is assigned to the needs of the Church, for ministries at home.

13. "Funding for Evangelism and Mission," Lausanne Occasional Paper No. 56, §2, https://www.lausanne.org/content/lop/funding-evangelism-mission-lop-56.

14. "Funding for Evangelism and Mission," §2.

15. This is a field ripe for research. One of the few extensive studies on money and mission in the twentieth century was Jonathan J. Bonk, *Missions and Money*, published in 1991. It has since been revised as Jonathan J. Bonk, *Missions and Money: Affluence as a Missionary Problem . . . Revisited*, rev. and exp. ed. (Maryknoll, NY: Orbis, 2006).

16. David B. Barrett and Todd M. Johnson, *World Christian Trends, AD 30–AD 2200* (Pasadena, CA: William Carey Library, 2001), 656.

17. "Five Great Commission Challenges," https://joshuaproject.net/assets/js/ppt /FiveCelebrationsChallenges/index.html.

The remaining amount ($15 billion) supports world mission.[18] This means that the average church member, who gives $2.75 each week, provides $0.15 for missions.[19] However, at the time of their findings, the reality was even more troubling. Of that $15 billion to missions, $13 billion supported pastoral ministry in World C contexts (countries over 95% evangelized, with church members comprising 60% of the population), and $1.8 billion supported evangelism in World B (countries over 50% evangelized, with church members comprising less than 60% of the population). This left *only* $250,000,000 for outreach in World A contexts (countries less than 50% evangelized).[20] *Thus only 0.1 percent of the Church's annual income went to evangelize the unreached peoples!*[21] This statistic is an indictment of the Church's stewardship and convictions regarding the Great Commission. It reveals just how far the Church is from an apostolic imagination that includes a desire to leverage available resources for the kingdom.

The best research to date consists of approximations. It has been estimated that by 2050 the personal income of all the world's Christians will reach $70 trillion, up $10 trillion from 2019.[22] In 2020, Gina A. Zurlo, Todd M. Johnson, and Peter F. Crossing projected that by midyear the annual amount for "foreign missions" would have increased to $47 billion and was expected to soar to $60 billion by 2025.[23] The article reporting their research did not address how much was allocated to Worlds A, B, and C. It is likely that the percentages have changed little from the 2001 findings in *World Christian Trends, AD 30–AD 2200*.

18. Barrett and Johnson, *World Christian Trends*, 661, estimate that 5.6% goes to "foreign missions."

19. Barrett and Johnson, *World Christian Trends*, 600.

20. Barrett and Johnson, *World Christian Trends*, 52. The language of Worlds A, B, C is rarely used in missiological circles today.

21. Barrett and Johnson, *World Christian Trends*, 661.

22. Gina A. Zurlo, Todd M. Johnson, and Peter F. Crossing, "Christianity 2019: What's Missing? A Call for Further Research," *International Bulletin of Mission Research* 43, no. 1 (2019): 92–102, here 98. For more information on the research methodology behind financial statistics, see p. 100.

23. Gina A. Zurlo, Todd M. Johnson, and Peter F. Crossing, "World Christianity and Mission 2020: Ongoing Shift to the Global South," *International Bulletin of Mission Research* 44, no. 1 (2020): 8–19, here 18.

A 2001 survey of 810 North American mission agencies, published in *Mission Handbook*, found that although 94% of all US workers were being used for evangelism/discipleship activities, only 59% of the overseas money was applied to that category. However, 3% of the workers were engaged in relief and development and responsible for 35% of the income. Among Canadian agencies, 82% of workers were involved in evangelism/discipleship activities, receiving 31% of the overseas money. Just over 8% of the workers were engaged in relief and development, yet responsible for 67% of the income.[24]

Edition 22 of the *Mission Handbook* was published in 2017, the most current version at the time of this writing. The North American mission agencies surveyed had over $12 billion in annual revenues in the previous year.[25] It was reported for 1998 to 2016: "The percentage of all agencies indicating a primary activity in the Evangelism and Discipleship category has dropped significantly." A decline of almost nineteen points was observed, reducing the statistic from 63% to 44%. While evangelism, church planting, and discipleship remain as top priorities among mission agencies, the percent of agencies reporting a primary activity in the category of Relief and Development doubled from 1998 to 2016, increasing from 11% to 23%. The Education and Training category also increased by 10 points, from 8% to 18%.[26]

Funding apostolic teams. Although it is impossible to know how much money (and other resources) the first-century churches used

24. A. Scott Moreau, "Putting the Survey in Perspective," in *Mission Handbook: US and Canadian Christian Ministries Overseas 2004–2006*, ed. Dotsey Welliver and Minnette Northcutt, 19th ed. (Wheaton: Evangelism and Missions Information Service, 2004), 11–64, here 24, 47. The US Relief and Development Activities were categorized as development, communications, medicine, dentistry, public health, relief and/or rehabilitation, childcare/orphanage, medical supplies, agricultural programs, supplying equipment, disability assistance programs, justice and related, adoption (25–26). Canadian Relief and Development Activities were categorized as relief and/or rehabilitation, development, community and/or other, childcare/orphanage, medicine, dentistry, public health, disability assistance programs (44).

25. J. Ted Esler, Marvin J. Newell, and Michael VanHuis, "Mission Handbook Survey: Perspective and Dynamics," in *North American Mission Handbook: US and Canadian Protestant Ministries Overseas 2017–2019*, ed. Peggy E. Newell, 22nd ed. (Pasadena, CA: William Carey Library, 2017), 43–93, here 93.

26. Esler, Newell, and VanHuis, "Mission Handbook Survey," 58.

for apostolic work, it is safe to say that the modern Church lacks kingdom vision if measured by how much the Church allots to reaching the nations with the gospel. There is much room for improvement when it comes to funding apostolic teams.[27] The first-century apostolic teams were supported in their labors through at least three means.

Support through churches. First-century apostolic work was sometimes funded through financial support from local churches. Paul wrote to the Philippians to thank them for their partnership with him in the ministry. Epaphroditus, an *apostle* (Greek *apostolos*, usually translated "messenger") of the church (Phil. 2:25), ministered to Paul's needs and brought financial assistance (4:14–18). While writing to the Corinthians, Paul declared that the apostles had a right to such financial resources, though he and Barnabas gave up this privilege when serving in Corinth (1 Cor. 9:3–7, 11–12, 14).

Support through individuals. Hospitality was also a means of apostolic support in the first century (Rom. 12:13; 1 Tim. 3:2; Heb. 13:2). Individuals gave of their time, food, shelters, and likely financial resources. Paul's concluding exhortation to Titus was that Zenas and Apollos were to be sent from Crete, lacking nothing for their journeys (Titus 3:13). Paul had no reservations about asking for assistance. He instructs Philemon to "prepare a guest room for me"; he hoped to be released from prison and able to visit the church in Philemon's house (Philem. 22). His Letter to the Romans concluded with the notice of a forthcoming partnership in the apostolic work (15:24).

Support through work. Paul was a tentmaker (Acts 18:3); at times he used this trade to support himself and even to finance his team. When he first entered Corinth, he stayed with fellow tentmakers Aquila and Priscilla while he began his work in the synagogue "every

---

27. Conversations on funding often ask, Should Western churches support nationals or workers sent to their countries? More research needs to be conducted on this topic. See also Michael Pocock, Gailyn Van Rheenan, and Douglas McConnel, *The Changing Face of World Missions: Engaging Contemporary Issues and Trends* (Grand Rapids: Baker Academic, 2005), 279–98. For a brief evaluation of these two models, see Scott Klingsmith, "The Past and Future of Funding Missions: From Everywhere to Everywhere? National Workers vs. Missionaries," presentation to the Evangelical Missiological Society, October 9–10, 2020.

Sabbath" (Acts 18:1–4).[28] Luke's comments on Paul's work coincide with Paul's statements found in 1 Corinthians 9 regarding his work in the city. Paul refrained from financial support from the Ephesians while he was present with them for nearly three years (Acts 20:33–35). A similar situation was likely the case in Thessalonica, where the team modeled a godly work ethic (1 Thess. 2:9; 4:11–12; 2 Thess. 3:7–9).

In many areas of the world, apostolic teams need to be fully funded. Jobs are either unavailable or restricted to nationals. Given a team's background, community employment may be next to impossible to arrange. Teams may lack the skills desired by potential employers. Churches and agencies would do well to evaluate their present budgets and assess whether or not they are allocating a large enough portion of their finances to reflect the apostolic imagination.

Some churches and agencies need to rethink support development. Scott A. Bessenecker has much concern with the approach requiring persons to obtain funding as a prerequisite for being sent. The need to raise personal support as an "entrance requirement automatically leaves at the front door those who do not have relationships with middle-class people and churches that are accustomed to supporting missionaries this way."[29] Hesselgrave likewise calls agencies to "rethink, and perhaps retool" paradigms that require missionaries to raise their own financial support: "Rather than requiring harried candidates to 'sell' themselves and their worthiness for service to potential supporters who do not even know them, perhaps missions-minded Christians who have experience in business, finance, and sales could help alleviate the difficulties of raising personal support. These volunteers could make contacts with potential donors, introduce candidates and their projected ministry, make presentations on their behalf, and otherwise help them in this most time-consuming and difficult aspect of missionary service."[30] Some churches and agencies may find they will have a greater kingdom impact by increasing

28. For a comprehensive study on tentmaking, see Kurt T. Kruger, *Tentmaking: A Misunderstood Missiological Method* (Eugene, OR: Wipf & Stock, 2020).

29. Scott A. Bessenecker, *Overturning Tables: Freeing Missions from the Christian-Industrial Complex* (Downers Grove, IL: InterVarsity, 2014), 61.

30. David J. Hesselgrave, *Paradigms in Conflict: 10 Key Questions in Missions Today* (Grand Rapids: Kregel, 2005), 229–30.

their financial contributions to a few apostolic teams as opposed to providing a small amount to many missionaries doing a variety of ministries.

Tentmaking, bivocational, and covocational[31] ministries need to be encouraged and supported. Ministry "success" needs to be reconsidered to accommodate apostolic teams who choose to serve in such capacities. In many areas of the world, apostolic teams need to be in the marketplace. Without this option, many will not be permitted into the country or will be looked upon with suspicion. Nationals will wonder if the foreigners are either rich, lazy, or criminals because they do not have jobs in the community.

The funding model for church planting throughout North America is based on a pastoral missiology and is inadequate for sustained apostolic labors. The church planter is expected to become the pastor of the newly planted church and serve for an indefinite period of time.[32] It is expected that the new church will provide the pastor's income. Frequently the established churches, networks, and mission agencies will provide the church planter with funding for two or three years until the church is planted. North American financial structures are not built from an apostolic imagination. In order for the Church to consider funding and sending apostolic teams into such contexts, radical changes need to be made to this long-held model.

As with Paul's teams, contemporary workers may need to float between funding models, depending on their contexts. Churches and agencies should not expect that a one-size-fits-all funding model is the norm and should encourage teams to consider a variety of approaches. Of course, part of this approach to rethinking financial support requires that churches equip their members to understand the

31. *Covocational* is a term that has developed recently in the US to describe church planters who intentionally seek employment in the marketplace as a strategic option rather than funding by agencies, which have limited funds. See Brad Brisco, *Covocational Church Planting: Aligning Your Marketplace Calling and the Mission of God* (Alpharetta, GA: North American Mission Board, 2018), 21. Some understand this to be a variation of tentmaking.

32. This is the opposite of an apostolic paradigm. On their first missionary journey, Paul and Barnabas did evangelism to make disciples, who were gathered as local churches. The last step of the process involved their appointing pastors over those churches (Acts 13–14). See J. D. Payne, *Apostolic Church Planting: Birthing New Churches from New Believers* (Downers Grove, IL: InterVarsity, 2015), 40–52.

kingdom value in obtaining marketable skills and college degrees to best position themselves for taking the gospel to the nations, across the street and around the world.

Train Pastors to Develop an Apostolic Imagination

I hold two seminary degrees and have spent over two decades in the classroom training ministers and nineteen years in pastoral ministry. Although there are exceptions, the traditional Western approach to theological education is to train pastors to be managers of the status quo, not to lead churches for global disciple making. Maintaining ministry structures is the standard. Limited training, if any, is offered for leading a church through change.[33]

The Church has assumed that maintaining "the faith . . . once for all delivered to the saints" (Jude 3) is to occur within ecclesiastical structures that have existed for centuries. But what happens when the world does not play by the Church's rules? What occurs when contexts shift and global realities develop that were unknown to Aquinas, Luther, and Schleiermacher? Ministerial training is far more than education in biblical studies, theology, history, and homiletics. Educators need to recognize at least two things. First, seminaries and colleges, while undergoing declining enrollments, are still viewed by most as the leading models for ministerial training, both in North America and throughout the world. For better or worse, what is modeled in the West still has major influence throughout Majority World contexts.[34] Second, theological institutions must train their students to develop an apostolic imagination. This does not mean that they educate only those going to lead apostolic teams. Rather, everyone is taught to study the Scriptures with a missional hermeneutic and

33. This is greatly needed in North America, where the overwhelming majority of churches are declining in membership. The odds are likely that any graduate from a seminary who enters pastoral ministry will be joining a church in desperate need for change and not for a mere continuation of present activities.

34. I once knew a student from Nigeria who obtained an accredited doctoral degree (DMiss) in the US. When he approached a school in Nigeria for possible employment, he was informed that the school was not satisfied with his doctorate since it was not a PhD!

to view the disciple-making potential wherever they serve. Students need to be trained for leading churches through change and equipping them for calling, developing, sending, partnering, and caring for apostolic teams in their communities and throughout the world. Some schools in the United States have already taken significant steps in this direction.

Apostolic teams need theological education too. However, many church planters choose to avoid such training, viewing it as irrelevant and not worth the time and cost. If someone's calling is not to pastoral ministry, then why would they want to study at an institution where the expectation is to train for ministry in established churches? Church planters and mission agencies often recognize this disconnect and either avoid formal training or only desire a minimal amount required to serve with a specific sending organization.

Though budgetary and accreditation challenges are ever present, change is desperately needed. Since some apostolic teams will be entering contexts where they need marketable platforms, why not consider an approach to education that allows the student to learn a profession, marketable skill, or trade while also studying theological education? This may require creative partnerships between Christian institutions and colleges and universities, or between seminaries and Bible colleges that offer some education in disciplines outside the Bible-related courses. Some schools in the United States have taken creative liberties with their programs. Instead of a degree in divinity, students graduate with a degree in divinity *and* business management, education, or some other marketable skill. Another possibility to consider is offering degrees while students obtain technological skills.

Partnerships

Scholars have noticed the growth and development of the Church throughout the Majority World.[35] Several countries have surpassed

---

35. While missiologists frequently use the term *Majority World*, *Global South* has become a popular, though less accurate, term to describe contexts outside the traditionally Western cultures. Many books exist on the growth and development of the Majority World Church; two influential ones are by Philip Jenkins, *The Next Christendom: The Coming of Global Christianity* (New York: Oxford University Press,

the evangelical percentage found in the United States.[36] The Church
is sending members "from everywhere to everywhere."[37] According
to Mary T. Lederleitner, cross-cultural partnerships "have become
a primary method in which churches and organizations engage in
global missions."[38] The apostolic imagination recognizes the importance of partnership. C. René Padilla writes, "Because there is one
world, one church, and one gospel, the Christian mission cannot be
anything other than mission in partnership."[39] While he is certainly
correct, developing healthy kingdom partnerships for global disciple
making is a challenging task. For most Western churches, partnership
is an unfamiliar concept. How should Western churches and agencies
approach partnerships with Majority World churches and agencies?[40]
This task requires stewarding the Church's power for apostolic work
and sharing that power to build partnerships throughout the world.[41]
The following are some general points for consideration. For detailed
study and practical actions, see the sources cited in the footnotes.

Do not neglect the past . . . or the present. Borthwick writes, "In order
to get to God's missional goal, the global church needs to work to-

2002); and Mark A. Noll, *The New Shape of World Christianity: How American
Experience Reflects Global Faith* (Downers Grove, IL: IVP Academic, 2009).

36. Evangelical percentages for select countries include Kenya, 49%; Uganda,
37%; Central African Republic, 32%; El Salvador, 32%; Zimbabwe, 31%; Nigeria,
31%; Nicaragua, 30%; and Burundi, 27%. See Mandryk, *Operation World*, 914. As
a point of comparison, the United States is 25% evangelical.

37. Mandryk, *Operation World*, 950–51.

38. Mary T. Lederleitner, *Cross-Cultural Partnerships: Navigating the Complexities of Money and Mission* (Downers Grove, IL: IVP, 2010), 21.

39. C. René Padilla, *Mission between the Times: Essays on the Kingdom* (Grand
Rapids: Eerdmans, 1985), 136.

40. This is a growing area of research in missiology, with literature frequently
being produced. For example, Daniel Rickett and Dotsey Welliver, eds., *Supporting
Indigenous Ministries: With Selected Readings* (Wheaton: Billy Graham Center, 1997);
William D. Taylor, ed., *Kingdom Partnerships for Synergy in Missions* (Pasadena,
CA: William Carey Library, 1994); Daniel Rickett, *Building Strategic Relationships:
A Practical Guide to Partnering with Non-Western Missions*, 3rd ed. (Minneapolis:
STEM, 2008); Lederleitner, *Cross-Cultural Partnerships*; and Paul Borthwick, *West-
ern Christians in Global Mission: What's the Role of the North American Church?*
(Downers Grove, IL: IVP, 2012).

41. Craig Van Gelder, "The Future of the Discipline of Missiology: Framing Current Realities and Future Possibilities," *Missiology* 42, no. 1 (2013): 39–56, here 48;
Borthwick, *Western Christians in Global Mission*, 104.

gether, incorporate our respective strengths, accommodate our re-spective weaknesses and move forward as a family."[42]

Colonialism and paternalism must be studied and acknowledged as not reflective of the apostolic imagination. Although there are unhealthy chapters in Protestant and Catholic history, such is not to result in poor kingdom stewardship in the present, including a laissez-faire approach to partnership, given an embarrassing history. Mistakes of yesteryears do not provide a pass for today. The Great Commission still applies to churches in the West.

Develop synergy, but avoid doctrinal, missiological, and philosophical compromise. Partnership involves sacrifice and allowing all parties to have a seat at the table. This is especially true in developing col-laborative leadership teams. Everyone must be considered an equal participant. Interdependence is necessary for healthy partnership. Unfortunately, certain partnerships are unhealthy and should be avoided. Doctrinal, missiological, and philosophical compromise is unwise. Everyone involved must understand the duration and pur-pose of the partnership, agree on the non-negotiables, develop clear communication, and deliver proper accountability.

Be a learner . . . and a teacher. Partnership means that all parties pro-vide and receive tangible and intangible contributions. Leadership and sharing must flow in both directions. The Church in the West has much to learn from the Church in the Majority World. This re-quires listening for understanding and a posture of servanthood. In general, Churches throughout the Majority World are theologically conservative. The West has much to learn from their high view of the Scriptures, which they have not demythologized, deconstructed, or denigrated. Their convictions of the reality of the supernatural in everyday life are often more akin to a first-century perspective than a Western worldview. Such is not a support of animistic beliefs, but rather embracing a more biblical view of God, miracles, demons, spiritual warfare, and signs and wonders, which sometimes accom-pany the Church's apostolic work. There is much to learn from a simplicity of faith and suffering and sacrifice for the kingdom.

As in the West, not everything that occurs in the Majority World is good and healthy. Sometimes those closest to the field—physically

42. Borthwick, *Western Christians in Global Mission*, 193.

and culturally—do not always make the best decisions. Indeed, an examination of many Western churches in their contexts also reveals this reality. False teachings and unhealthy ministries exist in the Majority World too. Churches in the West have much knowledge and experience to share with others and must be wise in the process.

QUESTIONS TO CONSIDER

1. Do you agree or disagree that the West is in need of apostolic teams? Explain.
2. What are the strengths and challenges of established church ministries and apostolic teams laboring in the same geographical context?
3. Why do you think the present amount of financial resources allocated to the unreached peoples is so low?
4. What challenges do you anticipate if your church enters a partnership with a church in another country?

Conclusion

A Word to Pastors

Although much of my time these days involves training ministers of the gospel, for many years I served as a pastor with churches in Kentucky, Indiana, and Alabama. These congregations reflected the traditional congregation, house church, cell church, and megachurch models. Some prized tradition and heritage, and others valued growth and innovation. My calling and ministry, even to this date, has been in the realm of pastor-teacher (Eph. 4:11). I share this information to report that I am not a missionary or apostle. I understand that for many of you much of the content of this book is new and perhaps even strange. Nothing was written to shock you, but to challenge the Church toward a more excellent way.

Shepherding a church to apostolic labors is a foreign practice for most pastors. Ministry-related thoughts and activities, including global disciple making, have traditionally been understood in view of the pastoral role. Such tradition, however, should not have the final say. Although pastors are to equip their people for the field, they also need to develop an apostolic imagination to complement their pastoral ministries. This conclusion is written to offer suggestions as you lead your church to develop an apostolic imagination and send teams to your community, across the country, and throughout the world.

Remain a Pastor

Whenever I share the contents of this book, a pastor usually responds by asking, "Should I change ministry direction, travel to the other side of the world, and lead an apostolic team?" I do think that some pastors should make this transition, but for most of you, the answer is no. Let that burden reside within your heart. If the Holy Spirit has made you an elder of an established church (Acts 20:28), then do not change your ministry. Take great delight in pastoral ministry. Remain in your calling, equip your church, and send apostolic teams to the unreached peoples. Much of overcoming the challenge of reaching the unreached is not for pastors to give up their callings, but to be pastors!

Pastors have one of the most important roles to play in making disciples of all nations. At the dawn of the twentieth century, John R. Mott expressed the urgency and significance of pastoral leadership to reaching the unreached. His words were relevant then and also now: "The secret of enabling the home Church to press her advantage in the non-Christian world is one of leadership. The people do not go beyond their leaders in knowledge and zeal, nor surpass them in consecration and sacrifice. The Christian pastor, minister, rector—whatever he may be denominated—holds the divinely appointed office for inspiring and guiding the thought and activities of the Church."[1]

Pastors are a critical part in God's mission. Your people need you to lead them to the nations. Discharge your pastoral duties, and the Spirit and the Word will do the rest.

Function Pastorally, Think Apostolically

Few pastors have developed an apostolic imagination. This is one of the reasons I wrote this book. Many may have the conviction of reaching the nations, are able to preach on the topic, and know that global disciple making is important, but lack apostolic experience. Because of this, leaders default to repeating their own experi-

---

1. John R. Mott, *The Pastor and Modern Missions: A Plea for Leadership in World Evangelization* (New York: Student Volunteer Movement for Foreign Missions, 1904), vii–viii.

ence. For pastors, this means that apostolic ministry is understood and expected to be carried out by a pastoral approach—a pastoral imagination.

The apostolic mindset and pastoral mindset operate two different paradigms of ministry, which do not need to be mutually exclusive. You need to learn to differentiate between these categories and express yourself accordingly. While these mindsets are similar in many ways, their contextual differences are often misunderstood. The mind of the pastor is on the established church. Such ministry is complex in nature. The apostolic imagination has a pastoral bent but operates initially in the context with no believers, no churches, no structures. Such ministry is simple in nature and consists primarily of basic tasks. The apostolic imagination sees ministry with one church as temporal and with planned role changes. Strategy is developed to begin the ministry with the end in mind and for contextualized leaders to become the overseers.

Pray, Pray, Pray

Leading your church to send apostolic teams requires much prayer and fasting. Pray for church leaders to catch the vision. Pray before you begin to cast such a vision for your church. Pray for the Spirit's guidance in your life and words. Pray that the Lord of the harvest would send out laborers (Luke 10:2). Pray for your people in understanding the mission of God and their place in that calling. Pray for unity. There will be great spiritual opposition. Pray against such evil.

Put Away the Wrecking Ball

A warning is necessary, lest zeal should lead to immediate destruction of present church structures. Alan J. Roxburgh is correct in stating, "The radical overthrow of deeply embedded ways of life results in profoundly destructive consequences for the great masses of ordinary people caught in the ideologies of change."[2] Part of the way forward is

2. Alan J. Roxburgh, *Structured for Mission: Renewing the Culture of the Church* (Downers Grove, IL: InterVarsity, 2015), 47.

not to scrap what the Lord has allowed to develop over the years with your church. Restructuring for the present and future is needed. Those present structures have brought about the sanctification of many people and continue to facilitate their growth. Immediate removal of them may create an environment in which people will not know how to respond. Their kingdom labors could come to a screeching halt. The perspectives and structures did not develop overnight and will not be changed overnight. Pastoral gentleness and patience are needed to lead for change.

Prepare for Conflict

Conflict is inevitable. Anticipate the tensions that will arise and humbly, but with conviction, lead for change. Be patient and give the church time to catch the vision; the Lord was patient with you and gave you time to obtain this vision and change your perspective.

Know Your Church Family

Leading your church to develop an apostolic imagination that results in teams commissioned and sent requires a healthy understanding of your faith family. Does an atmosphere of expectation exist when it comes to people going to make disciples? Or is it a shock to the crowd whenever someone says, "We're going to the nations"? If your church has never sent apostolic teams (or individuals to serve with other teams), it may take a while to create a culture that prays for and expects such actions. Knowing the church's general passions, values, vision, leaders, and organization is critical to leading your people across the bridge and into the world of unreached peoples.

Lead with the Scriptures

Above all, your people need to understand that the vision for such ministry comes from the Scriptures. What does God have to say about *his* mission? The church needs to have the big picture, Genesis to

Revelation, for understanding the mission of God.[3] In your expositional preaching—yes, I am expecting that your preaching is Word-based, Word-organized, and Word-driven—make certain that a missional hermeneutic comes through in your outline, points, and words. In no way am I saying that you are to force something into the text. Rather, just as we should preach the text and *always make a beeline to the cross*, we should make certain that we always point out along the way that if it were not for God's apostolic mission, then there would be no cross at the end of that beeline.

Teach the Difference between Cultural Preferences and Biblical Requirements

Have the courage to return to the Bible and evaluate your church's ecclesiology. Ask your people, What are the biblical requirements for any local church to be a local church? Assist the church in understanding the differences between biblical prescriptions and cultural preferences. Teach them that while preferences are not necessarily bad, they are not necessary and may not need to be replicated among other people groups.

Set the Example—at Least in the Short Term

Your example is powerful. What you say about reaching unreached peoples is cherished, but what you do makes an impact. A great place to start doing cross-cultural disciple making is in your community. Who are the unreached people groups living there? If you are in a small town or rural area and they cannot be located, then who are the groups living nearby? Take your people on a day trip to another community. Take an international trip each year. Make sure it is to a location with unreached peoples. Return with excitement in your voice, a burden within your heart, stories to share, and a challenge to your church family.

3. See J. D. Payne, *Theology of Mission: A Concise Biblical Introduction* (Bellingham, WA: Lexham, forthcoming).

Regularly Describe Global Lostness

Closely related to your understanding of unreached people groups in your community, across the country, and throughout the world is the importance of communicating those spiritual needs to the church. Most church members are unaware of the size of the global unreached population. Even if they are aware of unreached people groups throughout the world, most of them are unaware that such lostness exists within their own country.[4]

Challenge People to Go with Their Vocations

Develop a church culture in which parents are urged to help their children get marketable skills and degrees so that one day they may use them to reach the unreached.[5] Students need to be taught the value of preparing themselves for the global marketplace. This is not done simply because they might obtain a good income and comfortable living, but so that their vocations may be used by the Spirit to reach the unreached peoples across the street, the nation, and the world.

I remember meeting with a church member to discuss his burden to reach others with the gospel. After I shared an apostolic vision for reaching unreached peoples, he experienced an aha moment. "So, J. D.," he asked, "you are telling me that what I have been doing in Birmingham (evangelizing, leading a small group, raising up leaders) can be done in another location, only among an unreached people group, and that I can transfer my job and apply these skills elsewhere? Of course! It makes sense!" Twelve months later, after he accepted a job in another location, we commissioned and sent him and his family to join a team working among the unreached. Our people often do

4. Start by studying information on unreached people groups at joshuaproject .net, peoplegroups.org, and peoplegroups.info. Jason Mandryk, *Operation World: The Definitive Prayer Guide to Every Nation*, 7th ed. (Colorado Springs: Biblica, 2010), is an excellent resource as well.

5. While many Christian parents are open to their children going to the nations, many parents often serve as barriers according to Barna Group in *The Future of Missions: 10 Questions about Global Ministry the Church Must Answer with the Next Generation* (Ventura, CA: Barna Group, 2020), 87–93.

not know the possibilities because we do not help them understand how they can use their occupations to reach the nations.

Assess People for the Task

People need to be assessed before being sent from your faith family. Although your local church is capable of conducting these assessments, consider involving other church and agency resources in this process. A thorough assessment will help potential team members and the church to understand their strengths and limitations and how they can best be equipped and supported by the church. Members should be evaluated based on their doctrine, lifestyle, marriage, and commitment to the church. Do they have a history of being intentionally involved in personal evangelism, teaching, developing leaders? What about doing so within a cross-cultural setting? If not, why not? If not, how can the church best prepare them for serving unreached people?

This process should not be just between you and the individual or team. Involve as many church members as possible. Obtain wisdom from other church leaders. Talk with the team's small-group leaders and friends. Invite others into the assessment process.[6] Before members are sent, ask the church what they have seen, heard, and experienced in the lives of these prospective team members. Such input is not only valuable but also models the importance of community in developing and sending apostolic teams.

Train Members for Church Planting

People need to be equipped in strategic thinking, disciple making, and leadership-development skills. I recognize that most churches think this is beyond what they can accomplish. Part of the reason is because of our default assumption that such ministry is challenging

6. Among other strategies, our church had a small-group leader evaluate the potential church planter based on eight characteristics of the life of Barnabas. This was a tool I developed for my book *The Barnabas Factors: Eight Essential Characteristics of Effective Church Planting Team Members* (n.p.: CreateSpace, 2012).

and complex. All churches, however, can be involved in the process to some degree and should consider looking to others when assistance is needed. Numerous books, conferences, and online resources are available. Denominations, networks, and agencies can also help. Caution is needed, however, since the apostolic imagination is not widespread throughout many Western contexts, nor reflected in such resources. Until this reality changes, I recommend finding assistance from those who have a history of serving among unreached peoples, which often means consulting with those serving throughout the Majority World, though a few groups may be found in North America that are serving exclusively with unreached peoples.

Commission, Send, and Partner with Them

Use a portion of the church's worship gathering to recognize, pray over, and send people to the unreached. The commissioning is just the beginning of a partnership in the apostolic ministry. Teams remain members of the church family and thus in continual need of member care. They are not going to the unreached peoples to plant a church for themselves and their families. They are going to plant churches among the unreached peoples and for the unreached peoples. Teams sent from the church are extensions of your church's ministry and need the ongoing pastoral care, prayer support, visits, encouraging words, resources, and opportunities to return and share all that God is doing among the nations—through them . . . and your church (Acts 14:27)!

QUESTIONS TO CONSIDER

1. What are the three greatest challenges *now* preventing your church from developing an apostolic imagination?
2. If you and your church's leaders need assistance in becoming better prepared to equip, assess, and care for teams, who are some individuals and organizations to contact *this year* for assistance?

3. Which three suggestions made in this chapter will you commit to work on over *the next month*?

4. What will you commit to do throughout *the next year* to lead your church toward this paradigm of ministry?

Bibliography

Addison, Stephen Bruce. "The Continuing Ministry of the Apostle in the Church's Mission." DMin diss., Fuller Theological Seminary, 1995.

Agnew, Francis H. "The Origin of the NT Apostle-Concept: A Review of the Research." *Journal of Biblical Literature* 105, no. 1 (1986): 75–96.

Allen, Roland. *Discussion on Mission Education*. London: World Dominion, 1931.

———. *Missionary Methods: St. Paul's or Ours?* American ed. 1912. Grand Rapids: Eerdmans, 1962.

Andersen, Wilhelm. *Towards a Theology of Mission*. International Missionary Council Research Pamphlet No. 2. London: SCM, 1955.

Anderson, Gerald H., ed. *The Theology of the Christian Mission*. Nashville: Abingdon, 1961.

"Apostle." In *Nelson's New Illustrated Bible Dictionary*, edited by Ronald F. Youngblood, 91–92. Nashville: Nelson, 1995.

Ashcraft, Morris. "Paul Defends His Apostleship Galatians 1 and 2." *Review and Expositor* 69 (Fall 1972): 459–69.

Barna Group. *The Future of Missions: 10 Questions about Global Ministry the Church Must Answer with the Next Generation*. Ventura, CA: Barna Group, 2020.

Barnett, Mike, ed. *Discovering the Mission of God: Best Missional Practices for the 21st Century*. Downers Grove, IL: IVP Academic, 2012.

Barnett, P. W. "Apostle." In *Dictionary of Paul and His Letters*, edited by Gerald F. Hawthorne, Ralph P. Martin, and Daniel G. Reid, 45–51. Downers Grove, IL: InterVarsity, 1993.

Barrett, C. K. *The Signs of an Apostle*. Philadelphia: Fortress, 1972.

Barrett, David B., and Todd M. Johnson. *World Christian Trends: AD 30–AD 2200*. Pasadena, CA: William Carey Library, 2001.

Barrett, David B., and James W. Reapsome. *Seven Hundred Plans to Evangelize the World: The Rise of a Global Evangelization Movement*. Birmingham, AL: New Hope, 1988.

Bartlotti, Len. "Reimagining and Re-envisioning People Groups." *Evangelical Missions Quarterly* 56, no. 4 (October–December 2020): 46–50.

Bassham, Rodger C. *Mission Theology, 1948–1975: Years of Worldwide Creative Tension—Ecumenical, Evangelical, and Roman Catholic*. Pasadena, CA: William Carey Library, 1979.

Bavinck, J. H. *An Introduction to the Science of Missions*. Translated by David Hugh Freeman. Philadelphia: Presbyterian and Reformed, 1960.

Beaver, R. Pierce. "North American Thought on the Fundamental Principles of Missions during the Twentieth Century." *Church History* 21, no. 4 (December 1952): 345–64.

Belleville, Linda L. *2 Corinthians*. Downers Grove, IL: IVP Academic, 1996.

Bessenecker, Scott A. *Overturning Tables: Freeing Missions from the Christian-Industrial Complex*. Downers Grove, IL: InterVarsity, 2014.

Best, Ernest. "Paul's Apostolic Authority?" *Journal for the Study of the New Testament* 27 (1986): 3–25.

Betz, Hans Dieter. "Apostle." In *The Anchor Bible Dictionary*, edited by David Noel Freedman, 1:309–11. New York: Doubleday, 1992.

Blauw, Johannes. *The Missionary Nature of the Church: A Survey of the Biblical Theology of Mission*. London: Lutterworth, 1962.

Blomberg, Craig. *1 Corinthians*. Grand Rapids: Zondervan, 1994.

Bonk, Jonathan J. *Missions and Money: Affluence as a Missionary Problem . . . Revisited*. Rev. ed. Maryknoll, NY: Orbis, 2006.

Borthwick, Paul. *Western Christians in Global Mission: What's the Role of the North American Church?* Downers Grove, IL: IVP, 2012.

Bosch, David. "Theological Education in Missionary Perspective." *Missiology* 10, no. 1 (January 1982): 13–34.

———. *Transforming Mission: Paradigm Shifts in Theology of Mission*. 20th anniversary ed. New York: Orbis, 2011.

Bowers, Paul. "Fulfilling the Gospel: The Scope of the Pauline Mission." *Journal of the Evangelical Theological Society* 30, no. 2 (June 1987): 185–98.

Braaten, Carl E. *The Flaming Center: A Theology of the Christian Mission.* Philadelphia: Fortress, 1977.

Brisco, Brad. *Covocational Church Planting: Aligning Your Marketplace Calling and the Mission of God.* Alpharetta, GA: North American Mission Board, 2018.

Bruce, F. F. *The Epistle to the Hebrews.* Rev. ed. Grand Rapids: Eerdmans, 1990.

———. *Paul: Apostle of the Heart Set Free.* Grand Rapids: Eerdmans, 1977.

Caldwell, Larry W. *Sent Out! Reclaiming the Spiritual Gift of Apostleship for Missionaries and Churches Today.* Pasadena, CA: William Carey Library, 1992.

Cannistraci, David. *Apostles and the Emerging Apostolic Movement: A Biblical Look at Apostleship and How God Is Using It to Bless His Church Today.* Ventura, CA: Renew, 1996.

Carson, D. A. *The Gospel according to John.* Grand Rapids: Eerdmans, 1991.

———. "Matthew." In *The Expositor's Bible Commentary: Matthew, Mark, Luke.* Edited by Frank E. Gaebelein. Grand Rapids: Zondervan, 1984.

Clarke, Andrew D. "The Source and Scope of Paul's Apostolic Authority." *Criswell Theological Review* 12, no. 2 (Spring 2015): 3–22.

Cole, Neil. *Organic Church: Growing Faith Where Life Happens.* San Francisco: Jossey-Bass, 2005.

Cole, R. Alan. *Galatians.* Grand Rapids: Eerdmans, 1989.

———. *Mark.* Grand Rapids: Eerdmans, 1961.

Coleman, Robert E. *The Master Plan of Evangelism.* 1964. Reprint, Old Tappan, NJ: Revell, 1972.

Costas, Orlando E. *The Church and Its Mission: A Shattering Critique from the Third World.* Wheaton: Tyndale, 1974.

Cranfield, C. E. B. *A Critical and Exegetical Commentary on the Epistle to the Romans.* Vol. 2. Edinburgh: T&T Clark, 1979.

Culver, Robert Duncan. "Apostles and the Apostolate in the New Testament." *Bibliotheca Sacra* 134 (April–June 1977): 131–43.

Darragh, Neil. "Hazardous Missions and Shifting Frameworks." *Missiology* 38, no. 3 (July 2010): 271–80.

Datema, Dave, and Leonard N. Bartlotti. "The People Group Approach: A Historical Perspective." *Evangelical Missions Quarterly* 56, no. 4 (October–December 2020): 8–11.

Dayton, Edward R. *That Everyone May Hear: Reaching the Unreached.* Monrovia, CA: MARC, 1979.

Dayton, Edward R., and Ted W. Engstrom. *Strategy for Leadership: Planning, Activating, Motivating, Elevating.* Old Tappan, NJ: Revell, 1979.

———. *Strategy for Living: How to Make the Best Use of Your Time and Abilities.* Glendale, CA: Regal, 1976.

Dayton, Edward R., and David A. Fraser. *Planning Strategies for World Evangelization.* Rev. ed. Grand Rapids: Eerdmans, 1990.

Dent, Donald T. "The Ongoing Role of Apostles in Missions." DMiss diss., Malaysia Baptist Theological Seminary, 2009.

———. *The Ongoing Role of Apostles in Missions: The Forgotten Foundation.* Nashville: Westbow, 2019.

DeYoung, Kevin, and Greg Gilbert. *What Is the Mission of the Church? Making Sense of Social Justice, Shalom, and the Great Commission.* Wheaton: Crossway, 2011.

DuBose, Francis M. *God Who Sends: A Fresh Quest for Biblical Mission.* Nashville: Broadman, 1983.

Dunn, James D. G. *The Theology of Paul the Apostle.* Grand Rapids: Eerdmans, 1998.

Effa, Allan. "The Greening of Mission." *International Bulletin of Missionary Research* 32, no. 4 (October 2008): 171–76.

Esler, J. Ted, Marvin J. Newell, and Michael VanHuis. "Mission Handbook Survey: Perspective and Dynamics." In *North American Mission Handbook: US and Canadian Protestant Ministries Overseas 2017–2019*, edited by Peggy E. Newell, 43–93. 22nd ed. Pasadena, CA: William Carey Library, 2017.

Ferdinando, Keith. "Mission: A Problem of Definition." *Themelios* 33, no. 1 (2008): 46–59.

Flemming, Dean. *Recovering the Full Mission of God: A Biblical Perspective on Being, Doing and Telling.* Downers Grove, IL: IVP Academic, 2013.

Flett, John G. *Apostolicity: The Ecumenical Question in World Christian Perspective.* Downers Grove, IL: IVP Academic, 2016.

France, R. T. *The Gospel of Mark: A Commentary on the Greek Text.* Grand Rapids: Eerdmans, 2002.

Frost, Michael, and Alan Hirsch. *The Shaping of Things to Come: Innovation and Mission for the 21st Century Church.* Peabody, MA: Hendrickson, 2003.

"Funding for Evangelism and Mission." Lausanne Occasional Paper No. 56, §2. https://www.lausanne.org/content/lop/funding-evangelism-mission -lop-56.

Gill, Brad. "A Church for Every People: A Retrospect on Mapping Peoples." *Evangelical Missions Quarterly* 56, no. 4 (October–December 2020): 43–45.

Gründer, Horst. "Christian Mission and Colonial Expansion: Historical and Structural Connections." *Mission Studies* 12, no. 1 (January 1995): 18–29.

Hadaway, Robin Dale. *A Survey of World Missions.* Nashville: B&H Academic, 2020.

Harrison, E. F. "Apostle, Apostleship." In *Evangelical Dictionary of Theology,* edited by Walter A. Elwell, 70–72. Grand Rapids: Baker, 1984.

Herron, Robert W., Jr. "The Origin of the New Testament Apostolate." *Westminster Theological Journal* 45 (1983): 101–31.

Hesselgrave, David J. *Paradigms in Conflict: 15 Key Questions in Christian Missions Today.* Edited by Keith E. Eitel. 2nd ed. Grand Rapids: Kregel Academic, 2018.

Hirsch, Alan. *The Forgotten Ways: Reactivating the Missional Church.* Grand Rapids: Brazos, 2006.

Hirsch, Alan, and Tim Catchim. *The Permanent Revolution: Apostolic Imagination and Practice for the 21st Century Church.* San Francisco: Jossey-Bass, 2012.

Hirsch, Alan, and Dave Ferguson. *On the Verge: A Journey into the Apostolic Future of the Church.* Grand Rapids: Zondervan, 2011.

Hocking, William Ernest. *Re-thinking Missions: A Laymen's Inquiry after One Hundred Years.* New York: Harper & Brothers, 1938.

Hoekstra, Harvey T. *The World Council of Churches and the Demise of Evangelism.* Wheaton: Tyndale, 1979.

Huttar, David. "Did Paul Call Andronicus an Apostle in Romans 16:7?" *Journal of the Evangelical Theological Society* 52, no. 4 (December 2009): 747–78.

Glasser, Arthur F., and Donald A. McGavran. *Contemporary Theologies of Mission.* Grand Rapids: Baker, 1983.

Goheen, Michael W. *Introducing Christian Mission Today: Scripture, History, and Issues.* Downers Grove, IL: IVP Academic, 2014.

———. *A Light to the Nations: The Missional Church and the Biblical Story.* Grand Rapids: Baker Academic, 2011.

Green, Michael. *Evangelism in the Early Church*. Grand Rapids: Eerdmans, 1970.

———. "Methods and Strategy in the Evangelism of the Early Church." In *Let the Earth Hear His Voice: International Congress on World Evangelization*, edited by J. D. Douglas, 165–66. Minneapolis: World Wide Publications, 1975.

Grudem, Wayne. *Systematic Theology: An Introduction to Biblical Doctrine*. Grand Rapids: Zondervan, 1994.

Grunlan, Stephen A., and Marvin K. Mayers. *Cultural Anthropology: A Christian Perspective*. 2nd ed. Grand Rapids: Zondervan, 1988.

Guder, Darrell L. *Missional Church: A Vision for the Sending of the Church in North America*. Grand Rapids: Eerdmans, 1998.

Guthrie, Donald. *Hebrews: An Introduction and Commentary*. Downers Grove, IL: InterVarsity, 1983.

Herron, Robert W., Jr. "The Origin of the New Testament Apostolate." *Westminster Theological Journal* 45 (1983): 101–31.

Jackson, Walter C. "A Brief History of Theological Education Including a Description of the Contribution of Wayne E. Oates." *Review and Expositor* 94 (1997): 503–20.

Jenkins, Philip. *The Lost History of Christianity: The Thousand-Year Golden Age of the Church in the Middle East, Africa, and Asia—and How It Died*. New York: HarperOne, 2008.

———. *The Next Christendom: The Coming of Global Christianity*. 3rd ed. New York: Oxford University Press, 2011.

Johnson, Alan R. *Apostolic Function: In 21st Century Missions*. Pasadena, CA: William Carey Library, 2009.

———. "Foundations of Frontier Missiology: Core Understandings and Interrelated Concepts." *Evangelical Missions Quarterly* 56, no. 4 (October–December 2020): 12–15.

Johnston, Arthur P. *The Battle for World Evangelism*. Wheaton: Tyndale, 1978.

Johnstone, Patrick. *The Future of the Global Church: History, Trends, and Possibilities*. Downers Grove, IL: IVP, 2014.

Kee, Doyle. "Who Were the 'Super-Apostles' of 2 Corinthians 10–13?" *Restoration Quarterly* 25 (1980): 65–76.

Kirk, J. Andrew. "Apostleship since Rengstorf: Towards a Synthesis." *New Testament Studies* 21, no. 2 (1975): 249–64.

———. *What Is Mission? Theological Explorations*. Minneapolis: Fortress, 2000.

Klingsmith, Scott. "The Past and Future of Funding Missions: From Everywhere to Everywhere? National Workers vs. Missionaries." Presentation to the Evangelical Missiological Society, October 9–10, 2020. Abstract: https://www.emsweb.org/wp-content/uploads/2021/02/Abstract_Booklet _2020.pdf.

Köstenberger, Andreas J. "The Place of Mission in New Testament Theology: An Attempt to Determine the Significance of Mission within the Scope of the New Testament's Message as a Whole." *Missiology* 27, no. 3 (July 1999): 347–62.

Köstenberger, Andreas J., and Peter T. O'Brien. *Salvation to the Ends of the Earth: A Biblical Theology of Mission*. Downers Grove, IL: InterVarsity, 2001.

Kruger, Kurt T. *Tentmaking: A Misunderstood Missiological Method*. Eugene, OR: Wipf & Stock, 2020.

Kruse, C. G. "Apostle." In *Dictionary of Jesus and the Gospels*, edited by Joel B. Green, Scot McKnight, and I. Howard Marshall, 27–33. Downers Grove, IL: InterVarsity, 1992.

Ladd, George Eldon. *A Theology of the New Testament*. Rev. ed. Grand Rapids: Eerdmans, 1993.

Lambert, J. C. "Apostle." In *The International Standard Bible Encyclopedia*, edited by James Orr et al. Chicago: Howard-Severance, 1915.

Langmead, Ross. "Ecomissiology." *Missiology* 30, no. 4 (October 2002): 505–18.

Lausanne Diaspora Leadership Team. *Scattered to Gather: Embracing the Global Trend of Diaspora*. Rev. ed. Vernon Hills, IL: Parivar International, 2017.

Lederleitner, Mary T. *Cross-Cultural Partnerships: Navigating the Complexities of Money and Mission*. Downers Grove, IL: IVP, 2010.

Lewis, R. W. "Clarifying the Remaining Frontier Mission Task." *International Journal of Frontier Missiology* 35, no. 4 (October–December 2018): 154–68.

———. "Fog in the Pews: Factors behind the Fading Vision for Unreached Peoples." *Evangelical Missions Quarterly* 56, no. 4 (October–December 2020): 28–31.

Lightfoot, J. B. *St. Paul's Epistle to the Galatians*. 2nd ed. London: Macmillan, 1866.

Lin, Yii-Jan. "Junia: An Apostle before Paul." *Journal of Biblical Literature* 139, no. 1 (2020): 191–209.

Little, Christopher R. "The Case for Prioritism: Part 1." *Great Commission Research Journal* 7, no. 2 (Winter 2016): 139–62.

———. *Mission in the Way of Paul: Biblical Mission for the Church in the Twenty-First Century.* New York: Lang, 2005.

Longchar, Wati. "Rethinking Mission in Asia: Looking from Indigenous People's Experience." *Theologies and Cultures* 6, no. 2 (December 2009): 188–202.

Lyon, David. *The Steeple's Shadow: On the Myths and Realities of Secularization.* Grand Rapids: Eerdmans, 1987.

Magda, Ksenija. *Paul's Territoriality and Mission Strategy.* Tübingen: Mohr Siebeck, 2009.

Malphurs, Aubrey. *Advanced Strategic Planning: A New Model for Church and Ministry Leaders.* 2nd ed. Grand Rapids: Baker Books, 2005.

Mandryk, Jason, ed. *Operation World: The Definitive Prayer Guide to Every Nation.* 7th ed. Downers Grove, IL: IVP, 2010.

Marshall, I. Howard. *The Acts of the Apostles: An Introduction and Commentary.* Grand Rapids: Eerdmans, 1980.

McGavran, Donald A. *Understanding Church Growth.* Grand Rapids: Eerdmans, 1970. 3rd ed., 1990.

———. "Yes, Uppsala Betrayed the Two Billion: Now What?" *Christianity Today* 16, no. 19 (June 23, 1972): 16–18.

McMahan, Alan. "Ferment in the Church: Missions in the 4th Era." *Evangelical Missions Quarterly* 56, no. 4 (October–December 2020): 36–38.

McQuilkin, Robertson. "The Missionary Task." In *Evangelical Dictionary of World Missions,* edited by A. Scott Moreau, 648–50. Grand Rapids: Baker Academic, 2000.

Mercer, Calvin. "Jesus the Apostle: 'Sending' and the Theology of John." *Journal of the Evangelical Theological Society* 35, no. 4 (December 1992): 457–62.

Moo, Douglas J. *The Letters to the Colossians and to Philemon.* Grand Rapids: Eerdmans, 2008.

Moreau, A. Scott. *Contextualization in World Missions: Mapping and Assessing Evangelical Models.* Grand Rapids: Kregel, 2012.

———. "Putting the Survey in Perspective." In *Mission Handbook: US and Canadian Christian Ministries Overseas 2004–2006,* edited by Dotsey

Welliver and Minnette Northcutt, 11–64. 19th ed. Wheaton: Evangelism and Missions Information Service, 2004.

———. "Short-Term Missions in the Context of Missions, Inc." In *Effective Engagement in Short-Term Missions: Doing It Right*, edited by Robert J. Priest, 1–33. Pasadena, CA: William Carey Library, 2008.

Moreau, A. Scott, Gary R. Corwin, and Gary B. McGee. *Introducing World Missions: A Biblical, Historical, and Practical Survey*. 2nd ed. Grand Rapids: Baker Academic, 2015.

Morris, Leon. *The Epistle to the Romans*. Grand Rapids: Eerdmans, 1988.

———. *The First Epistle of Paul to the Corinthians*. Grand Rapids: Eerdmans, 1975.

Mosbech, Holger. "Apostolos in the New Testament." *Studia Theologica* 2 (1948): 166–200.

Mott, John R. *The Pastor and Modern Missions: A Plea for Leadership in World Evangelization*. New York: Student Volunteer Movement for Foreign Missions, 1904.

Mounce, Robert H. *Romans*. Nashville: Broadman & Holman, 1995.

Munck, Johannes. "Paul, the Apostles, and the Twelve." *Studia Theologica* 3, no. 1 (1949): 96–110.

Murray, Stuart. *Post-Christendom: Church and Mission in a Strange New World*. 2nd ed. Eugene, OR: Cascade, 2018.

Myklebust, Olav Guttorm. *The Study of Missions in Theological Education: An Historical Inquiry into the Place of World Evangelisation in Western Protestant Ministerial Training with Particular Reference to Alexander Duff's Chair of Evangelistic Theology*. 2 vols. Oslo: Forlaget Land og kirke, 1955–57.

Nässelqvist, Dan. "Apostle." In *The Lexham Bible Dictionary*, edited by John D. Barry et al. Bellingham, WA: Lexham, 2016. In Logos Bible Software.

Neill, Stephen. *Creative Tension*. London: Edinburgh House, 1959.

Newbigin, Lesslie. *The Gospel in a Pluralist Society*. Grand Rapids: Eerdmans; Geneva: WCC Publications, 1989.

———. *The Open Secret: An Introduction to the Theology of Mission*. Rev. ed. Grand Rapids: Eerdmans, 1995.

Nguyen, Minh Ha. "Globalization, Urbanization, Migration, and Rethinking the People Groups Concept." *Evangelical Missions Quarterly* 56, no. 4 (October–December 2020): 32–35.

Nicholls, Bruce. *Missionary Strategy*. London: Evangelical Missionary Alliance, 1962.

Noll, Mark A. *The New Shape of World Christianity: How American Experience Reflects Global Faith*. Downers Grove, IL: IVP Academic, 2009.

Nottingham, William J. Review of *Transforming Mission: Shifts in Theology of Mission*, by David J. Bosch. *Mid-Stream* 33, no. 1 (January 1994): 125–30.

Ott, Craig, and Stephen J. Strauss, with Timothy C. Tennent. *Encountering Theology of Mission: Biblical Foundations, Historical Developments, and Contemporary Issues*. Grand Rapids: Baker Academic, 2010.

Owens, H. P. "Resurrection and Apostolate in St. Paul." *Expository Times* 65, no. 11 (August 1954): 324–28.

Padberg, John W., ed. *The Constitutions of the Society of Jesus and Their Complementary Norms: A Complete English Translation of the Official Latin Texts*. St. Louis: Institute of Jesuit Sources, 1996.

Padilla, C. René. *Mission between the Times: Essays on the Kingdom*. Grand Rapids: Eerdmans, 1985.

Payne, J. D. *Apostolic Church Planting: Birthing New Churches from New Believers*. Downers Grove, IL: InterVarsity, 2015.

———. *The Barnabas Factors: Eight Essential Characteristics of Effective Church Planting Team Members*. N.p.: CreateSpace, 2012.

———. "Currents of Change: How Did Everything Become Missions?" *Mission Frontiers* 41, no. 6 (November–December 2019): 28–31.

———. *Discovering Church Planting: An Introduction to the Whats, Whys, and Hows of Global Church Planting*. Downers Grove, IL: IVP, 2009.

———. *Strangers Next Door: Immigration, Migration and Mission*. Downers Grove, IL: IVP, 2012.

Pelikan, Jaroslav Jan. *Acts*. Grand Rapids: Brazos, 2005.

Peters, George W. *A Biblical Theology of Missions*. Chicago: Moody, 1972.

Pew Research Center. "America's Changing Religious Landscape." May 12, 2015. https://www.pewforum.org/2015/05/12/americas-changing-religious-landscape/.

———. "In U.S., Decline of Christianity Continues at Rapid Pace." October 17, 2019. https://www.pewforum.org/2019/10/17/in-u-s-decline-of-christianity-continues-at-rapid-pace/.

Platt, David. "We Are Not All Missionaries, but We Are All on Mission." Interview in *Conversations on When Everything Is Missions: Recovering the Mission of the Church*, by Denny Spitters and Matthew Ellison, 97–105. N.p.: BottomLine Media, 2020.

Pocock, Michael, Gailyn Van Rheenan, and Douglas McConnel. *The Changing Face of World Missions: Engaging Contemporary Issues and Trends.* Grand Rapids: Baker Academic, 2005.

Polhill, John B. *Acts.* Nashville: Broadman, 1993.

———. "Paul: Theology Born of Mission." *Review and Expositor* 78 (1981): 233–47.

Priest, Robert J. "Introduction." In *Effective Engagement in Short-Term Missions: Doing It Right*, edited by Robert J. Priest, i–ix. Pasadena, CA: William Carey Library, 2008.

Rengstorf, K. H. "*apostellō (pempō), exapostellō, apostolos, pseudapostolos, apostolē*," in *Theological Dictionary of the New Testament*, edited by Gerhard Kittel and Gerhard Friedrich, edited and translated by Geoffrey William Bromiley, 1:398–447. Grand Rapids: Eerdmans, 1964.

Rickett, Daniel. *Building Strategic Relationships: A Practical Guide to Partnering with Non-Western Missions.* 3rd ed. Minneapolis: STEM, 2008.

Rickett, Daniel, and Dotsey Welliver, eds. *Supporting Indigenous Ministries: With Selected Readings.* Wheaton: Billy Graham Center, 1997.

Rightmire, R. David. "Apostle." In *Evangelical Dictionary of Biblical Theology*, edited by Walter A. Elwell, 33–35. Grand Rapids: Baker, 1996.

Robert, Dana L. "Mission Frontiers from 1910 to 2020." *Missiology* 39, no. 2 (April 2011 Electronic Issue): 5e–16e.

———. "'Rethinking Missionaries' from 1910 to Today." *Methodist Review* 4 (2012): 57–75.

Rogers, Everett M. *Diffusion of Innovations.* 5th ed. New York: Free Press, 2003.

Roxburgh, Alan J. *Structured for Mission: Renewing the Culture of the Church.* Downers Grove, IL: InterVarsity, 2015.

Scaer, Peter J. "Luke and the Foundations of the Church." *Concordia Theological Quarterly* 76, nos. 1–2 (January–April 2012): 57–72.

Scherer, James A. "Transforming Mission: Paradigm Shifts in Mission Theology; A Review Article Commemorating an Important Missiological Event." *Missiology* 19, no. 2 (April 1991): 153–60.

Schmithals, Walter. *The Office of Apostle in the Early Church.* Nashville: Abingdon, 1969.

Schnabel, Eckhard J. *Early Christian Mission*. Vol. 1, *Jesus and the Twelve*. Vol. 2, *Paul and the Early Church*. Downers Grove, IL: InterVarsity, 2004.

Schnackenburg, Rudolf. "Apostolicity—The Present Position of Studies." *One in Christ* 6 (1970): 243–73.

Schreiner, Thomas R. *Paul, Apostle of God's Glory in Christ: A Pauline Theology*. 2nd ed. Downers Grove, IL: IVP Academic, 2020.

Schütz, John Howard. *Paul and the Anatomy of Apostolic Authority*. Louisville: Westminster John Knox, 2007.

Scott, James M. *Paul and the Nations*. Tübingen: Mohr Siebeck, 1995.

Seifrid, Mark A. *The Second Letter to the Corinthians*. Pillar New Testament Commentary. Grand Rapids: Eerdmans, 2014.

Seumois, André. *Théologie missionnaire: Délimitation de la fonction missionnaire de l'Église*. Rome: Bureau de Presse O.M.I., 1973.

Shenk, Wilbert R. *Changing Frontiers of Missions*. Maryknoll, NY: Orbis, 1999.

———. "Introduction." In *Theology of Mission: A Believers Church Perspective*, by John Howard Yoder, 13–33. Edited by Gayle Gerber Koontz and Andy Alexis-Baker. Downers Grove, IL: IVP Academic, 2014.

Shimron, Yonat. "Is the Rise of the Nones Slowing? Scholars Say Maybe." *Religion News Service*, February 20, 2020. https://religionnews.com/2020/02/11/is-the-decline-in-religious-affiliation-slowing-some-scholars-say-maybe/.

Sinclair, Daniel. *A Vision of the Possible: Pioneer Church Planting in Teams*. Waynesboro, GA: Authentic Media, 2005.

Smither, Edward L. *Missionary Monks: An Introduction to the History and Theology of Missionary Monasticism*. Eugene, OR: Cascade, 2016.

Spitters, Denny, and Matthew Ellison. *When Everything Is Missions*. N.p.: BottomLine Media, 2017.

Steer, Roger. *Basic Christian: The Inside Story of John Stott*. Downers Grove, IL: IVP, 2009.

Stein, Robert H. *Luke*. Nashville: Broadman & Holman, 1992.

Stott, John R. W. *Christian Mission in the Modern World*. Downers Grove, IL: InterVarsity, 1975.

Stroope, Michael W. *Transcending Mission: The Eclipse of a Modern Tradition*. Downers Grove, IL: IVP Academic, 2017.

Sunquist, Scott W. *Understanding Christian Mission: Participating in Suffering and Glory*. Grand Rapids: Baker Academic, 2013.

Tasker, R. V. G. *The Gospel according to St. Matthew: An Introduction and Commentary*. Tyndale New Testament Commentaries. Grand Rapids: Eerdmans, 1961.

Taylor, Walter F. *Paul, Apostle to the Nations: An Introduction*. Minneapolis: Fortress, 2012.

Taylor, William D., ed. *Kingdom Partnerships for Synergy in Missions*. Pasadena, CA: William Carey Library, 1994.

Tennent, Timothy C. *Invitation to World Missions: A Trinitarian Missiology for the Twenty-First Century*. Grand Rapids: Kregel, 2010.

Terry, John Mark, and J. D. Payne. *Developing a Strategy for Missions: A Biblical, Historical, and Cultural Introduction*. Grand Rapids: Baker Academic, 2013.

Topf, Daniel. "The Global Crisis of Unemployment in an Age of Automation and Artificial Intelligence." *Occasional Bulletin of the Evangelical Missiological Society* 33, no. 2 (Spring 2020): 9–15, 36–37.

Van Engen, Charles. "Essay 1: 'Mission' Defined and Described." In *MissionShift: Global Mission Issues in the Third Millennium*, edited by David J. Hesselgrave and Ed Stetzer. Nashville: B&H Academic, 2010.

Van Gelder, Craig. "The Future of the Discipline of Missiology: Framing Current Realities and Future Possibilities." *Missiology* 42, no. 1 (2013): 39–56.

Vanhoozer, Kevin J. "5 Picks." *Christian Century*, October 3, 2010. https://www.christiancentury.org/reviews/2010-09/kevin-j-vanhoozer-5-picks.

Verkuyl, Johannes. *Contemporary Missiology: An Introduction*. Grand Rapids: Eerdmans, 1978.

Vicedom, Georg F. *The Mission of God: An Introduction to a Theology of Mission*. Saint Louis: Concordia, 1965.

Wagner, C. Peter. *Apostles and Prophets: The Foundation of the Church*. Ventura, CA: Regal, 2000.

Watson, Charles R. "Rethinking Missions." *International Review of Mission* 21, no. 1 (January 1932): 106–18.

Wilson, Andrew. "Apostle Apollos?" *Journal of the Evangelical Theological Society* 56, no. 2 (2013): 325–35.

Winter, Ralph D. "The Highest Priority: Cross-Cultural Evangelism." In *Let the Earth Hear His Voice: International Congress on World Evangelization, Lausanne, Switzerland*, edited by J. D. Douglas, 213–41. Minneapolis: World Wide Publications, 1975.

———. "The Meaning of Mission: Understanding This Term Is Crucial to the Completion of the Missionary Task." *Mission Frontiers*, March 1, 1998. https://www.missionfrontiers.org/issue/article/the-meaning-of-mission-understanding-this-term-is-crucial-to-the-completion.

———. "The Mission of the Kingdom." In *Perspectives on the World Christian Movement: A Reader*, edited by Ralph D. Winter and Steven C. Hawthorne, 572–73. 4th ed. Pasadena, CA: William Carey Library, 2009.

———. "Unreached Peoples: The Development of the Concept." In *Reaching the Unreached: The Old-New Challenge*, edited by Harvie M. Conn, 17–43. Phillipsburg, NJ: Presbyterian and Reformed, 1985.

Wolfe, Alan. *The Transformation of American Religion: How We Actually Live Our Faith*. Chicago: University of Chicago Press, 2005.

Wright, Christopher J. H. *The Mission of God: Unlocking the Bible's Grand Narrative*. Downers Grove, IL: IVP Academic, 2006.

Wright, N. T. "Paul and Missional Hermeneutics." In *The Apostle Paul and the Christian Life: Ethical and Missional Implications of the New Perspective*, edited by Scot McKnight and Joseph B. Modica, 179–94. Grand Rapids: Baker Academic, 2016.

Wrogemann, Henning. *Theologies of Mission*. Translated by Karl E. Böhmer. Downers Grove, IL: IVP Academic, 2018.

Yeh, Allen. *Polycentric Missiology: Twenty-First Century Mission from Everyone to Everywhere*. Downers Grove, IL: IVP Academic, 2016.

Zehner, Edwin. "On the Rhetoric of Short-Term Mission Appeals, with Some Practical Suggestions for Team Leaders." In *Effective Engagement in Short-Term Missions: Doing It Right*, edited by Robert J. Priest, 185–207. Pasadena, CA: William Carey Library, 2008.

Zurlo, Gina A., Todd M. Johnson, and Peter F. Crossing. "Christianity 2019: What's Missing? A Call for Further Research." *International Bulletin of Mission Research* 43, no. 1 (2019): 92–102.

———. "World Christianity and Mission 2020: Ongoing Shift to the Global South." *International Bulletin of Mission Research* 44, no. 1 (2019): 8–19.

Scripture Index

Subject Index

Printed in the USA
CPSIA information can be obtained
at www.ICGtesting.com
LVHW050035230823
755946LV00004B/140